The Private Pilot's Licence Course

Human Factors
Flight Safety

The Private Pilot's Licence Course

Human Factors
Flight Safety

Jeremy M Pratt

ISBN 1 874783 03 9

Published by

Airplan Flight Equipment Ltd

This book is intended to be a guide to the human factors element of the PPL course. It **does not** in any way overrule the instruction you will receive from a qualified Flying Instructor at a registered Flying Training Organisation (FTO). No part of this book overrules or supersedes the Air Navigation Order (ANO), the Aeronautical Information Publication (AIP), Aeronautical Information Circulars (AICs), the Joint Aviation Requirements (JARs) and other documents published by a competent authority. Nor does it overrule or supersede the flight manual/pilot's operating handbook for the aircraft being flown, the pilot order book/FTO syllabus and the general provisions of good airmanship and safe flying practice.

First Edition 2000

Reprinted 2001

The Private Pilot's Licence Course Human Factors and Flight Safety

ISBN 1 874783 03 9

Airplan Flight Equipment Ltd.,
1a Ringway Trading Estate, Shadowmoss Road, Manchester M22 5LH
Tel: 0161 499 0023   Fax: 0161 499 0298
email: enquiries@afeonline.com
www.afeonline.com

contents

Human Factors Introduction

contents

contents

Flight Safety Prologue

INDEX

editorial

AUTHOR: JEREMY M PRATT

Acknowledgments

This book would not have been possible without the invaluable assistance of many people and organisations, including:

Air Accident Investigation Branch

James Allan

Beaufort

Geoffrey Boot

Flightcom

Flyer Magazine

Mike Jerram

Dave Johnson

Ian Manfield

Peter R March

Chris Mathews

Ray Mitchell

John Nelson

Mike Nichols

Dr Brian Pickard

Pilot Magazine

Racal Aerad

RAF Coltishall

Randolph Engineering

John Ross

Rob Taylor – GDi studio

Mark Smith

Gill Stitt

Barry Tempest

Mike Vines

'Tugg' Wilson

Jeremy Pratt took his first flying lesson aged 14, paid for by weekend and holiday jobs at his local airfield cleaning aircraft and working in the hanger. Later he also worked in the air/ground station of the airfield and in the operations department of an air taxi company. He completed his PPL after being awarded an Esso/Air League scholarship and became a flying instructor at the age of 19. Since then he has taught students for the Private Pilots Licence and associated ratings and also applicants for professional flying licences. He has flown as a commercial pilot in a variety of roles and has also flown microlights, gliders and helicopters. He stays current by instructing and flying around Europe for business and pleasure.

He has been Managing Director of Airplan Flight Equipment since 1985, is author of the 'Pilot's Guide' series, the 'Questions and Answers' series; and has also co-authored, compiled and contributed to, a number of aviation books and publications.

TECHNICAL ADVISORS:

Bill Stitt – Chief Flying Instructor of Essex Flying School, Bill has been a flying instructor for over 20 years and is a delegated flight examiner. He has been training instructors for over 15 years and he is married to a flying instructor: their daughter also flies!

Phillip G Mathews – Chief Flying Instructor of Cotswold Aviation Services, Phil has over 10,000 hours experience of flying light aircraft. He gained his PPL at the age of 17 and went on to achieve an ATPL through the 'self-improver' route. Phil also runs his own business teaching applicants for the PPL and IMC rating technical exams and flies as a commercial pilot.

John Thorpe – John Thorpe started his aviation career as an apprentice in aircraft engineering with the Bristol Aeroplane Company, leading to a flight testing position on aircraft such as the BAC 1-11 and Concorde. He later joined the CAA as a design surveyor on light aircraft design requirements, obtaining his PPL in 1972. In 1977 he started the General Aviation Safety Information Leaflet (GASIL) which was the first safety publication of its kind in the UK. He later also started the Safety Sense Leaflets series. He held the first Safety Evening in 1986 and he personally hosted a total of 385 Safety Evenings at airfields around the UK. John was head of the Safety Promotion section until his retirement in 1999. He now hosts Safety Evenings on behalf of a commercial concern and remains an active PPL with around 123 airfields and 35 types in his logbook.

David Hockings – David joined the Air Training Corps at the age of 14, soloed gliders at 17 (he went on to obtain a silver C) and became a Rolls Royce aero-engine apprentice. He joined the aviation insurance department of Lloyds of London and gained his PPL in 1976. In 1987 David moved to the Civil Aviation Authority in the General Aviation section and became active in safety promotion, writing in the General Aviation Safety Information Leaflet (GASIL) and holding Safety Evenings. He now is now a CPL/IR and Flying Instructor with about 50 types flown, with his own business in aviation insurance loss adjusting, flying instruction, aerial photography, banner towing and air taxi. In his spare time he is also a CAA-licenced engineer and has an aircraft maintenance company!

Human Factors introduction

When the idea of 'human factors' training for pilots was first mooted, many saw it as an ideal opportunity to address a glaring omission in pilot education. After-all, it is an acknowledged truism that the majority of aviation accidents are caused by so-called 'human error', rather than straightforward mechanical failure or the like. And in general, as aircraft get smaller the proportion of 'pilot error' accidents becomes greater. With this in mind, what could make more sense than teaching pilots about the common pitfalls, the best-known examples of pilot error, and thus making for safer flying? Surely if pilots were to know more about how the mind works, about personality traits and how humans interact with each other, this would make it easier for pilots to avoid human errors – wouldn't it?

Like many things in life, the reality turned out to be not quite so simple. The human psyche is hardly a straightforward topic, and the experts in the field are wont to disagree amongst themselves on a regular basis about what is 'right' and what is 'wrong' – there is often no clear definition between established fact and popular belief. Human behaviour is complex, and there is no way of pretending that it can be discussed in anything other than the broadest terms. It is easier to talk about general principles and common theories rather than strict definitions and exact rules.

Of course, this presents a certain difficulty to an examiner. It is difficult to set questions in an exam paper with multi-choice answers if it can be argued that more than one answer could be correct! It is maybe for this reason that when the first Human Factors examination papers appeared, many felt that an opportunity had been missed, and that instead of gaining an insight into human behaviour in an aviation environment, candidates were instead being asked to be able to list parts of the body and recite lists of symptoms for common aviation-related medical conditions. Even if this is true (and this author is not about to take sides in the debate!), there is still much to be learnt in the Human Factors syllabus, not just about human behaviour but also about the body and how it works in an aviation environment. Furthermore, a knowledge of subjects often neglected in civil aviation, such as first aid, safety equipment and the principles of survival, can be invaluable. With that in mind the Human Factors section has been written in part to pass a test, and in part to give the reader a basic grounding in the subject. The second section, Flight Safety, is far more a personal discourse on how I believe accidents happen and how they could be avoided. It is not an attempt to cover any particular syllabus, and if you want to know more have a look at the 'prologue' to that section.

Now the traditional disclaimer. Until the English language finds an acceptable way of dealing with people regardless of sex, I will continue to use 'he' rather than a cumbersome 'he or she' in the text, and I ask all readers to read 'he' or 'she' as appropriate!

Finally, an extra disclaimer. Many of the photographs and illustrations used throughout this book have been culled over many years from noticeboards and internal publications on the coffee tables and notice boards of flying schools, crew rooms and briefing units around the world. We have done our best to trace and acknowledge the original copyright holder, but inevitably there are a few illustrations whose origin remains a mystery. We have used these in the belief that anything that might improve flight safety or help prevent an accident is worth publishing, so if any of the copyright holders read this I hope they will agree!

Jeremy M Pratt

August 2000

The Functions of the Body (Basic Physiology)

▶ **Composition of the Atmosphere**

▶ **The Breathing Machine**

▶ **Breathing Problems and Flight at High Altitude**

▶ **Light Aircraft Oxygen Systems**

▶ **The Ears**

▶ **The Eyes**

▶ **'G' Effects**

▶ **Revision**

*The Functions
of the Body
(Basic
Physiology)*

▶ Composition of the Atmosphere

We all live at the bottom of an ocean of air – the *atmosphere* – and as air-breathing creatures our existence is inextricably linked to its properties. A healthy human can survive weeks or months without food, and even several days without water. However, in the absence of oxygen, life expectancy is measured in minutes. So before we look at the functioning of the human body in relation to flying, we should remind ourselves of some properties of the atmosphere.

As you may well remember, the constituents of the atmosphere are as follows:

Nitrogen	78%
Oxygen	21%
Other gases	1%

*The percentage of gases
in the atmosphere*

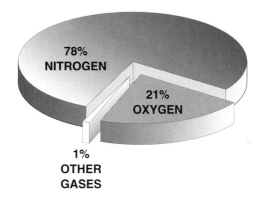

These proportions remain fairly constant with increasing altitude until well above the sort of levels conventional aircraft can reach. But temperature, density, and pressure – the latter especially important in this context – all change markedly as altitude increases. The reduction in pressure with increasing altitude does not occur at a constant rate but is greatest in the lower atmosphere, where a one-millibar reduction in pressure occurs around every 27ft of altitude increase. By the time you get to 30,000 feet, a one-millibar pressure reduction occurs after about 75ft of increased altitude.

*Approximate pressure
levels in the standard
atmosphere*

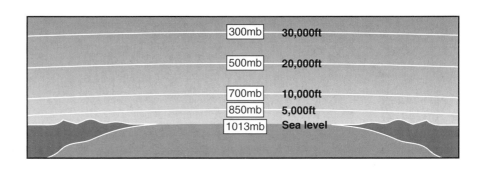

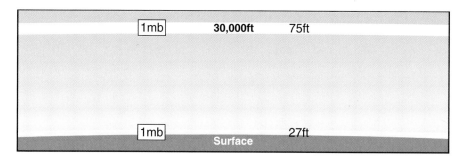

| 1mb | 30,000ft | 75ft |
| 1mb | Surface | 27ft |

Pressure reduces at the greatest rate in the lower atmosphere

1013mb = sea level

850mb = 5,000ft

700mb = 10,000ft

500mb = 20,000ft

300mb = 30,000ft

Although the *proportion* of oxygen within the air stays largely unchanged with increasing altitude, the *amount* of oxygen taken in by humans every time they draw breath reduces markedly with the decreasing pressure. The amount of oxygen within the air can be expressed by the term *partial pressure*. At sea level the partial pressure of oxygen is around 212mb (i.e. 21% of 1013mb). At 20,000ft the partial pressure of oxygen is closer to 105mb. For an air-breathing creature, this is clearly going to present problems.

▶ The Breathing Machine

Each time you breathe in, air is drawn through the mouth and/or nose into the windpipe (*trachea*) and down to the lungs. Within the lungs, air travels down passages which continually branch off and narrow, rather like the branches of a tree. At the end of these passages the air reaches millions of tiny air sacs (*alveoli*). These air sacs are surrounded by blood capillaries, and the pressure of the oxygen within the air allows oxygen to diffuse into the blood. More specifically, the oxygen combines with the *haemoglobin* in red blood cells. The oxygenated blood passes to the left side of the heart, which then pumps it out into the body via the arteries. The haemoglobin releases its oxygen to cells around the body and particularly

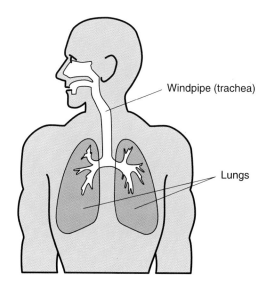

Windpipe (trachea)

Lungs

When you breathe in, air passes down the windpipe and into passages in the lungs

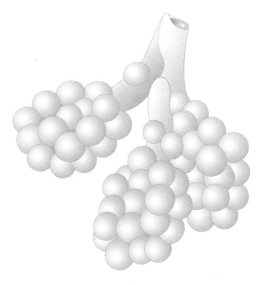

The alveoli

those in the brain: although the brain makes up only around 2% of body weight, it requires nearly 20% of the body's oxygen intake.

As haemoglobin gives up its oxygen, the blood collects carbon dioxide (CO_2) which is, in essence, the waste product of the breathing process. The deoxygenated blood travels along veins to the right side of the heart, which pumps it back to the alveoli. At the air sacs, the waste carbon dioxide diffuses into the lungs as fresh oxygen is transferred to the blood. This carbon dioxide is then expelled as you breathe out, although even exhaled air still contains significantly more oxygen than it does carbon

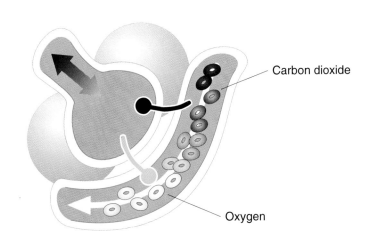

At the alveoli, oxygen diffuses into the blood, and carbon dioxide diffuses into the lungs

Carbon dioxide

Oxygen

dioxide. All this takes place without conscious effort. On average you breathe in and out around 15 times a minute, with the heart beating around 70 times a minute.

The body holds only a very small store of oxygen, hence the constant demand to bring oxygen in. By contrast, the body possesses a greater store of carbon dioxide (whose function is to help maintain the chemical balance within the body). The level of stored carbon dioxide affects the breathing rate; although this is also sensitive to oxygen levels, the body is more susceptible to CO_2 than oxygen in this respect. Breathing rate is also affected by exercise, stress, injury or illness.

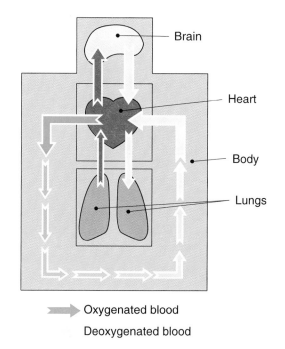

The breathing machine

Brain

Heart

Body

Lungs

Oxygenated blood
Deoxygenated blood

▶Breathing Problems and Flight at High Altitude

Any situation in which the body (and in particular the brain) is not getting sufficient oxygen may have serious consequences. The condition when the amount of oxygen available is insufficient to meet the needs of the body is called *hypoxia*. In an aviation context, hypoxia is associated with increasing altitude and thus decreasing partial pressure of oxygen.

Once above 10,000ft AMSL or so, the reduction in quantity of available oxygen within the air is such that the effects become noticeable. The higher you are, the more severe hypoxia will be. The problem is that the first part of the body to be affected by hypoxia is the brain, and consequently the thought processes. So the very mechanisms that you would otherwise use to recognise and react to hypoxia, i.e. the higher brain functions, are the first to be degraded.

The effects of hypoxia, starting first with the initial symptoms, are some or all of the following:

■ *Personality changes and impaired judgement.* The victim may have a false sense of well-being and feel euphoric, uninhibited or even intoxicated. He will accept errors and mistakes whilst believing that he is performing the task very well indeed. This state of mind, not unlike being mildly drunk or high, can be summed up as feeling 'dumb and happy'.

■ *Confusion and difficulty concentrating.* Even simple mental tasks, such as fuel or navigation calculations, become difficult or even impossible. The short-term memory is affected, so that an item such as a change of radio frequency might be forgotten before it can be written down.

■ *Loss of co-ordination.* Physical tasks requiring fine muscular control, such as setting the heading indicator or altimeter, become difficult to achieve as the victim becomes more clumsy.

■ *Drowsiness.* The victim will become drowsy, sleepy and lethargic.

■ *Headaches, dizziness and nausea* may occur.

■ *Blue/grey skin colour.* The skin may become pale and fingernails, lips and the tip of the nose may take on a blue colour (*cyanosis*).

■ *Hyperventilation* ('over-breathing') may occur as the victim tries to draw in more oxygen. Hyperventilation is described in more detail shortly.

■ *Loss of basic senses.* Vision is the first sense to be affected. Colour vision may be lost, and 'tunnel vision' can occur. Night vision is especially susceptible to hypoxia, and can be reduced at altitudes as low as 5000ft.

■ *Unconsciousness.* Ultimately hypoxia will lead to a loss of consciousness. At this stage the victim is no longer able to help himself, and in the absence of assistance the final outcome is death.

Unfortunately, the exact symptoms of hypoxia and how they will manifest themselves will vary from individual to individual. Nevertheless, the symptoms listed above are those most commonly associated with this potentially very nasty syndrome.

An ability to recognise the onset of hypoxia is vital to any pilot flying at high levels. As the problems become more severe with increasing altitude, the time available for the pilot to act – the time of 'useful consciousness' – is reduced. The table below assumes that at the outset, the subject is at sea-level pressure and receiving sufficient oxygen:

Altitude AMSL (feet)	Time of useful consciousness
20,000	5 to10 minutes
25,000	2 to 3 minutes
30,000	45 to 75 seconds
35,000	30 to 45 seconds
40,000	18 to 30 seconds
45,000	12 seconds

The times above should be taken as an approximate guide only, and should be viewed in the context of the confusion and alarm that will occur after a rapid decompression or sudden loss of oxygen supply at altitude.

The Functions of the Body (Basic Physiology)

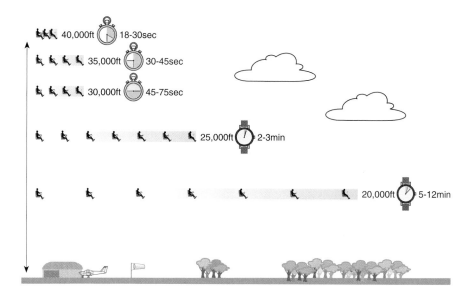

The time of useful consciousness reduces markedly with increasing altitude

Several factors other than altitude will affect the severity of and susceptibility to hypoxia. The list reads as follows:

- *Time*. The longer the exposure to altitude, the greater the effect of hypoxia.

- *Exercise*. Even a small amount of movement can significantly reduce the time of useful consciousness

- *Stress/workload*. High workload or significant stress can increase hypoxia symptoms.

- *Cold, illness and fatigue* all lower the threshold for hypoxia.

- *Alcohol* reduces altitude tolerance, so that hypoxia can set in at a lower altitude than otherwise.

- *Smoking*. A smoker will suffer more than a non-smoker from any degree of hypoxia; thus the symptoms may manifest themselves at a lower altitude in a heavy smoker.

If you suspect hypoxia at any time, the first action should be to descend to a lower altitude (below 10,000ft if at all possible) without delay. The use of supplemental oxygen systems is described later.

Hyperventilation or over-breathing is a condition where breathing is both deeper and more rapid than necessary. It is a condition most often associated with intense stress or anxiety, although it can also be caused by certain levels of vibration and turbulence, high *g*, hypoxia, pain or motion sickness. The symptoms of hyperventilation are:

- Dizziness, light-headed feelings and a sense of 'unreality'

- Tingling sensations, particularly in the fingers and hands, toes and feet

- Vision impairment such as blurring, tunnel vision or clouded vision

- Hot and cold feelings around the body

- Unconsciousness

The treatment for hyperventilation is to return the breathing rate to normal. The victim may be able to do this unaided by consciously slowing down the breathing rate. If this is not possible, re-breathing exhaled air (e.g. by breathing into and from a bag held over the nose and mouth) should help. This works because over-breathing lowers the body's carbon dioxide levels and rebreathing exhaled air helps return them to normal.

You may have noticed that the symptoms of hyperventilation and hypoxia are quite similar, so it is not easy to be sure from which one a person is suffering. The safest course of action is to check the altitude. If above 10,000ft, assume hypoxia and act accordingly (which normally means descending to below 10,000ft if at all possible). If already below that altitude, hyperventilation is more likely.

Breathing problems are not the only possible consequence of flight at higher altitudes. Even if the body is receiving sufficient oxygen, the reduction in atmospheric pressure can have other effects on its internal workings. With reduced external pressure, gases within the body will expand – notably those in the

Trapped gases expand in reducing external pressure

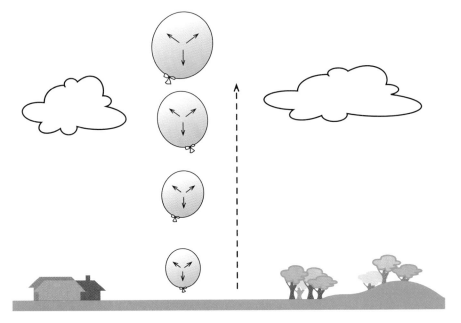

stomach and intestines. This can be very painful unless they can find some way to vent outside the body. No doubt you will be able to work out for yourself how this is most likely to occur and the reaction you are likely to receive from fellow aircrew and passengers. The problem can be largely circumvented before a flight at high altitude by not eating foods which might be especially gas-producing. Beer, beans, highly spiced foods and that special vindaloo menu from the local takeaway are all worth avoiding the night before you are due to fly above FL100 or so.

Reduced pressure also affects the store of nitrogen within the body, and the consequences can be quite serious. At sea-level pressure, nitrogen exists within the body in solution. During a climb to high altitude, the reduced atmospheric pressure allows nitrogen to come out of solution and form into bubbles. These are carried around the bloodstream and tend to congregate in the joints – shoulder, elbow, wrists, knees and ankles. The result can vary from mild discomfort to severe pain which may cause collapse. This pain is known in diving circles as "the bends" and is by far the most common symptom of decompression sickness (sometimes known as 'DCS'). Decompression sickness can also lead directly to collapse, usually preceded by nausea and headaches, without an intermediate stage of the bends. Other possible symptoms of DCS are skin irritation caused by nitrogen bubbles in the skin ("the creeps") which cause itching and a rash; respiratory difficulties ("the chokes"), making deep breathing difficult; visual problems such as blurred vision and partial blindness; and partial paralysis leading to "the staggers". If you suspect that you or somebody in the aircraft is suffering from decompression sickness, the first action should be to descend and land as soon as possible. The symptoms of DCS can continue for some time even after the descent, and medical advice should be sought immediately on landing.

The minimum altitude for the onset of decompression sickness is normally considered to be 18,000ft, with the likelihood of DCS increasing sharply once above 25,000ft. If you believe the nature of your aviation activities automatically excludes you from the possibility of DCS, think again before turning the page. Many turbocharged single-engine aircraft have service ceilings well in excess of 20,000ft, and gliders regularly reach these altitudes in mountain-wave conditions.

A number of factors will increase susceptibility to decompression sickness and the severity of its onslaught. The higher the altitude, and the longer the time spent there, the greater the chances of suffering from DCS. Moreover, anyone generally unfit, unwell or overweight is more susceptible to DCS and increasing age also leaves one increasingly vulnerable. Re-exposure to high altitude within a day or two increases the risk of DCS, and low temperatures and hypoxia (both associated with high altitude in themselves) increase the incidence and severity of decompression sickness.

There is one situation where the 'threshold' altitude for the onset of DCS is greatly reduced, and that is in relation to scuba or sub-aqua diving. The general advice is that you should **not fly at all with 24 hours of diving** using compressed air (or 12 hours if diving did not exceed 10m/30ft). This guideline applies not just to flying as a crew-member but also to flight as a passenger in a pressurised airliner. Contrary to

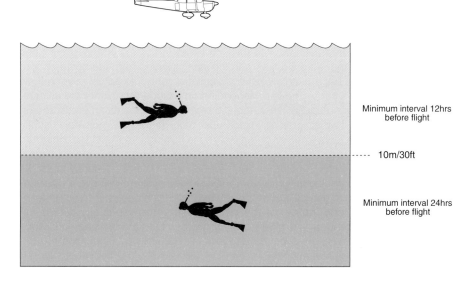

Minimum interval 12hrs
before flight

10m/30ft

Minimum interval 24hrs
before flight

You should not fly within 24 hours of diving with compressed air to in excess of 30ft/10m (or 12 hours if diving depth is less)

popular belief, a pressurised cabin does *not* maintain sea-level pressure inside it but instead embodies a pressure somewhat greater than that outside the aircraft. For an airliner cruising at high altitude, the cabin pressure may be the equivalent of 8,000ft or so. Each year a number of decompression-sickness cases occur as a result of an insufficient interval between diving and flying, and in such cases the onset of DCS has been known to occur at altitudes/cabin pressures as low as 6,000ft.

There are two other areas where the reduced pressure at high altitude can cause problems. Air trapped as a result of dental work (e.g. fillings) can expand under reduced pressure, and can be very painful. Trapped air can also cause pain in the *sinuses* and the middle ear, which we will consider in more detail shortly.

▶ Light Aircraft Oxygen Systems

A passenger aircraft designed to do most of its flying above 10,000ft invariably has a pressurised cabin. In simple terms this means that air from outside is pumped into the cabin, raising the pressure inside above that of the surrounding atmosphere. In a Boeing 747 cruising at 40,000ft or thereabouts, the passengers will be enjoying their gin-and-tonics in the comfort of a cabin pressure equivalent to around 7,000ft. The expense and weight of pressurisation systems and the associated structural considerations make it rare for single-engine light aircraft to be pressurised. Nevertheless, turbocharged piston-engined aircraft need to fly significantly above 10,000ft to achieve the highest airspeeds and most economic operation: typical maximum cruising altitudes for aeroplanes in this class are 20-25,000ft. It follows that their pilots (and passengers) will require some form of oxygen supply system. Some aircraft may be fitted with suitable equipment; alternatively the pilot may invest in a portable system. In either case it is **vital** that operation of the system is fully understood before using it for the first time for real. The design and use of oxygen systems can vary greatly, and the provision of adequate oxygen to the pilot is too essential to be neglected or taken for granted. What follows is some general advice; it is *not* a substitute for a thorough working knowledge of any system you intend to use for real.

For flight below 25,000ft or so a commonly used oxygen system is the 'Continuous Flow' type. Oxygen is stored either in a permanently installed bottle, which has fixed outlets in the aircraft, or in a portable equivalent. A lead runs from the bottle or fixed outlet to the mask, which normally has a bag attached. Oxygen is continuously supplied to the mask and bag, from where it is inhaled by the user. As the user exhales, some air flows out through holes in the mask and some goes back into the bag. From here it mixes with incoming oxygen from the bottle prior to being inhaled again. Each user will have a regulator control to adjust oxygen flow. A manual regulator is set by the user depending on altitude (the higher the altitude, the greater the oxygen supply). An automatic regulator senses cabin pressure and adjusts the oxygen flow accordingly. Each user also has a flow indicator, usually mechanical, which shows whether or not oxygen is flowing into the mask. Note that this indicator does not show how much oxygen is flowing and cannot reveal whether the user is getting enough oxygen for his or her needs; it merely indicates that some oxygen is getting through. Lastly the oxygen system will have a pressure gauge linked to the oxygen cylinder(s). It is worth noting that even if the cylinder is fully charged, the 'endurance' of the oxygen system – especially with a full complement of passengers – is highly likely to be less than the cruising endurance of the aircraft. However, the system handbook and operating instructions are the only reliable source of information.

Incidentally, the oxygen used in aircraft systems is not the same as oxygen used in other applications (such as 'medical oxygen'). Aviator's oxygen is at least 99% pure and also contains practically no water vapour. This last point is important because medical oxygen tends to contain more moisture, which may freeze at high altitude and block the oxygen system. Other available forms of the gas, such as 'welding oxygen', are nowhere near pure enough and should never be allowed anywhere near aeroplane oxygen systems.

Whenever intending to use an oxygen system, it is important not only to understand how it works and how to use it properly but also to test it before climbing above 10,000ft. The oxygen flow and quantity remaining must be checked regularly when the system is in use. As with other vital aircraft systems, any components associated with the storage and distribution of oxygen require regular maintenance and servicing to work properly. Smoking is **absolutely not** permitted when oxygen is in use, as an oxygen-rich atmosphere can encourage combustion even in normally harmless objects.

▶**The Ears**

The primary functions of the ears are hearing and balance. Sound travels as waves through the air. These pass the ear flap (*pinna*) and travel along the outer ear canal, causing the eardrum to vibrate. This motion is transmitted by the small bones of the middle ear to the *cochlea* of the inner ear. Here the resulting movements stimulate the minute hair cells by deforming them; in response they originate electrical signals which pass up the fibres of the auditory nerve to the brain.

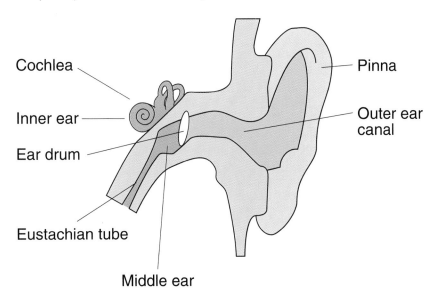

Cochlea

Inner ear

Ear drum

Eustachian tube

Middle ear

Pinna

Outer ear canal

The main components of the ear

In a light aircraft, the greatest concern regarding hearing is probably in relation to the noise level within the cockpit. The cockpit of an unpressurised piston-engined aeroplane is generally considered to be about as noisy as the inside of an aircraft can be. Many such aircraft have cockpit noise levels of around 100 decibels (dBa) in the cruise, and up to 115dBa in a full-power climb. To put this in perspective, prolonged exposure to sound levels in excess of 90dBa is considered capable of causing long-term hearing damage. When you consider this sobering fact, it is not surprising that nowadays the use of headsets in light aircraft is widespread. A headset not only reduces the noise levels reaching the ear (reductions of about 25-30dBa are claimed for most modern examples) but also makes radio messages much easier to hear and understand. Conversation between headset wearers via the intercom is also a lot easier than shouting across the cockpit! Many modern units allow the user to adjust the internal volume of the radio messages coming into the headset. It is worth setting this control carefully because over-loud radio messages can be just as damaging and distracting as background engine noise.

A headset should be considered essential to protect the hearing

Those who fly with passengers often provide headsets for them too (if the aircraft has enough intercom points) or just simple ear defenders (if not). The reduction in background noise not only protects the hearing of your passengers but also reduces fatigue and generally makes flight in a light aircraft a more civilised affair. If you regularly use headsets provided by the aircraft owner/operator, you are presumably sharing the headset with many other users. In this case you will not be comforted to learn that studies suggest many infections can be transmitted via a headset, causing inflammation of the outer ear or re-activating *otitis media* if the eardrum has been perforated. Most headsets have removable cloth earpiece covers, and changing these regularly is a good precaution against infection. Some headsets even have disposable paper covers for 'once only' use.

Buying your own headset(s) is a more expensive option, but well worth considering if you fly regularly. The latest developments in headset technology involve an electronic technique known as 'active noise reduction' (ANR) or 'dynamic noise reduction' (DNR), which dramatically reduces external noise levels within the headset. Reductions of up to 45dBa have been claimed. One possible disadvantage of such systems – other than the price – is that if you can hear too little external noise, certain danger signals such as an audible stall warner or a rough-running engine might be missed. This possible problem also demonstrates a basic law of aviation; give a group of pilots some brand-new technology and they will soon find a drawback with it!

Excessive noise outside the aviation context is also worth avoiding. Spectators and participants in noisy sports such as shooting and motor-racing are wise to use some form of hearing protection such as earplugs, and those using personal stereos should avoid excessive volume through the headphones (this also aids the sanity of other people in the vicinity). Headsets may reduce the possibility of hearing loss due to excessive noise, but nothing will prevent the natural loss of hearing that is a regrettable and inevitable feature of increasing age. This is why hearing is tested carefully during the medical examination, which itself becomes more frequent with increasing age.

Good hearing relies on the transmission of sound waves between the outer and middle ear, and for this to occur easily the pressure each side of the eardrum must be equal. The air cavity of the middle ear is connected to the nose and throat via the *Eustachian tube*. During a climb, the air pressure within the middle ear will be greater than the external pressure. This excess pressure should automatically vent via the Eustachian tube and is not normally a problem. However, the Eustachian tube contains a sort of one-way valve, to stop air travelling up the tube and back to the middle ear. So in a descent, when the pressure in the middle ear becomes less than the external pressure, there is no automatic venting of air back to the middle ear to equalise the pressure each side of the eardrum. This may lead to a painful stretching of the eardrum sometimes known as *barotrauma* – a term which covers the general problem of gases expanding within the body. Avoiding this should be simple: by swallowing or yawning, the one-way valve in the Eustachian tube is briefly opened and so pressure can be gradually equalised in the ear. Most experienced pilots find themselves doing this instinctively. However, if swallowing or yawning is not enough to equalise the pressure, pinching the nostrils and attempting to breathe out through the nose (known as "Valsalva's manoeuvre") should work.

A problem occurs when, due to illness or infection, the Eustachian tube becomes swollen or blocked. This most often happens if one is suffering from a cold, sore throat, rhinitis, sinusitis or hay fever, and can cause severe pain and ultimately bleeding into the middle ear or perforation of the eardrum. The *sinuses* (air-filled cavities within the skull) are also connected to the nose by tubes. Again, any illness or infection causing blockages here can lead to the generation of a pressure differential between the sinuses and the outside world. The result can be intense pain in the forehead and eyes, headache and watery eyes, any or all of which can

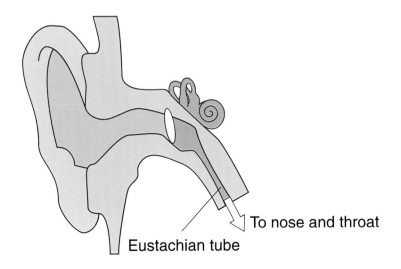

To nose and throat

Eustachian tube

The middle ear is connected to the nose and throat by the Eustachian tube

ultimately be incapacitating. In short, if you have a cold, the flu or any other condition that may lead to a blocked nose or sinuses, **do not fly.** It is important to remember that this advice applies equally to pressurised and unpressurised aircraft. Even in the cabin of a pressurised airliner, there is a significant reduction in pressure as the aircraft climbs to cruising altitude; remember that a typical cabin 'altitude' may be 7,000ft for a pressurised aircraft cruising at 40,000ft).

As well as being audio sensors, the ears also incorporate the balancing devices keeping us all upright most of the time. Within the inner ear there are two mechanisms that help the brain orientate itself – the *semicircular canals* and the *otoliths*, collectively known as the *vestibular apparatus*. The semicircular canals are three 'loops' filled with fluid. Within each canal are tiny hairs that sense movement

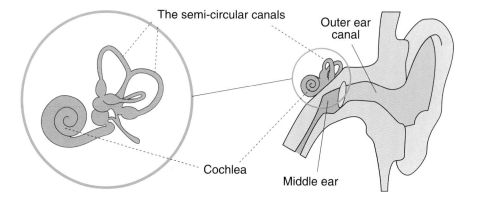

The semi-circular canals of the inner ear

of the fluid. If the head is rotated, inertia means that the hairs move relative to the fluid; their distortion produces impulses which are sensed by the brain and produce a sensation of rotation. Each loop is arranged to measure movement in one of the planes of movement – yaw, pitch and roll. The otoliths sense acceleration in the linear (fore and aft) axis and in the vertical (gravity) axis.

The vestibular apparatus is a biological marvel which has evolved over millions of years, whereas man has been capable of controlled flight for only around a century. This means that the signals the vestibular apparatus provide can sometimes be misleading or totally erroneous in an aviation context. There is no need to get airborne to prove the fallibility of the vestibular apparatus, however. Early on in life, most people will at some time have jumped off a rotating roundabout only to stagger across the playground, totally unable to walk in a straight line. This is simply because the balance signals from the vestibular apparatus have become totally confused. In an aircraft, the situation that can result from such conflicting signals is called *spatial disorientation*, and will be looked at in detail in a later chapter.

Because the signals from the inner ear can be so easily fooled, it is fortunate that the brain accepts input from a different set of organs which are far more sensitive than the ears and whose signals can 'override' conflicting information from other senses. Those organs are the eyes.

▶The Eyes

The eyes are the pilot's most important sensors, and the most sensitive and delicate. The outer covering of the front of the eyeball is the *cornea*, and this helps to focus light rays that then pass via the *pupil* to the *lens*. The lens further focuses the light

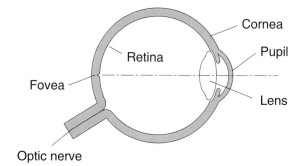

The main components of the eye

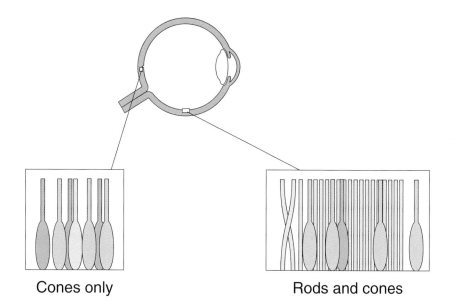

The cones are concentrated around the fovea

rays on to a point on the back of the eyeball (*retina*). The retina has two types of light-sensitive cells. These are *rods*, which are more sensitive in poor light conditions, but only give black and white vision; and *cones*, which work best in bright light and give colour vision. The central part of the retina on to which the lens focuses light rays is called the *fovea*, and the cones are concentrated at this central point. To see an object in the greatest detail, the eye must be moved so that the image falls upon the fovea (the ability of the eye to resolve detail is called *visual acuity*).

Moving away from the fovea there are progressively fewer cones and more rods. This part of the eye can resolve little detail in an object, but human 'peripheral' vision is good at detecting movement and the general position of other objects. Nerve fibres run from the rods and cones and combine to become the optic nerve which connects the eye to the brain. At the *optic disc*, where the nerve and vessels enter the retina, there are no rods or cones and so there is in effect a 'blind spot'. This is not normally noticeable because when both eyes are open, one will compensate for the blind spot of the other. To demonstrate the blind spot, cover your right eye and focus on the spot in the picture below. Move the page towards your face and at some point the aircraft on the left will disappear:

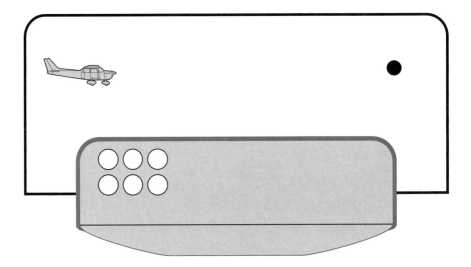

You probably don't normally fly around with one eye closed. However, if the field of vision of one eye is blocked – by a door pillar or strut, perhaps – an approaching aircraft appearing in a certain place might just fall on the blind spot of the unobstructed eye. Furthermore, you can only focus on objects when the eyes are stationary. So if you look-out by trying to move your eyes smoothly to cover a large area, you may miss a lot. Different lookout techniques are discussed in detail later, but consciously moving the eyes in a series of short movements, with a definite stop in-between, is a good method of lookout scan.

Door pillars and windscreen posts can block a large area of your lookout scan

The Functions of the Body (Basic Physiology)

The human optical system has to be able to cope with an enormous variety of lighting conditions and cover a wide range between exceptionally bright and totally dark. Very bright light can be harmful, especially at high altitude, because of the amount of damaging ultraviolet (UV) wavelengths. The best defence against UV is some sort of filtering, and sunglasses are the most popular devices for this. As with other safety equipment, the general advice is to buy the highest quality you can afford. Many (although surprisingly not all) good-quality sunglasses will have 100% UV protection and you should look for lenses made from optical-quality glass. The lenses should also be impact-resistant, and thinner frames reduce the amount of lookout area blocked to the eye. It used to be recommended that pilot's spectacles and sunglasses should have plastic lenses, but this has been rescinded because there is no evidence that plastic lenses reduce the risk of eye injury in an accident. Any spectacles used for flying should be familiar to the wearer, to avoid the alteration of sense of distance noticeable when wearing a new pair. The exact lens colour and characteristics are largely a matter of personal preference, differing lenses being capable of reducing glare in bright conditions or increasing contrast in dim and hazy situations. Photosensitive lenses are not recommended for flying because they are generally not able to react quickly enough to rapidly changing lighting conditions, for example flying from full sunlight into a cloud shadow. Some people consider that polarised lenses may not a good idea either because they tend to show up stress patterns in some transparent materials such as car windscreens. However, it is not clear whether this is a particular problem in aviation applications.

Quality sunglasses offer 100% UV protection

At the other end of the spectrum, very low-light conditions will make the resolution of objects quite difficult. To improve vision in dim light, the eye has two devices. The diameter of the pupil enlarges to let in more light (this can happen very quickly) and chemical changes in the retina adapt the rods and cones to lower lighting conditions (this takes several minutes). In all the eye can take up to 30 minutes to adapt fully to low-light conditions. So if at night you go straight from a brightly-lit room to an aircraft directly outside, you might be taking-off well before your eyes have fully adjusted to the dark conditions. Avoiding bright lighting conditions immediately before night flying is therefore a sensible precaution. Staying with night flying, anything that affects vision in general, such as hypoxia, will have a more marked effect at night. Even mild hypoxia, such as might be experienced below 10,000ft, can markedly reduce night vision. The cones, which are best at resolving detail and colour, dramatically lose effectiveness in dim light. As a result it is sometimes impossible to see a distant object such as a faint light at night by looking directly at it, because the light rays are focusing on the fovea and its concentration of cones. Instead, try looking about 10 degrees to the side of the object. It may now become visible because its light is falling on an area of the retina with more rods – which work better in poor light. Try this technique on a clear night for seeing faint stars; you may be impressed with the results. A final night-flying tip. If for any reason you have to use a bright light at night (to check a map detail or badly lit instrument) or the bright backlighting of most GPS displays, close one eye *before* turning on the light. This way at least some of your night vision will be preserved. Better still, stick to red lights in the cockpit. Colours at the red end of the spectrum have a lot less effect on retinal night vision than blues and greens, and a bright white light is bad news after dark. You do have a red filter for your night-flying torch, don't you…?

The ability of the eye to focus on both nearby and distant objects is called *accommodation*. The ability of the eye to accommodate varies from individual to individual. Some people are naturally short-sighted, meaning that their eyes cannot focus on distant objects. The medical fraternity calls this condition *myopia*. Those who are long-sighted have difficulty on focusing on nearby objects. Long-sightedness (*presbyopia*) commonly occurs with increasing age, especially beyond about 45 or so, and is often first noticed as difficulty in reading small print in poor light. Glasses can rectify both conditions but the problems of bifocal contact lenses have not been completely resolved. Full-lens reading glasses should not be used for flying, because constant changes from near to distant vision are a feature of piloting and distant vision will be blurred by reading lenses. Half-moon glasses, 'lookover' glasses or lenses with a neutral upper segment can be used, subject to medical advice. Glasses to correct both near and far vision (bifocals) are sometimes used by pilots, again subject to medical advice, but varifocal glasses are not normally advised for flying. Non-bifocal contact lenses may be used, subject to meeting certain requirements, although the pilot is required to carry a 'standby' pair of spectacles too (which incidentally is also a requirement if the pilot wears glasses for flying, in case of breakage or loss).

Surgical procedures are now available to correct curvature of the cornea and thereby reduce or eliminate the need for corrective spectacles, but you should contact an Aviation Medical Examiner (AME) before contemplating this procedure. The AME may well advise against surgery because of the interval between the operation and fitness to fly, the uncertainty of the result and the risk of blurred vision in poor light.

As a general rule, the vision standard required for aviators is the equivalent of being able to read a car number plate at 40m (23m is the UK driving-test requirement).

▶ 'G' Effects

The human body has evolved over hundreds of thousands of years of earth-bound existence, and the world of flight has opened up all sorts of conditions for which it is not ideally suited. One such condition is that of increased or decreased *g*. It is almost certain that as you read this, you will be experiencing the normal force of the earth's gravity – in other words 1*g*. This is also the force you would expect to experience in normal straight and level flight. If you now get airborne and set up a steep turn at 60 degrees of bank, you will feel an additional force; in relation to aerodynamics, this condition can be called a load factor of 2. In relation to the body, it would more often be called 2*g*. In a simple training aircraft, a positive flight load

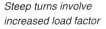

Steep turns involve increased load factor

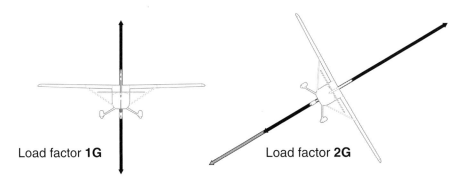

Load factor **1G**   Load factor **2G**

limit of 4 is common; an aircraft cleared for aerobatics might have an upper limit of 6. So even in a small aircraft you can experience forces of several *g* – for example in a steep turn or pulling out of a dive – without exceeding the limits of the airframe.

As positive *g* builds up, the most noticeable manifestation is that the head becomes heavy and the limbs more difficult to move. As *g* increases further the internal organs are displaced. However, the most serious effect of *g* is the change in blood circulation. Under increasing positive *g* the blood pressure in the brain will reduce, and blood will begin to pool in the lower body unable to return to the heart against the

From normal flight, pulling back on the control column increases positive 'g', and the pilot is forced down in the seat

increased *g*. The reduced flow of blood is first apparent as a loss of peripheral vision ("greying out") which can develop into marked 'tunnelling'. If *g* continues to increase, vision may be lost altogether. Ultimately, with the cessation of blood flow to the head, loss of consciousness may occur. This condition, known technically as 'G-Induced Loss of Consciousness' or G-LOC is of great concern to those such as aerobatic and fighter pilots whose daily flying activities subject them to high values of *g*.

Most healthy people will begin to experience greying-out at around 3 to 4*g*. As you will probably have induced this by pulling back on the control column, relaxing the back pressure is the quickest way to reduce *g* and so stop the greying-out. If you must pull extra *g*, the onset of its effects can be delayed a bit by tensing the stomach muscles. Tolerance to *g* can be built up over a period of time by constant exposure to large quantities of it; the average military fast-jet pilot can probably cope with 6 or 7*g* without too much trouble. However, anything that adversely effects your general state of health (alcohol, smoking, being ill or unfit) will rapidly reduce your *g* tolerance, as does hypoxia and excessive heat.

Most pilots find increased positive *g* quite tolerable, especially with increasing experience. By contrast, negative *g* is agreed by the majority of aviators to be quite unpleasant and even alarming, especially if it occurs unexpectedly. As negative *g* builds up, the sensation increases from merely being 'light' in your seat, being weightless and then being forced up against your safety belt/harness. *In extremis* you may even feel that you are being thrown out of the aircraft. Most people will have experienced negative *g* at some time, perhaps by driving too fast over a hump-backed bridge or being in a lift when it starts a sudden descent, usually accompanied by a collective "Oohhh!". Passengers who have flown through turbulent conditions may recollect a dropping sensation which left 'the heart in the mouth and rising stomach', and recall this experience far more vividly than a positive *g* event of equal force.

The sensations of negative *g* tend to be far more apparent to the pilot than other physical symptoms. Nevertheless it is worth noting that blood flows to the upper body in negative *g* conditions and blood pressure in the head increases. The face may become flushed and even painful, small blood vessels in the cheeks and eyes might burst and the lower eyelid can push up to cause a visual effect called 'red-out'. The heart rhythm is likely to be disturbed, and loss of consciousness is likely to occur at a much lower '*g*' value and after a much shorter duration than for positive *g*. In all, the effect is far more uncomfortable than positive *g*. The negative *g* limit for most aircraft is less than its positive flight load limit and negative *g* manoeuvres are often not permitted. By the same token, a pilot who may be able to endure 7 or even 8*g* before losing consciousness may be only able to tolerate a maximum of -3*g* and even then only for a very short period.

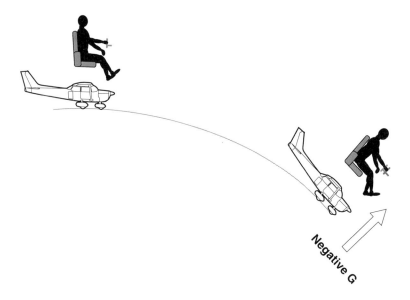

From normal flight, pushing forward on the control column increases negative 'g', and the pilot is forced up out of the seat

Negative *g* in flight is often associated with an outside loop or push-over (sometimes called a *bunt*). However, the sensation of negative *g* may first be experienced during the recovery from the stall in early training. Such an unexpected and perhaps unpleasant sensation may explain many pilot's aversion to stall training. This theme has been explored in detail by Derek Piggott, the highly experienced light-aircraft and glider pilot and well-known author of gliding textbooks. His work has established that negative *g* – or more accurately, pilots' reactions to negative *g* – may be a significant factor in gliding accidents. It appears that some individuals are particularly sensitive to negative *g* and react to the 'falling' sensation it causes by moving their head back and pushing their hands forward. This natural reaction to a fall becomes dangerous in an aeroplane when one of the hands is probably pushing the control column forward, pitching the aeroplane nose-down. That the same problem may be relevant to powered aircraft is not generally accepted at present, and it is true to say gliders generally have much lower stick forces than powered aircraft. So it is easier to 'push' negative *g*. Nevertheless, a dislike or aversion to stalling and stall practice can often be traced to a sensitivity to negative *g*, although tolerance can be built up over a period with the help of a perceptive instructor. Gentle stall entries, rather than pulling the control column hard back into the stomach and waiting for the fall from an extreme attitude, also help.

An aversion to negative *g* might also go some way to explaining the classic landing accident where an inexperienced pilot bounces on landing and then proceeds to make a number of further bounces (normally around three) directly on the nosewheel until it gives up and collapses. Imagine if after the first bounce the pilot pushes forward on the control column, either in fear of stalling or to pitch the

A series of bounces on landing, contacting the nosewheel each time, is almost certain to lead to the collapse of the nosewheel

aircraft to a level attitude. A hard push can lead to a 'bunt', and in extreme situations the 'falling' sensation of negative *g,* which is very uncomfortable for some people. Of course, pushing the control column forward pitches the aircraft nose-down and can bring the nosewheel into hard contact with the runway, forcing another (maybe bigger) bounce. The pilot reacts by pushing the control column forward again…and so on. The pilot's reactions can even become out of phase with the aircraft, leading him or her to push forward on the control column when the aircraft is already pitching nose-down. Moreover, the force of the bounce on the runway can even throw the pilot's hand/arm forward, applying a down-elevator input at precisely the wrong moment! All this can happen too quickly to digest, and it is not uncommon for the hapless aviator to be later unable to explain how or why he reacted as he did after the first bounce. That said, it is generally accepted that the correct reaction is to go around – but more of that later.

It could well be that a sensitive approach to early stall training, an awareness of the effects of the sensation of negative *g* and a willingness to learn from the experience of non-powered pilots could all reduce the number of broken nosewheels and embarrassed aviators featuring in the annual accident statistics.

▶Revision

Revision questions are found at the end of each chapter in this section of the book. Their aim is to enable you to test your knowledge of the chapter subject material, and to help you retain the essential elements of each subject.

Once you have read through a chapter a few times, and are satisfied that you understand the main points, attempt these questions without reference to the text. When finished, you can check your answers against those at the end of the 'Human Factors' section. You should aim for a 'success rate' of not less than 80%.

1 What is the approximate proportion of oxygen in the atmosphere at 15,000ft?

2 The levels within the body of which gas are primarily responsible for regulating breathing?

3 List at least six symptoms of hypoxia, starting with the earliest symptoms likely to occur.

4 What is the approximate time of useful consciousness at 35,000ft?

5 Name at least three factors (other than altitude) that will effect the severity and susceptibility to hypoxia.

6 Rapid over-breathing, possibly accompanied by some or all of the following symptoms: (dizziness, light-headed feelings and a sense of 'unreality'; tingling sensations; vision impairment; hot and cold feelings); could be symptoms of what condition if they occur at low altitude?

7 Fill in the blanks: "A condition caused by .... coming out of solution in the bloodstream at altitude is known as .... One method of avoiding this condition is not to fly within .....[time] of diving to more than 30ft/10m using compressed air."

8 The air cavity of the middle ear is connected to the nose and throat via what body part?

9 You are suffering from a heavy cold, which has led to a blocked nose and sinuses. Under what circumstances is it safe to fly?

10 In principle, how should the eyes be moved during a good lookout scan?

11 During a night flight, you notice that it is easiest to see a faint light when looking slightly to one side of it. Why is this?

12 Other than hypoxia, "greying-out" of the vision can be caused by what flight condition?

Answers at page HF115

Health and Flying

▶ **Diet and Health**

▶ **Heart Disease**

▶ **Alcohol and Drugs**

▶ **Incapacitation**

▶ **Common Ailments and Medication**

▶ **Toxic Hazards**

▶ **IMSAFE**

▶ **Revision**

▶ Diet and Health

It is generally acknowledged that major factors in the general state of human health are diet, lifestyle and weight. Being aviators, we should perhaps be referring to the last item as mass, but we'll stick with the more common usage for the moment.

As far as weight is concerned, the most common problem is that of being overweight or obese. Definitions of obesity vary but as a practical guide, an average person's ideal weight is probably the weight they achieved in their early 20s – at which stage the growth process is completed. For those of us who don't wish to think back that far, an alternative guideline is the 'Body Mass Index' (BMI). The formula for calculating it is:

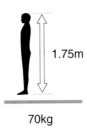

1.75m

70kg

$$\frac{70kg}{1.75m^2} = 22.80$$

The calculation of Body Mass Index (BMI)

BMI = weight (in kg) divided by height (in metres) squared.

For example, someone who weighs 70kg and is 1·75m tall would have a BMI of:

$$70/1\cdot75^2 = 22\cdot80$$

A BMI of about 25 is generally considered to be the upper limit of 'normal', with the risk of certain diseases, such as diabetes and high blood pressure, increasing rapidly once the BMI is in excess of 30.

If you do decide to lose some body mass, the bad news is that there seems to be no magic formula other than the most obvious course of action – eating less. The good news is that the other processes usually involved in losing weight, such as altering your diet and taking more exercise, have their own significant benefits.

Doctors, dieticians and TV advertisements regularly trumpet the importance of a healthy and balanced diet, although the ideal composition of such a diet appears to alter with alarming regularity. About the only indisputable fact appears to be that an excess of any one particular foodstuff is likely to have some unfortunate side-effects, but for more information you are directed to the overburdened bookshelves in the health and diet section of your local bookshop. Even better, avail yourself of some proper medical advice.

Regular exercise is not a very efficient means of losing weight on its own, but a combination of a restricted diet and walking one mile quickly each day will lead to greater weight loss than the diet alone. Where regular exercise is considered beneficial is in reducing the risk of heart disease, of which more in a moment. To be of benefit, the exercise has to raise the pulse to about double its resting level for at least 20 minutes, and such exercise should occur at least three times a week. The usual caveat applies in that if you are not accustomed to regular exercise, you should proceed with caution and preferably with the benefit of professional advice.

In terms of general health and fitness, most pilots fall somewhere between the extremes of the couch potato dedicated to a lifestyle of all-round health abuse and the fitness fanatic who runs up several mountains each day before consuming a vegan breakfast. There are capable aviators in both camps. That said, it is worth noting that certain medical hazards associated with aviation such as the effects of *g* present greater problems to those who are generally unfit or in poor health.

▶ Heart Disease

Heart disease is probably the most common cause of loss of a medical certificate. So, if you enjoy your flying (and life in general, for that matter) it pays to look after your heart.

The heart is the muscle responsible for pumping blood around the body. It needs its own blood supply to operate, which is furnished by the coronary arteries. Any hardening or narrowing of these will effect the action of the heart muscle (hence the term *coronary disease*). Narrowing or hardening of the coronary arteries can lead to pain in the chest or shoulders and neck during exercise or exertion, which subsides on resting. Such pain may be *angina*, and a precautionary visit to a doctor is essential. A sudden blockage of a coronary artery more often results in severe chest pain, collapse and even heart stoppage – the classic heart attack or *cardiac arrest.*

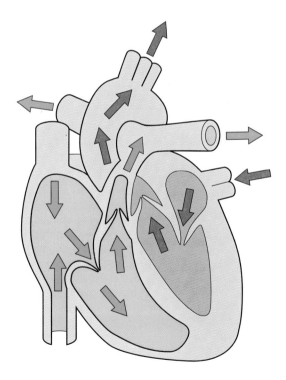

The heart is a muscle which pumps blood around the body

Major factors in assessing the risk of heart disease are age and family history, neither of which you can do very much about. Factors which probably can be addressed include high blood pressure, raised blood cholesterol, diabetes, obesity and a lack of exercise. Other items that can influence heart disease are stress, alcohol and drug use.

▶ Alcohol and Drugs

It remains a fairly safe assumption that if someone is talking about a drug used socially or recreationally (as opposed to medicinally, i.e. to cure an illness) the subject is some type of illicit substance – cannabis, cocaine, LSD, ecstasy and so on. The altered state of consciousness produced by drugs such as these is clearly incompatible with being around aeroplanes in any way, shape or form. However, it is now widely accepted that an extensive variety of substances, some of which are in daily use, can also have effects on thought processes and perceptions or reduce reaction times and co-ordination. Candidates in this context include tobacco and caffeine. However, probably the greatest danger in this respect comes from the oldest socially acceptable drug of all – alcohol.

When you consume alcohol, it is absorbed into the bloodstream and quickly carried to the brain. It makes itself evident here by affecting the higher thought processes. Rather like hypoxia, alcohol initially has an adverse effect on mechanisms such as behaviour and mood. A feeling of well-being and increased confidence is common, and risk-taking behaviour increases. As Shakespeare wrote in *Macbeth* "...it provokes the desire but it takes away the performance". The Bard wasn't referring to flying, but the principle is the same. And all this occurs even at a level of consumption that many consider quite moderate – two units of alcohol, i.e. the equivalent of one pint of beer, two glasses of wine or two measures of a spirit.

Skill errors approximately double after consumption of just two units of alcohol – that is a pint of beer, two (standard) glasses of wine or two small measures of a spirit

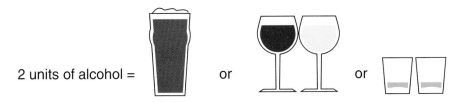

2 units of alcohol =   or   or

Even with this very modest intake, studies have shown that the likelihood of having an accident increase sharply. In an experiment using a Cessna 172, pilots were asked to fly an instrument approach after consuming various amounts of alcohol. They were accompanied by a sober safety pilot who noted their errors. At the equivalent of two units of alcohol, errors approximately doubled in comparison with the performance of the same pilot when sober. By the time the equivalent of eight units of alcohol was reached, errors had increased six-fold. In fact, during the experimental flights at this level of alcohol consumption, the safety pilot had to take over control on half the approaches flown!

Skill errors increase rapidly with increasing alcohol consumption

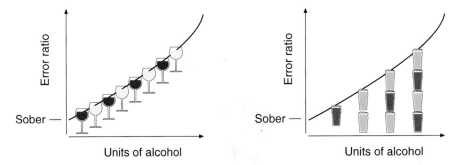

Health and Flying

The message that flying and drinking do not mix is well understood within the aviation community. In the UK, the traditional guideline regarding alcohol consumption and flying is "eight hours bottle to throttle". In other words, allow at least eight hours between last drinking alcohol and getting into an aeroplane. In some other countries the recommended time interval is 12 hours. The problem is that after drinking larger amounts of alcohol, even these time limits can be quite inadequate. At the time of writing, the law in respect of alcohol and flying states only that a person must not act as flight crew if they are under the influence of alcohol or a drug "...to such an extent as to impair his capacity so to act." There is a proposed change to the legislation that would introduce a requirement for a blood/alcohol test to be taken from a pilot following an accident or incident, or if there was reasonable cause. The maximum 'acceptable' alcohol level in a pilot's blood is expected to be 20mg/100ml (a blood/alcohol concentration of 0.02%). This compares with the present UK driving limit of 80mg/100ml (0.08%).

The rate at which alcohol is absorbed by the body will vary according to the type of the alcoholic drink and whether any food eaten at the same time. By contrast, the rate at which alcohol leaves the body seems to be solely related to time, because 90% of alcohol disposal is processed by the liver, which works at a constant rate. There is no evidence that anything else (black coffee, exercise, etc.) will speed up the process. The best advice that can be offered is in the form of a very approximate guide to the time it takes for alcohol to leave the body. After commencing drinking it is assumed that no alcohol leaves the body for the first hour, it then leaves at the rate of one unit of alcohol per hour. As discussed above, one unit is the equivalent of half a pint of beer, a standard (small) glass of wine or a single measure of a spirit.

Let's look at an example. A pilot begins drinking at 2100 and consumes six pints of beer (or 12 small glasses of wine or 12 measures of spirit) by 0100. At this time he stops drinking, having consumed 12 units of alcohol. When will his body be free of it?

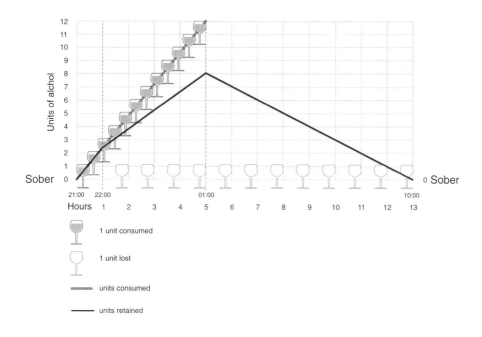

If drinking starts at 2100, alcohol starts to leave the body one hour later at 2200. Twelve units of alcohol will take 12 hours to leave. So theoretically the pilot's body is not free of alcohol until 1000 the next morning. In practice, most non-teetotallers will know from hard-won experience to avoid mixing certain drinks, and that some types of alcohol give them longer-lasting effects than others. The emphasis is very much on the individual to treat the guidelines above as an absolute minimum, and increase the time interval between drinking and flying as necessary to reflect his or her own experience. It is worth noting that it has never been proved that any of the favoured 'hangover cures', such as a cold shower, actually works. As a recent article about flying and alcohol noted, if you have a hangover a cold shower is only likely to result in a cold wet pilot with a hangover. And flying whilst in possession of a hangover can be as dangerous as flying immediately after consuming alcohol.

As well as the direct effect of alcohol on a pilot's performance, excessive drinking can have longer-term health implications even if the pilot is not actually dependent on alcohol. Once again, the guidelines are only very approximate but they state that the safe limits for regular drinking are in the region of 14-21 units per week for a woman and 21-28 units per week for a man.

As was stated earlier, the use of illicit drugs is not remotely compatible with aviation. This is not a social judgment but a simple medical fact. Quite apart from their effects on the mental processes, illicit drugs may contain all sorts of impurities and additional substances that make their use particularly dangerous to general health. Moreover, a single encounter with even a so-called 'soft' drug can produce life-long side effects that will preclude holding a pilot's licence. And even a single dose of an illicit drug can be fatal, thus permanently ruling-out any flying ambitions.

The dangers of illicit drug taking were emphasised by a fatal accident investigation which found the presence of cannabis and amphetamine in the accident pilot's body, probably taken within 24 hours of the accident. The pathology report noted that "...*pilot performance can be impaired for as long as 24 hours after smoking a moderate dose of marijuana and the user may be unaware of the drug's effects. Marijuana impairs those mental activities requiring conscious thought such as retention of information and reasoning. Flying an aircraft under difficult conditions is a task which is limited by the memory's capacity to process and respond to the information. The introduction of a drug such as marijuana, that impairs or disrupts this capacity reduces the pilot's performance. The effect of low to moderate social doses of marijuana may produce significant impairment for as long as 24 hours and the effects are more profound when difficult tasks are attempted.*

Amphetamine is a central nervous system stimulant and leads to insomnia, restlessness, irritability and excitability, nervousness, euphoria and sometimes dizziness. Amphetamines have many other effects but these are the most important central nervous system effects. It is unlikely that the presence of amphetamines would impair the pilot's ability to fly the aircraft properly. However, the euphoria that is sometimes induced by the amphetamines may have been such to make him over-confident in a difficult situation."

Tobacco is a drug which is becoming less and less socially acceptable as time passes. If you are a hardened smoker, you may be relieved to know that this book will not attempt to catalogue all the serious diseases and health hazards associated with the smoking habit. However, you should know that there's a lot of them, and that some aviation situations are particularly relevant to smokers. Oxygen is transported around the body by haemoglobin within the blood. Unfortunately, haemoglobin has a much greater affinity for carbon monoxide than it does for oxygen, and carbon monoxide is found in tobacco smoke. Hence the haemoglobin within a smoker's bloodstream tends to contain more CO than that of a non-smoker, meaning that a smoker can absorb much less oxygen than a non-smoker. The practical outcome is that a smoker's body is, in effect, operating as if it is at a higher altitude. At sea level, even a moderate smoker may be experiencing a physiological altitude of around 6-7000ft. For a heavy smoker, the figure may be nearer 10-12,000ft. This has obvious implications for that person's tolerance to higher altitudes and susceptibility to hypoxia. Smokers should also consider the effects that their habit can have on non-smokers in the vicinity. A non-smoker can find exhaled tobacco smoke quite distracting and even nauseating. More seriously, the 'side-stream' smoke (the smoke that arises directly from the cigarette or cigar without being inhaled) contains a much higher concentration of the various toxins that are found in exhaled tobacco smoke. So it can be much more damaging to the health of the 'passive' smoker.

Smoking is prohibited during refuelling, when oxygen is in use and generally when a 'No Smoking' notice is displayed

There are a few aviation situations where smoking is banned. Refuelling operations are perhaps the obvious case, although smoking is also forbidden when oxygen is in use and often generally within hangars and on the apron. A 'No Smoking' sign in an aircraft, or a no-smoking instruction by an aircraft commander, has the force of law. Many light aircraft have a permanently affixed 'No Smoking' notice. This is often done not just for the benefit of non-smoking pilots and passengers using the same aircraft, but because many of the materials found in light aircraft – especially the seat materials of older aeroplanes – are flammable and give off highly toxic fumes once burning.

Caffeine is a prime ingredient in tea and coffee, and general aviation is an activity in which the amount of coffee consumed is second only to the amount of AVGAS. It is unfortunate then that caffeine is considered to have certain harmful effects on users when taken in excess. Caffeine has certain beneficial side effects up to a point. It is a stimulant capable of increasing alertness and also acting as an anti-depressant. However, large doses can lead to insomnia, fatigue, anxiety, depression and increased reaction times. There are also questions as to the long-term health risks of excessive caffeine consumption. So once again, the scientists have managed to find hazards in what many of us considered a relatively harmless social activity! The good news is that as common sense dictates, moderation is the key.

The amount of caffeine found in an average cup of various common drinks is:

Coffee*	100mg
Tea	75mg
Cola	60mg

*the amount of caffeine in coffee can vary widely, from 60mg in instant coffee to 140mg in 'dripped' filter coffee.

Tea? Coffee? Or maybe something with less caffeine, for a change...

The general rule is that an 'average' safe consumption limit is around 400mg per 24 hours. If you find you're regularly consuming more than this, you should perhaps be thinking about moderating your intake. Otherwise there is no doubt that in moderation a caffeine drink can be a useful 'perk up' at times. The only additional word of caution is that, as you might have noticed, GA aircraft are not usually endowed with onboard toilets and caffeine consumption will increase your desire for one. This is worth remembering, especially before setting off on a long flight. Few things are more distracting *en-route* than an ever more urgent need to empty your bladder with no opportunity to do so…

▶ Incapacitation

Total incapacitation of a pilot whilst in flight is an exceptionally rare event. It might occur under certain circumstances already discussed (hypoxia and the effect of *g*) but the commonest cause of in-flight pilot incapacitation is gastroenteritis. Gastroenteritis is a general term for an infection of the stomach or intestines, which can cause acute abdominal pain, nausea, vomiting and diarrhoea. 'Food poisoning' is a general term including infections and toxins produced by bacteria in food (those old *Airport* films got that one right). Although total incapacitation through gastroenteritis is happily rare, it is a serious condition in the context of flying an aircraft and certainly renders the sufferer unfit to act as a pilot. In the airline world the captain and first officer eat different meals to reduce the risk from food poisoning. For single-pilot operations, a simple precaution is to avoid unaccustomed or 'risky' foods ahead of a flight.

Other possible causes of in-flight incapacitation include heart problems, alcohol withdrawal and kidney problems.

▶ Common Ailments and Medication

Before looking in detail into illnesses, medication, and how these might affect your ability to act as a pilot, there is a simple adage to keep in mind. This is "If you're ill enough to need medication, you're probably too ill to fly." This statement is rather sweeping and might not apply in all cases. But from the safety point of view it has a lot to recommend it, especially if you require medication in the form of antibiotics.

Two common illnesses have already been mentioned. A cold or flu can cause congestion within the sinuses and Eustachian tubes. That is reason in itself to stay on the ground because of the risk of barotrauma, caused by the differential between the external pressure and the pressure inside the middle ear or sinus cavities. If you think that you might avoid this problem simply by not flying very high, it is worth remembering that the greatest change in pressure with altitude takes place in the *lowest* levels of the atmosphere. Climbing from 1000ft to 2000ft will cause a much greater pressure change than climbing from 11,000ft to 12,000ft. Those who have been unfortunate enough to suffer barotrauma whilst airborne, can attest to the intense pain it can cause, especially in the sinuses. Incidentally, you will not get around the problem by flying in a pressurised aircraft. The cabin pressure of a pressurised aircraft *does* reduce as the aircraft climbs. It's just that it doesn't reduce as much as the outside pressure. You may remember from an earlier chapter that an airliner at high altitude (say 40,000ft) may have a cabin pressure equivalent to about 7000ft, leaving the cold or flu sufferer liable to the same effects as someone flying at this height in an unpressurised aircraft. As well as the risk of barotrauma, most people will recognise the lethargy and difficulty in concentrating that often accompanies a cold or flu. This is another good reason for staying earthbound. Medication to treat a cold, sickness, allergy or hayfever often takes the form of an *anti-histamine*. A disadvantage of this class of drugs is that they can cause drowsiness – not something associated with safe flying. By the same token, drugs to control bowel spasms caused by gastroenteritis can themselves cause blurred vision.

A very common over-the-counter medication (i.e. available without a prescription) is *paracetamol*, often used to counter fairly minor aches and pains. But even though this is such a well-known and apparently benign substance, caution must be advised. In a fairly recent incident, an airline pilot used a painkiller that was not the type he usually took. Unfortunately it caused some side effects which to all intents and purposes incapacitated him. Even more unfortunately, he was a member of the crew of a transatlantic flight at the time. The story has a happy ending insofar as the other pilot successfully landed the airliner single-handed (as airline pilots are trained to do), and the afflicted aviator made a full recovery. Nevertheless, the moral for a general-aviation pilot flying 'single-crew' is obvious.

In a different context, it is recommended that if you have been subject to a local anaesthetic, you should not fly within 24 hours. Please note that contrary to the conventional wisdom (as habitually propounded at the bar of many a flying club), this stricture *does* apply to a dental anaesthetic. A minimum interval of 48 hours is recommended after a procedure involving general anaesthetic. The anaesthetist should be asked to advise how long should elapse before flying – bearing in mind that an operation in itself will usually be a bar to flying until the medical department of the authority has approved re-certification, usually on the recommendation of the surgeon. It is also recommended that pilots should not fly within 24 hours of donating blood or plasma, and indeed the RAF does not permit its aircrew to fly until no less than seven days after giving blood. If donating bone marrow (which involves general anaesthetic) pilots should allow at least 48 hours before next flying. On a different note the American FAA have recommended that pilots should not fly within six hours of using Viagra, apparently because of possible visual disturbances…

You should not fly within 24 hours of receiving a local anaesthetic

All this leads to the straightforward suggestion that before mixing medication and flying, you should take appropriate medical advice. Ask your Authorised Medical Examiner (AME) for his opinion before getting airborne.

A dangerous condition that can affect the health is that of an abnormally high or low level of blood sugar. The initial symptoms of low blood sugar (known as *hypoglycaemia*) are those of a general malaise, sleepiness and difficulty in concentrating. Ultimately the sufferer may become confused and even lose consciousness. The problem is that the condition first affects judgment and the ability to make decisions. If the sufferer is then subjected to stress, anxiety or physical exercise, the severity of the symptoms can increase rapidly. There are processes to maintain a proper blood sugar level in a healthy person, but in a diabetic these processes are impaired and the condition is controlled by diet or medication.

Although a non-diabetic should not technically experience hypoglycaemia, a long and very busy day with no proper meal breaks, a disrupted and late-running flying schedule or even just pre-flight nerves could all lead you to skip a meal or two. This is an unwise decision, as hunger (the physical need for food) and appetite (the desire for food) can be incredibly distracting. You should find time to eat *something*, even if it's only a sandwich or a chocolate bar. A cup of coffee is no substitute for adequate food. Hunger and fatigue often seem to go together and there is no doubt that this can be a dangerous combination, likely to adversely affect a pilot's ability to deal with a problem when placed under stress.

The subject of fatigue is covered in some detail in material aimed at professional pilots, largely on the assumption that it is they who will be flying long sectors and crossing many time zones on a regular basis (the latter in particular leading directly to the well-known problems associated with 'jet lag'). Indeed, the confidential reporting system used by professional pilots to report problematic situations rarely fails to include at least one hair-raising account of errors caused by excessive fatigue on the flight deck. Primary culprits are heavy workloads coupled with night flights, unsympathetic scheduling of flights by the airline, long working days and irregular resting patterns. All are exacerbated by the effect of crossing and re-crossing time zones on a daily basis.

You might initially think that such factors are irrelevant to a private pilot, but this is far from the case. Long days, working at unsociable hours and irregular resting patterns are not confined to pilots; ask anybody with young children! Jet lag certainly affects pilots of long-range aircraft. It also affects their passengers, some of whom might have been working much longer hours. In other words, individuals can suffer fatigue from events quite unrelated to piloting an aircraft. They will then be just as much at risk from the effects of fatigue if they step into an aircraft with the intention of going flying.

Most of us have no difficulty in recognising the effects of fatigue and tiredness. We also probably have some appreciation of their adverse effects on reaction times, decision-making and judgment. However, one of the important differences between those who fly for a living and those who fly for pleasure is that the private pilot can easily decide not to fly at a particular time or on a particular day. If you feel you are fatigued or tired, this is a privilege you should not hesitate to exercise. After all, you can always fly another day.

Apart from the question of fatigue, flying at unsociable hours of the day (such as late night or early morning) can have other implications even if you are adequately rested. The internal temperature of the body varies through the day around a mean of about 37°C. A daily fluctuation of this kind is known as a *circadian rhythm*. In terms of body temperature, the minimum occurs at around 0400 or 0500 in the morning and the maximum at about 1700 in the afternoon. Many people will find that the small hours of the morning are the time when they are most likely to fall asleep. Certain other functions such as reaction times and performance of manual tasks also tend to follow a rhythm similar to that of body temperature. Other rhythms, such as those for mental reasoning, also tend to peak in late afternoon and then decline sharply to an early-hours low. There is considerable variation between individuals, but most people have some feeling for their own daily rhythms and describe themselves as 'morning' or 'afternoon' persons, 'night owls' and so on. Whatever your particular pattern, its daily peaks and troughs should be considered if you are planning a particularly challenging flight.

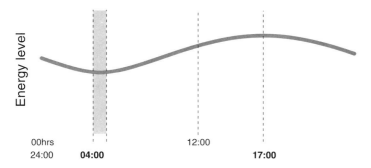

The 'average' circadian rhythm

Long-duration sorties are not the sole preserve of professional pilots. Many touring aircraft have a full-tanks endurance stretching into six or seven hours. Whether you want to stay airborne for this length of time is another question. The task of hand-flying a light aircraft as a single pilot for such a period is not something to be undertaken lightly. Unless you are practised in long-duration flights, a realistic maximum for one flight is around three to four hours, with a suitable break before getting airborne again. Apart from fatigue and general comfort considerations, most people will find their own flight endurance limited to about four hours by their bladder capacity!

Although pregnancy is not an illness in itself, as a condition it does have implications for someone acting as a pilot. Any pilot who believes that she is pregnant must inform the authority (which is the CAA in the UK) in writing, as soon as possible. As a general rule a medical certificate will be revoked for the first three months of a pregnancy, but may be re-instated for the 'middle' three months. However, this is a general guide only, and guidance from the authority must be sought.

If you suffer an injury likely to prevent you from acting as a pilot, you must also inform the authority in writing as soon as possible. If you suffer an illness preventing you from acting as a pilot for a period of 21 days or more, you must also inform the authority in writing as soon as 21 days of illness have passed. In all cases the authority will then decide what action to take, but you should consider that your medical has been suspended from the date of injury or confirmation of pregnancy, or the 21st day of illness. It is important to follow these rules because medical expertise may be necessary to understand the full implications of a particular injury or illness or medical condition in terms of flying. This principle also applies to any other circumstances which leave you in any doubt as to your fitness to fly. The problem of post-traumatic stress in the aftermath of an accident, disaster or life-threatening event is well known. It is perhaps less well appreciated that the effects may not manifest themselves until some time after the event and can include flashbacks, reduced confidence and sleep problems. Clearly a person suffering such problems is not in a good position to make safe piloting decisions.

Because there can be a long time interval between medicals, there is a heavy responsibility on the pilot to monitor his own health and seek medical advice where appropriate. In the flying context, doctors are especially concerned about injuries to the head – no matter how minor – and any episodes of fainting, fits and so on. Your AME is not just somebody who examines you for a medical every so often, but also an expert available to be consulted just as you might consult a flying instructor about a technical point involved in flying an aircraft, or an engineer regarding a serviceability issue.

►Toxic Hazards

Numerous substances found in and around aircraft present toxic hazards. The best-publicised toxic threat is that of carbon monoxide (CO) poisoning. Carbon monoxide is a by-product of combustion: it is a colourless and odourless gas which is lethal even in very low concentration. If carbon monoxide is breathed in, it quickly attaches to the haemoglobin within the blood (you might remember that haemoglobin has a much greater affinity for CO than it does for oxygen) and poisons the brain by reducing the oxygen reaching it. As the concentration increases, symptoms of CO poisoning include headaches, dizziness and nausea. These are often accompanied by poor judgment, impaired vision and difficulty in mental reasoning. Ultimately carbon monoxide poisoning can lead to a bright pink skin colour, loss of muscular co-ordination, unconsciousness and death.

As we have seen before with other medical hazards, one of the principal dangers of CO poisoning is that at the initial stage it affects the higher brain functions such as judgment. Hence it can lead to an accident caused by poor decision-making by the pilot, the consequences of which could be more serious than the level of poisoning itself. In one episode several years ago, a number of witnesses saw an aircraft on a dual training flight make a very poor approach, landing well short of the runway. The aircraft reached the parking spot, where the instructor and student disembarked. The instructor then watched apparently unconcerned as the student staggered across the apron and fell over whilst trying to get into his car. Help was fortunately at hand and both made a full recovery, although they remembered little of the incident. In a more recent CO poisoning event, a pilot described the final stages of a flight in which he was sure that he was dreaming, such was the sense of unreality. Nevertheless he managed to make a go-around when the first approach went wrong and just about landed safely from the second approach. Happily the pilot made a full recovery in due course.

As already stated, carbon monoxide is a by-product of the combustion process. The most likely way for aviators to experience its effects at first-hand is if exhaust gases from the engine enter the cockpit – as might happen if the heater system has a crack or hole. Although CO itself is colourless and odourless, other exhaust gases can certainly be seen and smelt and you should take this as a warning sign.

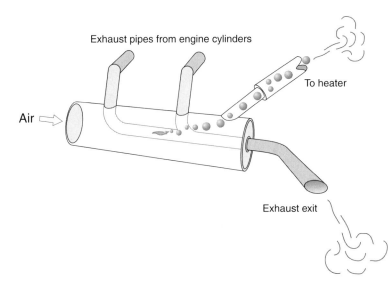

A leak in an exhaust pipe can lead to exhaust fumes, containing CO, entering the cockpit when the heater is in use

Exhaust pipes from engine cylinders

To heater

Air

Exhaust exit

To guard against the possibility of carbon monoxide poisoning, the exhaust and cabin heater system should be carefully maintained and checked at regular intervals. It is also possible to buy a CO detector, the most common type being a light-coloured disc mounted on a plastic backing. This is placed within the cockpit and darkens in colour if exposed to carbon monoxide. These detectors are a simple and inexpensive form of insurance against CO poisoning, but they do not last indefinitely – indeed, some operators replace them every thirty days. The detector itself should state its useful life, and there is usually a place for marking the date when it was put in place.

A common CO detector. If the central spot turns dark, CO is present

Although a short exposure to significant amounts of carbon monoxide is enough for symptoms to occur, the effect is cumulative. So a repeated exposure to small amounts of CO over a number of days or weeks can be just as dangerous as one encounter with a high CO concentration.

Whenever using the cabin heater, some air from the fresh-air vents should be mixed in too. This will help in reducing a potential CO concentration. Also, as winter is logically the time when the cabin heater will be used the most, this is the time to be especially vigilant for warning signs. If carbon monoxide poisoning is suspected at any time, you should shut off the heater system and vents immediately and close any possible path for exhaust fumes to enter the cockpit. For this reason alone, carrying spare clothing in case of a heater malfunction is always wise in winter and when flying at high altitude. Open the fresh-air vents and, if possible, open the windows too. Anything that will ventilate the cabin with fresh air and reduce the concentration of CO is vital at this stage. If oxygen is available on board, use it. You should land at the earliest available opportunity, and have the aircraft (and yourself and any passengers) properly examined. If you have been exposed to exhaust gases in the cockpit, it may be several days before you are fit to fly. So seek proper medical advice before flying again, even if the mechanical problem is sorted out.

Although CO poisoning is the best-publicised toxic hazard in aviation, there are several other less well-known dangers. Aviation fuels such as AVGAS (and AVTUR, if you're that sort of aviator) give off fumes which are not particularly pleasant, as do de-icing fluids. Perhaps more seriously, a spillage of aviation fuel on to bare skin can cause damage to the skin and should be washed off as quickly as possible. Some of the furnishing and materials used inside the aircraft cabin give off lethal gases if they burn, and indeed these can present a much greater hazard to the occupants than the flames themselves. Unfortunately, the gases given off by some older fire extinguishers are themselves a hazard if used in a confined space. This is discussed in more detail later. The pilot must also be aware of toxic hazards that might be loaded on-board the aircraft as baggage or cargo. Possible toxic substances are acids (such as in lead-acid batteries), corrosive liquids, compressed-gas containers, radioactive materials and disabling devices such as Mace and CS gas.

These compressed-gas containers, and the battery, present serious toxic hazards in an aircraft

▶**IMSAFE**

By now, you will appreciate that your own health and physical condition is a major factor in flight safety. There is a lot to think about and, added to the other pre-flight duties such as flight planning and other associated paperwork, you might feel that by the time you have pondered all the possible medical considerations there won't be any time left to go flying!

To keep things simple, a short mnemonic to check through at some time before you reach the aircraft is in order. The most common such checklist is 'I'm safe':

I **Illness**. Am I suffering from an illness, or do I have any appreciable symptoms?

M **Medication**. Am I taking any medication? If so, what are the side effects?

S **Stress**. Am I under particular pressure or undue stress?*

A **Alcohol**. Have I had any alcohol within the last eight hours (remember, eight hours bottle to throttle)? For a significant amount of alcohol, will it have left my system by now? Do I have a hangover?

F **Fatigue**. Am I well rested?

E **Eating**. Have I had adequate nourishment before starting this flight?

*The subject of stress is looked at in more detail shortly.

The simple 'I'm Safe' mantra should be enough to highlight the majority of potential aeromedical problems that occasionally afflict pilots. If you cannot be certain of a safe response to any of the 'I'm Safe' points, *do not fly*. It really is as simple as that.

In this respect you can draw comfort from the well-known flyer's motto which perhaps should be printed in large type on every pilot's licence:

"It's better to be down here wishing you were up there, than to be up there wishing you were down here!"

▶Revision

13 One unit of alcohol is the equivalent of what measure of beer, wine and spirits?

14 What is considered to be the 'safe' limit, in terms of units of alcohol per week, for men and women?

15 A pilot begins drinking at 2200, and consumes fourteen units of alcohol until 0200 when he stops drinking. In theory, by what time will all the alcohol have been eliminated from the blood?

16 To which gas does haemoglobin have the greater affinity, oxygen or carbon monoxide (CO)?

17 Which pilot will have a lower altitude 'threshold' for the onset of hypoxia, a regular smoker or a non-smoker?

18 What is the most common cause of in-flight incapacitation?

19 What are the recommended minimum times between the following and being considered safe to fly:
A   receiving a local anaesthetic;
B   receiving a general anaesthetic;
C   donating blood or plasma.

20 You suffer an injury that will prevent you from flying. Do you need to inform anybody and if so by what means?

21 If you suspect that exhaust gases are entering the cockpit in flight, and you are feeling drowsy, how should you act and why?

Answers at page HF115

The Functions of the Mind
(Basic Psychology)

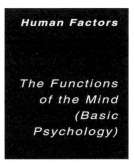

▶ **Human Information Processing**

▶ **Memory**

▶ **Perceptions, Central Decision-Making, Motor Skills**

▶ **Spatial Disorientation and Visual Illusions**

▶ **Lookout**

▶ **Behaviour: Skill-based, Rule-based and
   Knowledge-based**

▶ **Situational Awareness, Confirmation Bias**

▶ **Revision**

Human Factors

▶ Human Information Processing

The human body is armed with an impressive array of sensor devices to detect what is going on in the world around it. Sights, sounds, smells, touch, taste, sense of balance and position sense, in skin, muscles and joints all contribute to each individual's understanding of his or her surroundings and situation. However, as a whole all of these stimuli can be overwhelming, confusing and even contradictory. The portion of the human being we usually refer to rather loosely as the *mind* has to find a way of filtering these stimuli and organising them into a recognisable pattern. It can then compare them with past experience and expectations, make a decision about how to react to them and then monitor the results.

It is worth knowing something about this process if only because it can highlight the factors underlying some common human shortcomings and perhaps highlight areas where there is the greatest potential for error. However, the subject is enormous and in some ways still rather poorly understood; ideally it would have a book to itself.

It is convenient to compare the process outlined above to a process in a simple machine such as a computer, but it can be seriously misleading to push the comparison too far. However, it is reasonable to think in terms of a flow of information in and resultant actions out:

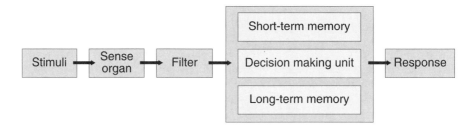

When a stimulus is received at the brain, it is *stored* for a very short period (about one second for a sight, about five seconds for a sound). This store gives us the ability to 'replay' a stimulus, such as a fragment of conversation, when you realise only after a few seconds that someone is speaking to you.

Once sensed, the stimulus is then *filtered*. Most people will be familiar with the phenomenon of *selective attention*. For example, if you are concentrating very hard on a book, a TV programme or a piece of work, you might well lose track of other things happening around you. Somebody might call your name quite loudly and yet apparently you do not hear them because that stimulus is not directly relevant to the task in hand. After filtering the incoming stimulus, it is then *perceived*. Perception is an organisation of the incoming data and an interpretation of it. The perception process, and thus the way in which decisions are made, is heavily influenced by our experience of the world and how we expect it to be. A good example of perception in the aviation world is the use of the radio. To the student pilot, an incoming radio message might sound like a stream of nonsense even though he or she is fluent in the language being used. To the instructor, however, the very same message makes perfect sense. His experience gives him the ability to *interpret* the message, and his anticipation of what he expects to hear at that time allows him to *comprehend* the meaning of the message and make a rapid response. One message, two perceptions. Experience comes from our memory, so we now need to consider that part of the information process

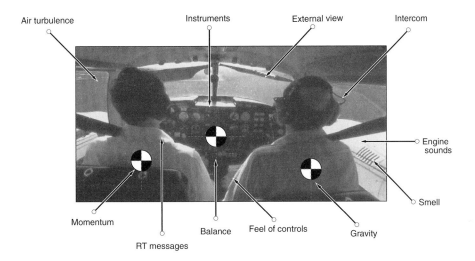

Air turbulence

Instruments

External view

Intercom

Engine sounds

Smell

Momentum

Balance

Feel of controls

Gravity

RT messages

The pilot has to filter and interpret a mass of incoming stimuli all the time

▶ Memory

For our purposes there are two types of memory – long-term and short-term. Short-term memory is used to hold information for a short period. For example if somebody gives you a telephone number, you can retain it for a short time until you find a pen and paper to write it down. If you have taken in a piece of information, it will remain available for recall from your short-term memory for around 15 seconds. To keep this information for a longer period, you will need to repeat it to yourself, a process known as *rehearsal*. The more often a piece of information in short-term memory is rehearsed, the longer it will be retained.

The number of unrelated items capable of retention in short-term memory is limited to about seven, and this number of items will only be retained if full attention is devoted to rehearsing the items. Once the limit is exceeded, items will soon be confused or pass beyond recall. One way to increase the number of items that can be retained is *chunking* of the information. For example, look at this group of 11 numbers:

0 1 6 2 5 9 4 8 3 7 2

Now look away from the page. Can you recite the numbers in sequence? Probably not.

However, if this was a French telephone number, it might appear as:

01 62 59 48 37 2

Look away and try again. Any better? That should be easier already. If it was a UK telephone number, it might be reduced to:

01625 948 372

Thus a set of 11 numbers has now been chunked into three pieces of information. Together with the three rehearsals above, this means that the information now stands a much better chance of being retained.

Another example of chunking, which is very relevant to aviation, is the *checklist*. For example, most pilots of general-aviation aircraft use cruise checks which include the following items:

Altimeter, Radio, Fuel, Direction, Engine.

Taking the first letter of each item makes the information more manageable:

A R F D E

However, a subtle re-arrangement of the letters comes up with a name:

FREDA – or "Freda".

Now we just have a single 'chunk' of information to recall, which is associated with the items needing to be checked.

One can achieve the same end by arranging the initials of the checks into an order forming the initials of a memorable sentence. The result is called a *mnemonic*. For example, pilots of the Chipmunk will probably have had the pre-landing checks of Mixture, Fuel, Flaps, Harness, Hood, Brakes drummed into their memory. The standard way of remembering these is 'My Friend Fred Has Hairy B***s', which you probably didn't want to know. However, it's a time-honoured example of the mnemonic technique at work, and there are many other examples – which all seem to be equally crude.

Despite these tricks and aids, short-term memory is a very volatile and rather unreliable information store. A string of unrelated information coming in – airfield joining instructions, for example – can easily exceed the nominal limit of seven items. What's more, if you are doing something other than simply listening to the radio (like flying the aircraft) these items are highly unlikely to be recalled successfully. There is one simple solution; write it down!

Nothing could be simpler. The act of writing down (and reading back) the information acts as rehearsal, and so helps retention. More importantly, if there is any subsequent doubt, there is a physical record of the information which does not need constant rehearsal and will be available for as long as the written record is in view of the pilot. Many pilots develop a form of 'short-hand' to quickly jot down incoming information and instructions. There is nothing complicated about this. Take the following message:

"G-AB, cleared to the airfield VFR, not above 2500ft on the QNH of 1025. Runway in use 24 left hand, QFE 1019".

The short-term memory is not prefect, so write it down!

DISTRESS 121.50			TRANSPONDER DISTRESS 7700 COM FAIL 7600 CONSPICUITY 7000
STATION	SVC	FREQ.	CLEARANCE/OBSERVATIONS
MCR	GND	121.70	**VFR 2500 1025 24LH 1019**
MCR	TWR	118.625	
MCR	APP	119.40	
SHAWBURY	LARS	120.775	
COSFORD	TWR	122.10	
H GREEN	AFIS	123.00	
GLOSTER	ATIS	127.475	
GLOSTER	APP	125.65	
GLOSTER	TWR	122.90	
BRIZE	LARS	134.30	

A pilot might write this as VFR 2500 1025 24LH 1019. Now there is written confirmation of the data, and again the chunking of information makes a big difference to how easily it can be interpreted and recalled.

Long-term memory holds our store of knowledge, and recollection of specific past events. Knowledge stored in long-term memory is generally considered to be there for good, although whether or not it can be recalled at will is another matter. It is generally accepted that information becomes more difficult to recall if it is rarely rehearsed. This is why it is necessary to practice some procedures regularly – airborne emergencies, for example – to be able to recall the correct information without difficulty if you ever really need it.

Our recollections of specific events do not remain untainted but can be influenced by what we think *should* have happened, or even what we would have *liked* to happen. This makes recall of certain events – especially traumatic ones such as accidents – extremely prone to error. Any accident investigator will tell you that eye-witness accounts of the same event often vary greatly. The eye-witnesses are not being deliberately unhelpful; they are just describing the event as they remember it. This phenomenon is not unique to so-called unqualified observers. An 'expert' witness may well have an erroneous recall of events simply because he or she has a much greater expectation of what should have happened.

Recall of past events is useful to a pilot, which is why such emphasis is placed on experience in the form of hours flown. Such experience is also far better developed as a result of first-hand encounters with reality than anything else. For example, you might carefully read a book chapter about the importance of good lookout and fully agree with the author's conclusions. However, should you ever have a 'near-miss' (or *airprox* as the authorities like to call it), the memory of the event is likely to remain considerably more vivid than any amount of written words, and will probably have much more long-term effect on your lookout technique.

▶ Perceptions, Central Decision-Making, Motor Skills

The subject of perception has already been briefly touched upon. We draw conclusions about incoming information based on how we perceive it. This process is unique to each individual, and two individuals may draw entirely different conclusions and take different decisions on the basis of the same incoming information. Imagine a soldier and a car mechanic walking together alongside a road. A passing car backfires loudly. The soldier immediately drops to the ground, convinced that the noise is a gun being fired. The car mechanic calmly analyses the sound and forms an opinion as to what is wrong with the car.

For our purposes, the perceived incoming data flows into the central decision-maker along a single channel. The significance of this is that no matter what we might think, we can only make one decision at a time. If a number of pieces of data arrive simultaneously at the decision-making machinery, only one can be dealt with straight away. The others will go into short-term memory, awaiting recall when the decision department is ready to take them. Of course, if the data stays in the short-term memory without being rehearsed for too long, it will be lost – or in human terms forgotten. If a person is faced with a lot of incoming data, there is a strong temptation to concentrate on one piece of information and ignore the others. Moreover, once a conclusion has been drawn about a piece of incoming information and a decision made, it can be very difficult to recognise that the initial conclusion was wrong and correct it. In other words, humans have a strong inbuilt predisposition to be *irrational*.

An everyday example of this occurs in visual navigation. Let's assume we are flying from A to B and see a town ahead. Based on the expectation of what it should be, we decide "That is Newtown". Once that decision is made, even direct evidence to the contrary – such as a railway line where no railway line should be, the distinct absence of what should be a large lake to port and so on – might well be ignored or discarded. It will then require a complete re-think of the situation to reach the correct conclusion, and make a decision accordingly.

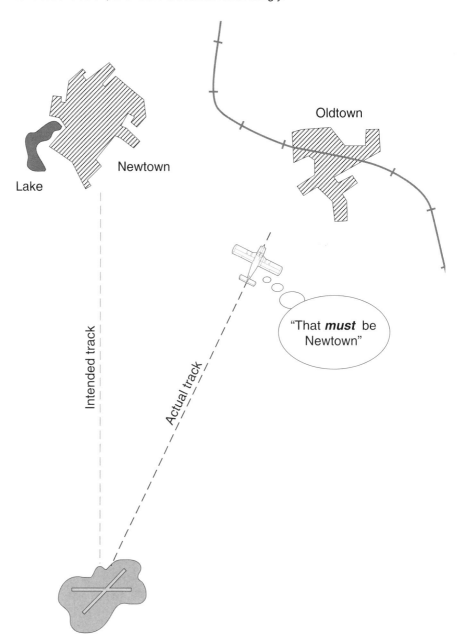

Seeing what you expect (or want) to see is more common than most pilots like to admit!

Along with this regrettable human tendency to avoid accepting what's staring you in the face, there is also a natural inclination to want to believe good news and disregard bad news. For example, if you are 'weathered in' and waiting to make a flight home, you might collect a number of weather reports and forecasts. Unless you are very careful, your own desire for flyable weather can lead you to seize on any good news you find (such as a single favourable weather report) and actively ignore bad news (such as all the other reports, which are unfavourable). It takes a certain amount of will-power to make an impartial and detached decision; it is much easier to use data selectively to back up the outcome you desire. This concept is explored in more detail shortly.

Although we have said that only one decision can be made at a time, we might often feel able to do more than one thing simultaneously. This might be the case if you change gear in a car and talk on a mobile phone at the same time, or type instructions into a computer whilst having an unrelated conversation. This can be accomplished because of the ability to develop *motor skills*, also sometimes known as *motor memory*. Motor skills allow us to carry out an action with minimal use of the central decision-maker. Let's take the example of changing gear in a car. When a learner driver first tries to do this, almost all the available concentration is likely to be required. With practice, however, the task becomes easier and requires less attention. And changing gear ultimately becomes a virtually automatic action requiring no real attention at all. In other words, it becomes a function of what an analytic psychologist would call the *unconscious*.

In terms of flying an aeroplane, motor skills are essential if a pilot is to 'juggle' the many decisions and actions that need to be taken in the course of a flight. Although use of motor skills allows attention to be directed to other things, they embody a trap into which it is remarkably easy to fall. Operating controls and switches often vary even between individual aircraft of the same type. So you might believe that you have just applied carburettor heat to 'hot' whereas in fact you have selected mixture to fully lean. If the action is not monitored at a conscious level, heart-stopping moments may ensue! In a similar way, car manufacturers seem to be unable to decide on whether the indicator controls should be on the left or the right of the steering column. The result will be familiar to anybody who regularly drives more than one type of car. Either the windscreen washers start operating as you change lane or you get a windscreen full of screen wash instead of a flash of the headlights.

*The training aircraft on the left has 'plunger' type throttle and mixture controls, with the carburettor heat control to the **left** of the throttle. The training aircraft on the right has a 'quadrant' type throttle and mixture control, with the carburettor heat control to the **right** of the throttle, beyond the mixture control*

Going back to the example of changing gear in a car, your motor skills can catch you out here too. If you have been used to a right-hand drive car, the first time you encounter a left-hand drive model can be an interesting experience! You will find yourself having to monitor your actions consciously and very carefully to make sure that you don't try to change gear with the wrong hand, for example. Something similar happens if you decide to become an instructor and have to learn to fly from the right-hand seat; it can take a while to get used to the new situation. The point is that even if an action can take place without conscious effort, it should be monitored to ensure that it is appropriate. This is never more vital than when you are operating in unfamiliar surroundings – flying a new aircraft type being an excellent example.

▶ Spatial Disorientation and Visual Illusions

As we've already seen, the brain is continually coping with a mass of incoming information which it sorts into a picture of the world and what is happening. Problems can arise when this incoming data becomes contradictory, or the wrong conclusions are drawn from it. There are several situations in flying which can lead to visual illusions or disorientation, and being aware of these and how they arise is the surest defence against falling victim to them.

A general description of any false perception of the aircraft's attitude is *spatial disorientation*. Pilots sometimes refer to flying "by the seat of their pants" – in other words by sense of balance rather than by relying on the instruments. The incoming information comes from the vestibular apparatus of the inner ear and sensors distributed throughout the body which sense the force of gravity.

If an aircraft is flying straight and level at a constant speed, the force of gravity acts straight down. However, if the aircraft accelerates, there is now an additional force, *inertia*, which is sensed by the otoliths in the inner ear. The resultant of these two

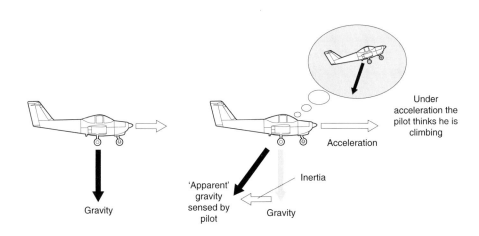

When an aircraft accelerates, the pilot senses a false 'pitch-up'

Gravity

'Apparent' gravity sensed by pilot

Inertia

Acceleration

Gravity

Under acceleration the pilot thinks he is climbing

forces can make the pilot feel that the aircraft has pitched up when in fact it is still flying level. The instinctive reaction is to pitch nose-down. This only increases the acceleration and the sensation of a pitch up, leading the pilot to pitch further nose-down and so on. In the same way, a deceleration can lead to the sensation of pitching down, leading to a reaction of pitching nose-up. So the airspeed decays further, leading to the temptation to pitch more nose-up. Clearly there is the danger of a stall in this scenario.

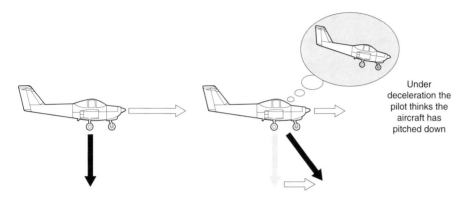

Under deceleration the pilot thinks the aircraft has pitched down

When an aircraft decelerates, the pilot senses a false 'pitch-down'

Changes in roll can also be confusing. If a turn is entered gently enough, it will not be sensed by the semi-circular canals in the inner ear. In a properly balanced turn, the resultant of the gravity and centrifugal force still acts through the aircraft's (and the pilot's) vertical axis. As far as the aviator is concerned, he is still sitting vertically. If the pilot realises that the aircraft is in a turn, he will roll out of it quickly enough for the semi-circular canals to sense the change in attitude. Having assumed that they were level before, they will now assume that the aircraft is turning even though it has come back to level flight. This sensation is sometimes called the *leans,* and it can afflict the multi-thousand hour pilot with the same regularity and frequency as the novice.

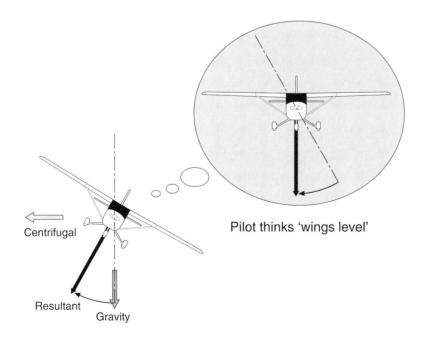

Pilot thinks 'wings level'

Centrifugal

Resultant

Gravity

In a properly balanced turn, there is no sensation of bank; the pilot senses that the aircraft is 'wings level'

Spatial disorientation is unlikely to occur in good visual flying conditions because the pilot has overwhelming evidence derived from his eyes to confirm the 'real' attitude. This visual input overwhelms the more subtle information coming from the balance and gravity sensors, However, if a good visual reference is not available, the danger of disorientation is very real. The classic situation for spatial disorientation to occur is when a pilot without proper instrument-flying qualifications attempts to fly in IMC (i.e. in cloud or in conditions of very poor visibility). If the pilot is unable to interpret the instruments properly, or trust the information they are giving, loss of control of the aircraft is almost inevitable. In a study carried out some years ago it was found that, on average, non-instrument qualified pilots lost control of an aircraft in IMC in around three minutes. Food for thought…

Apart from non-instrument qualified pilots attempting to fly by instruments, other dangerous situations – even for experienced pilots – are the transition from VMC to IMC flight; trying to fly visually when the conditions are actually IMC; night flying; and attempting to fly on instruments when not in current instrument-flying practice. Spatial disorientation is responsible for a number of accidents each year. Two general pieces of advice to avoid this dangerous situation are:

■ Keep out of cloud and poor weather unless you are properly trained and current in instrument flying

■ When flying on instruments, trust the information they give you and don't give way to conflicting physical sensations.

Even in good visual conditions, *visual illusions* are possible. Visual illusions are mostly caused because the brain has a strong expectation of what something **should** be, or **should** look like. Look at the picture below. The aircraft is above a cloud bank, and is apparently flying wings-level.

Now look at the fuller picture. Because the cloud bank is sloping (by no means a rare phenomenon) the aircraft is actually banked; the pilot will no doubt be wondering why the aircraft keeps wandering off heading! Similarly, if an aircraft is flying low over sloping terrain and the distant horizon is not in view, the aircraft may

be banked when thought to be level. Another visual illusion happens when a single stationary light is viewed against a dark background. After a while the light will appear to move; if you focus on it, the apparent movement becomes greater. This is known as an *autokinetic* illusion.

The most common (and dangerous) visual illusions relating to flying are associated with the approach. During a visual approach, most pilots rely heavily on the appearance of the runway to judge the approach angle, especially if the approach is over water or featureless terrain. In the diagram below, each aircraft is at the same height at the same distance from the threshold in all three cases. On approach to the down-sloping runway the aircraft appears to the pilot to be low. Approaching the up-sloping runway, the aircraft appears to the pilot to be high. This may well result in too shallow an approach. Additionally, an upsloping runway will appear to be longer than it really is whilst a downsloping runway will appear to be shorter.

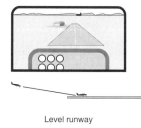

Level runway

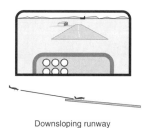

Downsloping runway

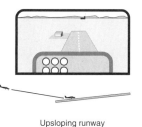

Upsloping runway

The slope of a runway will affect the pilot's judgment of approach slope and runway length. In all three diagrams the runway is the same length and the aircraft is at the same range and height

Human Factors

Equally, the shape of the runway can alter the pilot's perspective. In the diagram below, the pilot on approach to the wide runway might believe that he is too low. The pilot on approach to the narrow runway might believe that he is too high. In much the same way, a runway (or other object) that is smaller than expected will be perceived as being further away than it actually is and *vice versa*.

The shape of a runway will affect the pilot's judgment of approach slope. In all three diagrams the runway is the same length and the aircraft is at the same range and height

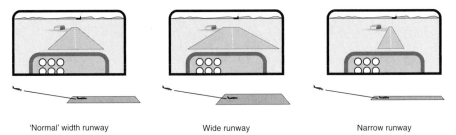

'Normal' width runway   Wide runway   Narrow runway

Judgment of the approach will be aided by taking in all the visual cues available. The touchdown point can be anticipated because it is the one point which remains at a constant angle to the horizon. This is one reason why the *approach perspective* is taught to students. If the touchdown point at which the pilot is aiming moves up towards the horizon, the aircraft is undershooting. If it moves down from the horizon, the aircraft is overshooting. As the aiming point is approached, other objects around it should appear to move away. If this does not happen, the aircraft is not going to touch down where the pilot wants it to. For example, if an obstruction on the approach moves up to obscure the desired aiming point, it is highly likely that the obstruction will be hit by the aircraft before reaching the aiming point.

When approaching at a constant angle, the aiming point will stay the same distance below the horizon and surrounding objects will appear to move away as the aiming point is approached

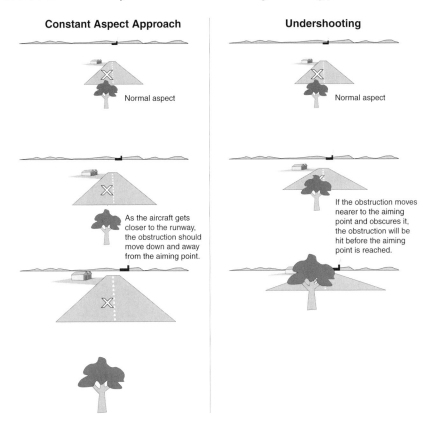

Constant Aspect Approach

Normal aspect

As the aircraft gets closer to the runway, the obstruction should move down and away from the aiming point.

Undershooting

Normal aspect

If the obstruction moves nearer to the aiming point and obscures it, the obstruction will be hit before the aiming point is reached.

There are two other 'landing' illusions worth noting. If a night approach is being flown to a runway with dark and featureless surrounds, there is a strong tendency for the approach to be flown too low and shallow. The aircraft may even fly into the ground some distance short of the runway threshold, and serious accidents have occurred as a result of this illusion. Rain on the windscreen will also affect judgment of height above the ground, especially in the final part of the approach. It is impossible to predict exactly how depth perception will be affected, but as a general rule the ground will appear to be further away than it really is (in other words the pilot will think that the aircraft is higher than it is in reality). This illusion is believed to have been responsible for more than one heavy landing by airliners.

Another (and extremely common) visual illusion which can catch out the unwary occurs when flying in hazy conditions. Objects at the limit of visible detection, perhaps partly clouded by haze, will appear further away than they really are. In other words you are closer to them than you think. So mountains or obstructions can apparently suddenly loom up out of the haze when you thought at first glance that they were a safe distance away.

It is not possible to list all the visual illusions that may occur in flight, and rather pointless trying to memorise them. It is more important to be aware that visual illusions can easily occur, especially in certain situations, and to recognise the importance of taking information from as many sources as possible rather than fixating on one visual cue.

▶Lookout

All flying textbooks, all flying instructors and all examiners stress the importance of good lookout. And we all like to think we have eyes like hawks and see everything else in the sky as a matter of course. In reality all of us miss many aircraft that we might otherwise have seen, either as a result of a poor lookout technique or because we were looking in the wrong place. Some of the factors reducing the effectiveness of lookout, such as the limitations of the eye itself and obstructions such as posts and struts which reduce the field of vision from the cockpit itself, have already been discussed, but there are others factors also worth a thought.

In the course of a flight you might well see other aircraft moving across your field of vision. As a general rule, an aircraft that moves relative to yourself is one that you are not going to hit (although that's not to say that it won't come close enough to give both of you a fright). An aircraft that does *not* move across your field of vision is much more dangerous. Such an aircraft is likely to be on a collision course with yourself. As the old adage puts it, *constant bearing = constant danger*.

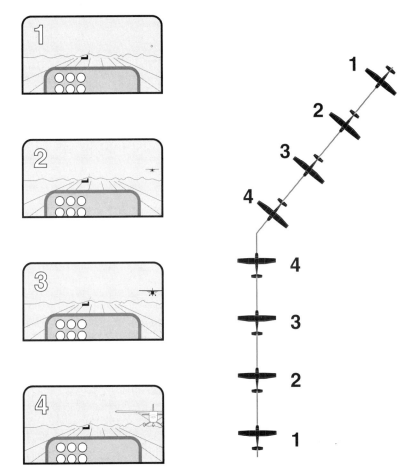

Try to spot the object that doesn't move across the windscreen: constant bearing = constant danger

The problem is that an aircraft remaining in a constant place on your field of vision is much less likely to be spotted, because there is no relative movement to give it away. Instead it grows in size, slowly at first and then much faster – in fact with frightening rapidity, as the closing distance reduces to a dangerously small figure. It is not always appreciated how little time may be available to spot an aircraft approaching head-on. Remember that at 60kts an aircraft covers one nautical mile in one minute. So if a microlight is flying in one direction at 60kts and a military fast jet is coming the other way at 420kts, the closing speed is 480kts – which is 8 x 60. In other words the aircraft are closing at eight miles per minute (or a mile every seven and a half seconds or so). So if these two aircraft spot each other at range of two miles they have just 15 seconds to avoid a collision. Furthermore, given the obstacles to clear vision in many aircraft – door frames, struts, canopy arches and so on – the occasional near-miss isn't perhaps too surprising.

To spot other aerial traffic, it is necessary to search an area around the aircraft. When the eyes move, they do not do so smoothly, but in a series of jerks (*saccades*). The eyes can only pick up information when they are at rest, so trying to smoothly scan over a wide area is no use. Instead you need to move the eyes with defined rests to look at a distant object such as a cloud or the horizon. Pausing on the 'hours of the clock' is one technique. Equally, left to its own devices the human eye tends to focus only a metre or two ahead, which is not the sort of distance at which you want to spot an oncoming aircraft! Focussing on the wingtip before starting the lookout scan helps, as does making a distinct effort to focus on a distant object during the 'rests' in the lookout scan. In the diagrams below, two possible techniques are summarised.

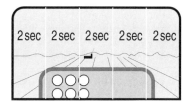

Block method

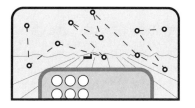

Wandering method

Two possible scanning techniques, with a regular 'rest' allowing the eyes to focus on a distant object

The UK Airprox Board publish regular summaries of their investigations of reported near-misses (airproxes). These reports tend to form a pattern. Outside controlled airspace, airproxes – if that's the proper plural – are normally caused by 'late sighting of traffic'. In other words, one or more of the pilots was not looking out very well. Conflicts between powered aircraft and gliders are normally caused by the powered aircraft flying into an area marked on charts as a gliding launch site. Whilst not illegal, such action is rather foolhardy – especially when you remember that gliders being 'winch-launched' may carry their cables to heights in excess of 2000ft! These cables are quite capable of downing an aircraft. Similarly flying through known parachuting, hang-gliding, parascending and microlighting areas is not very helpful to anyone.

These freefallers could ruin the day of a pilot passing overhead the airfield below them (above right of centre)

Many incidents within controlled airspace are caused by aircraft that were not meant to be there. The most commonly used phrase in describing the cause of an airprox in controlled airspace is, " Unauthorised penetration of the [controlled airspace] by the [aircraft type] pilot". Incidents close to an airfield are usually caused by one of the pilots being in the wrong place, or engaging in some dubious flying practice. In these cases the assessment of cause often carries the words, "Incorrect joining procedure by the [aircraft type] pilot", or "Unauthorised penetration of the [airfield] ATZ by the [aircraft type] pilot", or even "Failure of the [aircraft type] pilot to integrate safely into the existing circuit pattern". Airproxes also occur when aircraft fly through notified danger areas, especially when they do not make use of a crossing or information service.

If we're being brutally honest, we have to admit that all of the above stem from a basic lack of airmanship. Whether not looking out properly, getting lost, flying through hazardous areas which are marked on charts or not joining a circuit properly, at the end of the day there's really no-one responsible for this but the pilot. And whilst addressing these issues might stop you endangering somebody else, stopping yourself becoming the victim of somebody else's error really needs a high standard of lookout. As the airprox reports show, being inside controlled airspace and/or receiving a radar service is emphatically *not* a cast-iron guarantee against a fright from another aircraft. Likewise, even if you join the circuit properly and stick to the rules of the air, another pilot might not.

The importance of a proper lookout scan has already been stressed. In addition, there are certain other situations when an extra lookout check should be made. These should be practised until they become almost automatic – a motor skill if you like:

- Visually search a runway and its approaches both ways before entering or crossing a runway (even if you believe it to be inactive)

- Check under the nose periodically when climbing. Look in the direction of an intended turn before turning. Check beneath before descending.

- Be especially vigilant around airfields, VRPs, low-level corridors, radionavigation beacons or other 'bottlenecks'.

- Check the extended centreline before you turn on to finals, to ensure that you are not cutting ahead of somebody already established.

The importance of a good lookout really cannot be over-emphasised. If you practice your lookout scan, regularly review your lookout technique and practice basic good airmanship, you vastly improve your chances of avoiding fifteen minutes of fame as the star of an airprox or accident report.

▶ Behaviour: Skill-based, Rule-based and Knowledge-based

Broadly speaking, and again acknowledging that we're only scratching the surface of the subject, human behaviour can be divided into three basic types: skill-based, rule-based and knowledge-based. Each has its own implications for the business of piloting an aircraft.

Skill-based behaviour consists of actions which have been learnt as *motor skills*. In other words you learn that to achieve a certain result, certain actions are required. For example, when learning to fly you will learn that moving the flap control switch down lowers the flaps. You will also learn that doing this may tend to cause the aircraft to pitch nose-up and the airspeed to reduce. As a result, a new nose attitude will be needed, together with the necessary re-trimming, if level flight is to be maintained.

At first, mastering these things will require a certain amount of conscious mental application. With practice, the skill is learnt so that it can be applied without conscious thought. Skill-based behaviour is required if a pilot is to integrate the other facets of flying an aircraft (engine management, navigation, forward planning, radio communication and so on) without constantly having to suspend the thought processes to attend to a relatively simple operation.

This type of behaviour is extremely useful, but can catch out the unwary when a skill learnt in one situation is inappropriate for a different one. Taking the above example, let's assume our pilot goes on to fly an aircraft that pitches nose-down when flap is lowered. In these circumstances, trimming nose-down – as our pilot was accustomed to doing originally – is now inappropriate, and the skill will have to be re-learnt to avoid a dangerous situation. Even when the new skill has been learnt, however, a lapse on the part of the pilot – such as being overloaded with other tasks, being in a hurry, being tired, complacent or pre-occupied with non-flying thoughts – could lead to the wrong skill being used. Accident and incident reports frequently turn up the consequences of errors in skill-based behaviour. Thorough training and the conscious monitoring of skill-based actions are the best safeguards against this pitfall.

Another related skill-based glitch is the tendency of humans under stress to revert to the behaviour learned initially. So even if our man has flown several hundred hours on the aircraft which pitches nose-down when the flaps are lowered, he's quite likely to revert to trimming nose-up on the approach when it's a rainy night with a strong crosswind, the fuel state isn't all it might be and the oil temperature is a shade high. Aviation psychologists call this *retroactive interference.*

Over the years, *rule-based* behaviour has made a major contribution to flight safety. An example might be a procedure laid down for flying visual circuits. Instead of the pilot arriving at the airfield and then simply heading straight for the nearest into-wind runway, a known pattern, with defined procedures and manoeuvres is followed. These are practised in training, defined in aviation publications and the standard 'Rules of the Air' are followed to resolve possible conflicts. By observing these procedures, a pilot makes his own life easier by following a pattern with which he is familiar. And when several aircraft are in the circuit, safety is vastly enhanced because each pilot can reasonably predict what other pilots are going to do.

Approach airfield at 2,000 feet
above airfield elevation

Join the circuit,
maintain good
lookout

*Rule-based behaviour, in
this case a standard
overhead join and circuit*

Observe signals square
and windsock.
Lookout for other aircraft.
Maintain height until on
'deadside'

Existing circuit
pattern

Pass over the 'upwind'
end of the runway,
level at circuit height

Make a descending
turn (in the circuit
direction) to circuit
height on the deadside

Professional flying is largely governed by rule-based behaviour. For example, all commercial flights are subject to strict rules regarding minimum fuel reserves. As a result it is (almost) unheard-of for a commercial aircraft to run out of fuel. In the UK, private flights are not covered by the same strict rules. Arguably this is part of the reason why accidents caused by private aircraft running out of fuel are depressingly common.

IFR flight contains many examples of the importance of rule-based behaviour. It is mandatory for such flights that a minimum *en route* altitude is observed. In essence, the aircraft must be at least 1000ft above any obstacle within five miles

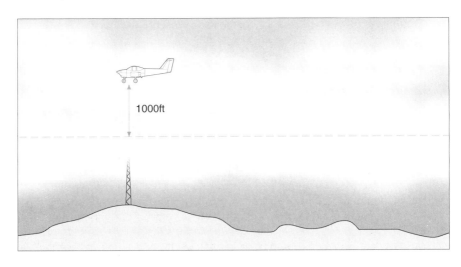

*Rule-based behaviour;
minimum heights for IFR
flight*

1000ft

either side of track. If a pilot fails to adhere to this rule-based behaviour ("If I just go a bit lower, I'm sure I'll see the ground"), safety is compromised and risk is vastly and unnecessarily increased.

Rule-based behaviour is also used to deal with emergencies. For example, to deal with an engine fire, a defined set of actions is set down. The pilot practices these and revises them until they are committed to the long-term memory. Periodically they are reviewed and practised, to ensure that they are available for recall. For reasons discussed above, the periodic review of rule-based behaviour is essential if a pilot is to be competent to deal with both the everyday and the 'once-in-a-lifetime' eventualities connected with piloting an aircraft.

Knowledge-based behaviour occurs when a pilot uses knowledge stored in the long-term memory to assess a situation and make decisions based on that assessment. This knowledge can have been acquired through the learning process ("I remember reading a book that said...") or by direct personal experience ("The last time this happened, the result was..."). The aviation world puts great emphasis on knowledge in all its forms, chiefly because our store of knowledge has a major influence on decision-making and therefore our judgment. It is generally perceived that a pilot with a large store of knowledge is in a much better position to make safe decisions than one with a lesser knowledge. As we mentioned earlier, this is why some importance is placed upon a pilot's licence, ratings and flying hours.

A pilot who has a modicum of appreciation of the interaction of skill-based, rule-based and knowledge-based behaviour is in a good position to improve the safety of his or her own flying. Take the example of a conversion from a fixed-undercarriage aircraft to a retractable one. Our aviator learns the **skill** of raising the flaps after landing using the flap lever. However, **knowledge** tells him that it is possible to raise the undercarriage by mistake, and that such an incident happens several times every year to unwary pilots. So he develops a **rule**, for example "I will not raise the flaps until clear of the runway after landing, and I will check that I am holding the correct control before operating it". This pilot is far less likely to join the ranks of those who have rounded off a perfectly good landing by raising the undercarriage instead of the flaps.

▶ Situational Awareness, Confirmation Bias

Situational awareness is a concept known to many in aviation but its definition is somewhat elusive. It is not the sort of phrase that turns up in any aviation dictionary or glossary; it is more a concept, a goal for a good pilot to aim for. To say that a pilot has good situational awareness is to say that he or she knows what is going on both in the aircraft and around it, and thus can make safe and accurate decisions and exercise good judgment based on all available information.

The words "all available information" perhaps sum up the art of developing good situational awareness. At any one time the pilot is at the heart of an incoming mass of material. This includes the aircraft's flight path, performance and general state of health based on the instruments and gauges in front of him; what he can see (or not) out of the window; navigational data from instruments, the view outside and its relationship to the map; ATC instructions and other pilot's messages on the radio; rules of the air and laid-down procedures; weather reports and forecasts, and so on. All of this information has to be processed to allow the pilot to build up a picture of what is going on at that instant and – just as importantly – what is likely to happen in the next few moments, minutes and hours. As a general rule, pilots do not like surprises. Good situational awareness allows the pilot not only to make decisions about what occurs and is likely to occur, but also to prepare alternative plans in the event that something different happens.

Let's take a hypothetical example of someone inbound to a destination airfield where the weather is close to limits for landing. A pilot *without* situational awareness will plough on regardless, **hoping** that the weather will be good enough to land, trusting that **luck** will be on his side. A pilot *with* good situational awareness may continue, but will prepare an alternative. He will **assess** the weather trend and check the weather reports; is it getting better or worse? He will **consider** his alternatives if the weather is too bad to land; will he hold or divert? Where can he divert to and what is the weather like there? Is the remaining fuel sufficient for the hold or diversion?

Even when you have arrived at a conclusion or decision, it is important to keep assessing incoming information to see whether it confirms your mental picture of the situation. Insofar as the limitations of the human psyche allow, your assessment must be rational and objective. Having decided on a course of action, or come to a conclusion about a situation, it is frighteningly easy to disregard anything that conflicts with that view. So a pilot who convinces himself that he is at point A may simply ignore massive evidence to the contrary. This state of affairs can continue for some time, usually until overwhelming evidence brings him to the conclusion that either he is actually at point B or he doesn't know exactly where he is. This situation will be familiar to most people who have practised visual navigation. "All available information"; we are back at that phrase again. If it can be difficult to pin down exactly how good situational awareness makes a flight safer, it is quite easy to show how poor situational awareness makes a flight less safe.

One evening in late December 1972, a Tri-Star airliner was approaching Miami International airport to land. It was flown by a highly experienced crew of three; the captain alone had around 30,000hr of flying experience. When the undercarriage lever was lowered, no green light appeared for the nose wheel. The crew decided to go-around and orbit at 2000ft over the Everglades whilst they investigated the problem. It is clear that the crew became engrossed in trying to sort out the problem with the nose wheel, to the exclusion of much else. At some stage, somebody accidentally disengaged the autopilot and none of the crew noticed that the aircraft had begun to descend. Thus it was that a perfectly serviceable aircraft, being flown by a highly experienced crew, crashed into the Everglades. Out of a total of 176 on board, 160 were killed or seriously injured.

What can happen when pilots lose situational awareness

Six years later, almost to the day, the crew of a DC-8 also failed to get green lights for the undercarriage as they neared their destination. Again they orbited near the airfield whilst they looked into the problem. It appears that the captain convinced himself that the undercarriage was not safe, despite the fact that indicators on top of the wings showed the gear to be down. Whilst they orbited for nearly an hour, the other two crew members made oblique references to the fuel state. These were not taken up by the captain, who remained fixated on the landing-gear problem and preparations for an emergency landing. As the crew prepared to make an approach, the fuel finally began to run out. The captain was taken by surprise:

First Officer	"We're going to lose an engine!"
Captain	"Why?"
First Officer	"We're losing an engine!"
Captain	"Why?"
First Officer	"Fuel!"

Even as the crew headed for the airport, with the imminent risk of losing the other three engines, the captain's mind was still on the undercarriage:

Captain	"Reset that circuit breaker momentarily. See if we get green lights."

The other engines failed as they ran out of fuel a few minutes later and the DC-8 crashed six miles from the airport. Miraculously, 179 of the 189 people on board survived. As with the Tri-Star six years earlier, there never was anything wrong with the landing gear. In each case the problem was a burnt-out indicator light bulb in the cockpit.

These accidents are perhaps extreme examples of what happens when pilots lose situational awareness, and indeed they are standard case-studies for those interested in human factors and flight safety. The second case, involving the DC-8, also highlights the danger of what is known as *confirmation bias*. The captain was convinced that the main undercarriage was unsafe, because there were no green lights. He had made up his mind about this. And yet the flight engineer had reported that the wing-top indicators showed the gear to be down and locked. Somehow, the captain disregarded this information; he just *knew* there was an undercarriage problem, and no information to the contrary could change his mind. Confirmation bias holds very real dangers in the aviation environment. Once we have formed a general model of the world, of our particular environment and situation, contradictory information will tend to be ignored or misinterpreted. We are only interested in information that confirms what we already believe. The desire to stand by a decision or conclusion, even in the face of evidence to the contrary, is very strong in all of us, and never more so than in an emergency or when we are under pressure. And yet, it is at these times above all others that the pilot must strive to maintain situational awareness, by being open to all the information he can manage and by periodically re-assessing the actual situation against his own mental model.

▶Revision

22 On average, what is the maximum number of unrelated items that can be retained in short-term memory?

23 How can a pilot help to ensure that information can be recalled from long-term memory?

24 What is the general term for a false perception of the aircraft's attitude?

25 When in level flight in poor visibility, the aircraft accelerates. How might a pilot interpret this acceleration and how should he react?

26 A pilot is approaching a runway that is wider than he is used to. In the absence of other references, how might he perceive his height on the approach to this runway?

27 A pilot is flying a night visual approach to a well-lit runway surrounded by total darkness. How might the approach be affected by this view?

28 In hazy flying conditions, you see an obstruction that you think is just far enough away for safety. Is this perception reliable?

29 Whilst looking out, you spot an aircraft which is not moving at all relative to yourself. What can you deduce from this lack of relative movement?

30 You are flying at a speed of 120kts, and you are warned of opposite-direction traffic in your 12 o'clock with a speed of 420kts three miles away. How long do you have from this moment to avoid a collision?

31 When presented with nothing in particular to focus upon (e.g. when flying at high altitude) where will a pilot's eyes naturally focus?

32 How might a pilot act to ensure that he has good situational awareness?

Answers at page HF116

Stress and Managing Stress

▶ **Stress, Arousal and Performance**

▶ **Environmental Stresses**

▶ **Life Stresses**

▶ **Coping With Stress**

▶ **Revision**

*Stress and
Managing
Stress*

▶ Stress, Arousal and Performance

What is stress? If you read a dozen different textbooks, you will probably find a dozen different answers. For our purposes, the simpler the better. The *Concise Oxford Dictionary* defines stress as "a demand upon physical or mental energy", which will do for now.

The first point to note is that not all stress is bad. When people talk about being "under stress" or "stressed-out", we can assume that they are suffering excessive mental stress. We all know people who seem to be able to tolerate much greater stress than others without apparent problems. For that matter, we all know people who seem to tolerate much *less* stress than most before they get into difficulty. We can therefore appreciate that mental stress is about the *perceived* ability to cope with the *perceived* situation. This is why an under-confident pilot may suffer great stress in a certain situation, even though his actual ability is greater than that of an over-confident pilot.

This leads us to an important concept about stress, namely:

There is no such thing as a stressful situation, only a stressful reaction.

To take an example, imagine a windy day giving a strong crosswind component on the only usable runway. To an inexperienced pilot, perhaps under-confident and not current in crosswind landings, this may present an excessively stressful situation. Such a pilot may become anxious, make unrelated mistakes because of excessive stress and wind up by making a poor approach and landing. An experienced pilot, landing exactly the same aircraft in exactly the same conditions, may not suffer excessive stress at all. He may actually welcome the opportunity to practice his crosswind landing skills and appreciate a change from the routine. It is quite possible that in this situation the little extra stress may cause the experienced pilot to make a *better* approach and landing than usual. This is because he is more 'keyed-up' or more alert than he might otherwise be.

One situation, two different reactions.

The response of the body to stress can be called *arousal* and can be thought of as a state of alertness, with deep sleep at one extreme of the scale and total panic at the other. Our arousal level has a marked effect on performance. A pilot who is under-aroused will probably become bored and lethargic, with no particular motivation to assimilate incoming information properly or maintain situational awareness. Most drivers will recognise this state of mind as being easily induced by the boredom of a long journey on a traffic-free motorway. Airline pilots may equate it to the cruise phase of a long-distance flight in a highly automated aircraft. The problem of staying alert (and even awake) in such a situation is well recognised.

*The classic
'arousal/performance'
curve*

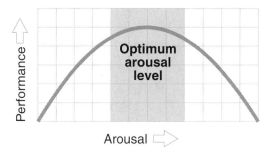

As arousal level increases – for example when driving on a busier road or during the intermediate departure and approach phases of flight – performance increases too. With a greater level of activity, both physical and mental, tasks are performed quicker and better.

Quite simply, the human mind needs stimulation to perform efficiently.

But if arousal increases too far, performance begins to suffer. This is the state which most people would recognise as being 'over-loaded'. It becomes difficult to handle tasks properly and some are missed, left unfinished or wrongly completed. The role of the pilot is to organise cockpit workload as much as possible, to reduce the number of tasks necessary at times of high arousal 'peaks', and slot non-essential tasks into the periods of low arousal. Thinking ahead and planning near-future tasks is a very good way to keep cockpit workload in the optimum section of the arousal/performance curve.

▶ Environmental Stresses

Environmental stresses are physical stresses caused by the pilot's surroundings. The most common in aviation terms are noise, temperature and vibration. The effect of excessive noise has already been discussed in earlier chapters. In essence, excessive noise tends to be both fatiguing and distracting, both of which are clearly undesirable factors. There is not much a pilot can do about the noise level inside an aircraft, although good headsets will reduce the noise levels reaching the pilot's ears. However, not all noise is to be avoided. Some aircraft warning systems (such as stall warners and undercarriage reminders) use noise to attract attention, although if the noise is too loud it can become a distraction. Thus arises the temptation amongst pilots to turn off any such alarms as first action in an emergency! There is also the ancient story about the pilot who landed wheels-up despite increasingly strident radio calls from ATC. Afterwards, he said that he couldn't hear the radio calls because of a blaring horn somewhere in the cockpit...

In normal clothing, the majority of people are at their most comfortable with an air temperature around 20°C. Most people start to get uncomfortable at temperatures much below 10°C, such as might be experienced in the cockpit of an aircraft flying at altitude if the heater fails. The ensuing discomfort and distraction should not be underestimated. Temperatures above 30°C will also cause discomfort to many people, but are rare in the cockpit of most light aircraft in flight because the fresh-air ventilation system should bring relief. That said, some light aircraft have fresh-air systems which could be described as inadequate at best, especially if they also have a large canopy area. High humidity merely increases the discomfort of a high temperature.

The effect of vibration can be difficult to quantify, but excessive vibration undoubtedly causes physical discomfort as well as fatigue. Those used to the smooth operation of jet aircraft are often unpleasantly surprised by the effects of the higher level of vibration present in propeller-driven machinery. Any multi-engine pilot can tell you that if the propellers are 'out of synchronisation', the resultant vibration is very wearisome for pilots and passengers alike.

Before leaving this subject, it is worth noting that the helicopter cockpit in particular has the potential for very high levels of environmental stress. The extra noise and vibration levels of a helicopter compared to a fixed-wing aircraft are well known. Less obviously, the very large canopy areas can give rise to a 'greenhouse' effect in the cockpit, leading to very high cockpit temperatures.

Inside the 'greenhouse' of a helicopter cockpit

▶Life Stresses

Life can at times be a very stressful business (it's also a terminal disease, but let's not get too depressed about it). Certain life events are considered to lead to stressful reactions in humans and a pilot – like any other human – may find it very difficult to separate one activity such as flying an aircraft from some stressful factor which is totally unrelated to the immediate task in hand. You will undoubtedly have at some time experienced the problems caused when you're preoccupied or worried about something that has nothing to do with your present task. Errors and omissions are far greater in this situation, and it is well established that it leads to a higher than normal risk of being involved in an accident.

Studies have shown that in general terms, certain events cause life stresses which can be arranged in an order of 'stress value'. The table below summarises some of these events and their value:

Event	Value
Death of spouse	100
Divorce	75
Martial separation	65
Jail sentence	65
Death of close family member	65
Injury or illness	55
Getting married	50
Dismissal at work	45
Retirement	45
Pregnancy	40
New family member	40
Death of close friend	35
Change in profession	35
Change in financial circumstances	35
Default on loan or mortgage	30
Child leaving home	30
Change in living conditions	25
Problems with boss	25
Change in working hours	20
Change in home	20
Change in sleeping habits	15
Change in eating habits	15
Holiday	15
Christmas	10

Little can be done about the stressful reaction suffered by a particular individual as a result of many of the above situations, but an appreciation of their effect on piloting ability is important. As already discussed, to a certain extent professional pilots have little say over when they fly; a private pilot is in a more fortunate position. If you have just had a major argument with your spouse or partner, you are unlikely to be in the best frame of mind to fly – not least as you re-run the argument and think of all the things you *could* have said! Basically, there are certain times when it is better to stay on the ground. You can always fly another day, and there is a fair body of evidence that points to serious piloting errors being committed by those under excessive stress as a result of life events.

▶ Coping With Stress

Most people whose lifestyle leads to stressful situations look for some way to alleviate that stress. One good strategy is *action coping* whereby the individual takes some direct action relating to the source of excessive stress, such as changing job. Of course this is not always possible and so *cognitive coping* may be called for. In this, the individual may rationalise or detach himself from the stress source and therefore reduce the perceived magnitude of the issue. A less productive form of cognitive coping is *denial*, where the individual simply refuses to acknowledge the problem (as comforting as denial is, we all know that problems tend not to go away on their own!) Meditation, regular exercise, and pastimes and hobbies unrelated to the source of stress are good examples of *symptom-directed* coping to reduce excessive stress. Over-use of alcohol or drugs (even 'acceptable' ones such as tobacco and caffeine) in the same context is less beneficial.

It is well recognised that certain stresses can build up over a long period, such as those that occur as the result of work or relationship problems. These can cause significant health problems as well as behavioural difficulties such as irritability or being short-tempered.

If you recognise that you are suffering from a stressful reaction, and devise a positive and constructive strategy for coping with it, you will be in a much better position to reduce the potential dangers that stress can bring. For many private pilots, flying in itself is an activity which reduces the stress they feel. There is nothing wrong with this, and many pilots can attest to the way in which a pleasant flight can leave you feeling more confident, more relaxed and generally more at peace with the world. The downside of this is that an unpleasant flight can have exactly the reverse effect. There are certain times when your physical or mental condition may make it inadvisable to go flying. You should be aware of this, and heed your own sense of when it would be better to stay on the ground instead.

▶Revision

33 On the diagram below, which area represents 'over-arousal' and reduced performance?

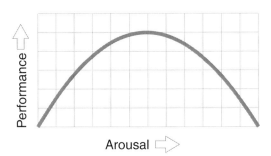

34 What is, on average, a comfortable temperature for a person wearing normal clothing?

35 Arrange the following life stresses in order of magnitude, starting with the highest value: new family member, divorce, change in home.

36 What is the term generally given to taking direct action relating to a source of excessive stress?

Answers at page HF116

Personalities and Cockpit (or Crew) Resource Management

▶ **Personality Traits**

▶ **Hazardous Attitudes**

▶ **Group Decision-Making**

▶ **Judgment and Risk Assessment**

▶ **Revision**

Human Factors

▶Personality Traits

The *personality* of individuals – their identity as seen by themselves or by others – has a significant impact on their actions and how they relate to those around them. There are many ways to think about personality, most of them of great interest but regrettably outside the scope of this book. We shall use an approach which is slightly outmoded and simplistic by modern standards but avoids some of the difficulties of analytically based treatments of the subject. It states that in general terms the individual can either be concerned about achieving a particular objective or concerned about the people he or she is interacting with. These can respectively be described as *goal-motivated* or *person-motivated*. Most people are in some sense a mixture of these two motivations, at least insofar as their conscious behaviour is concerned. A goal-motivated person can be described as 'G+' whereas someone who is not interested in achieving goals or targets can be described as 'G-'. Similarly, an individual who is person-motivated can be described as 'P+' and one who is not interested in other people's welfare or feelings can be described as 'P-'.

A person who is heavily influenced by wanting to achieve a certain goal, and will do so even if he offends or alienates those around him, can be described as 'P-G+'. Such a person may waste the talents of other people, who become unwilling to express their opinions or are not invited to do so. In its most extreme form we have the *authoritarian* personality, who may be likened to a mini-dictator. One interesting hazard associated with this type of personality is that if he or she makes an error, others may allow them to continue rather than risk the ensuing wrath.

By contrast, a 'P+G-' person is over-concerned about having good relations with those around him, to the detriment of the task in hand. Such a person may be too ready to give in to other's views, even if doing so reduces the chances of achieving the goal. In trying to establish friendly terms with all involved, this person may in fact be too democratic for the good of the task.

A 'P-G-' cares little for the task itself or those involved in achieving it. Such a person may appear to be simply 'not bothered', demotivated and even lazy.

You won't be surprised to learn that the ideal personality in this context is seen as

The idealised personality traits

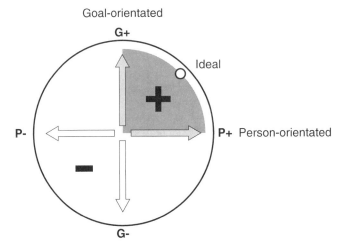

being somebody who is 'P+G+'. This person is motivated to attain the goal but involves those around him in achieving this and cares for their well-being. He creates an atmosphere where the 'team' around him feel that their contributions are recognised even if their ideas or views are not always used.

Although the 'P+G+' personality is seen as the ideal to work to, it is also true that there are times when a more dominant 'P-G+' personality has its advantages – notably in an emergency situation. In this case people may prefer 'strong' leadership, on the basis that they know exactly what is expected of them. They may also believe that despite a poor attitude to others, the leader is motivated to achieve an important goal such as saving their lives or property. This can work in the short term (the duration of the emergency) but in the longer term it tends to build up resentments and conflicts, no matter how good the 'P-G+' personality is at achieving targets.

The relevance of all this psychology – and we should again stress that no-one in their right mind would claim it to be the whole story of human behaviour – is that the pilot can usually only achieve a certain goal, such as making a safe flight from A to B, by involving other people – engineers, operations staff, meteorologists, ATC, other pilots, refuellers etc. All these people have a lot to offer in terms of expertise and practical aid. The better they understand the goal you are trying to achieve, and the better you recognise their own motivations and goals, the better your chance of achieving your goal with the maximum help and minimum hindrance.

▶ Hazardous Attitudes

None of us is perfect, and it is as well to recognise from the outset that we are all to a lesser or greater degree influenced by conscious or unconscious attitudes that can compromise safety. These attitudes may be long-term features of our own personality or short-term responses to a particular situation. An area of human-factors research called *cockpit resource management* (CRM for short) has defined a number of attitudes that are particularly dangerous in aviation. These are also known as hazardous thought patterns, and are generally grouped into five categories although they may well share common roots deep in the unconscious:

- Anti-authority

- Impulsiveness

- Complacency

- Machismo

- Resignation

An attitude of being *anti-authority* will lead a person to break rules and procedures regularly for no very obvious reason. He or she may resent being told what to do, or may simply feel that rules and regulations are unnecessary or should not apply to him as an individual. An anti-authority pilot may deliberately miss medicals, fail to keep his licence or aircraft paperwork in order or continually exceed his licence privileges. He generally dislikes any outside interference with what he sees as his 'right' to fly in any fashion he likes. All this ignores the simple truth that the vast majority of aviation rules and procedures are only enacted after a great deal of thought, and usually as a result of lessons learnt painfully by others.

Anti-authority, a hazardous attitude

'All right then, this photograph was taken from a high court judge's four-hundred feet high sun-lounger…'

A pilot who always acts with *impulsiveness* is probably one who feels the need to respond immediately to a situation for the sake of doing something – anything! His actions will be governed by the first thing that comes to mind, which is not always the best or most correct course. There are very few flying situations where instant reactions are required to avert a disaster. Usually there is time for the pilot to assess the circumstances, consider the possible courses of action and select the one best suited for the situation.

Complacency brings with it a feeling of invulnerability. All is well, the weather is perfect and the aeroplane fully functioning and just back from maintenance. Why bother getting the latest weather forecast and report? Do you *have* to check the pre-flight bulletins? Are all the pre-flight checks *really* necessary? Well, yes, of course they are. But once you start believing that accidents only happen to other people, or that "everything is going to be fine", you significantly increase the risk of proving yourself wrong.

A *macho* attitude is often associated with young male pilots, although it is now thought that males and females are equally susceptible. Such aviators are continually trying to prove their own abilities and skills, often by taking totally unnecessary risks or deliberately getting into hazardous situations. This attitude is at its most dangerous when the macho pilot has an audience, because then he has a chance to show off and impress on others what a splendid fellow he really is. Common symptoms of the macho pilot are reckless low flying and 'beat-ups', flying in poor weather and unnecessary abrupt climbs and steep turns just after take-off. A common result of such macho piloting is a crumpled aeroplane and a very public reassessment of the aviator's true abilities.

A macho attitude leads a pilot to 'show off'

"*...YOU GET SOME COCKY BASTARDS, DON'T YOU...*"

Resignation is a tendency for the person to believe he has little influence on the outcome of events. Such a pilot may press on into poor weather, hoping that things will get better and feeling resigned to his fate rather than making a positive decision to act. Even whilst he has the chance to change course, he may simply think "It's too late now" and just carry on. In essence, the resigned pilot in command is no longer in command of anything. He has abdicated his control of the situation and is merely a passenger, an interested observer of the events that follow. Resignation may be a fairly standard human reaction to an extreme emergency, where the person feels he has done all he can and then 'gives up'. However, there is some evidence that in situations that might be thought of as helpless, determined pilots have managed to avert disasters.

There is no point in me or anyone else trying to tell you not to have any or all of these attitudes if they're already buried in your unconscious and likely to emerge under the right (i.e. the wrong) circumstances. In fact there's evidence to the effect that *everyone* has them to a greater or lesser extent; the issue is merely one of how conscious we are of them and what particular circumstances will trigger them. But it's a fact that time and again, one or more of these hazardous attitudes results in a needless accident. Unfortunately, the pilot who has never been influenced, even for a few moments, by one or other of them has probably not yet been born.

If you think of the hazardous attitude as a sort of illness, it obviously needs an antidote. Short of intensive psychotherapy, the most practical treatment is probably a reminder of why the attitude is flawed and the substitution of a more realistic replacement. The table below summarises the attitudes described above and offers suggested antidotes:

Hazardous Attitude	Symptom	Remedy
Anti-authority	"They can't tell me"	"The rules are there for a reason"
Impulsiveness	"Do something now!"	"Think first, then act"
Complacency	"Nothing's going to happen to me"	"It could happen to me"
Macho	"I'll show them how good I am"	"Taking unnecessary risks is stupid"
Resignation	"What's the point?"	"I'm not helpless"

▶ Group Decision-Making

It is generally accepted that decisions reached by a group are usually of a better quality than decisions reached by an individual. Confusingly, it is also said that a group decision will rarely be better than a decision made by the most able member of the group. The point is that by reaching a decision in a group, you increase the chance of including a person most able to make the correct decision.

However, group decision-making is not all good news. People in a group tend to exhibit *conformity* – a pressure on each member of the group to conform with group decisions and behaviour. Tests have shown that when a group gives an incorrect answer to a problem, a member of the group is likely to go along with the rest even if he knows the answer to be wrong. Likewise, an individual may act in a way uncharacteristic of his normal behaviour, in order to conform with the behaviour of the rest of the group. Group decisions also tend to be more risky than a decision taken by an individual within the group, a phenomena sometimes known as *risk shift*.

This aspect of group decision-making may come as a surprise to those who regard group decisions as inevitably involving compromise. The reason for the increased risk in group decisions is unclear. The usual theories are that it occurs because the most dominant members in a group tend to be those who are more likely to accept risk, or perhaps because any blame or responsibility for the result of the decision can be shared amongst the whole group. This latter theory might also explain why people can behave as part of a group in a way that they would never do as individuals.

The cockpit of the commercial airliner is the classic aviation example of a 'group decision-making' situation

Within the cockpit, group decision-making can be an issue when there are two pilots on board. Even when each pilot's responsibility is clearly defined (as in a commercial operation with a designated captain and a designated co-pilot/first officer) there can be problems. Accidents have occurred in the past where the attitude of a particularly assertive or inflexible captain has persuaded a less experienced co-pilot not to voice doubts or concerns. One extreme example, already discussed, was the co-pilot and flight engineer who were apparently reluctant to stress to the captain that the aircraft was getting low on fuel whilst circling with a suspected undercarriage problem. Eventually the aircraft ran out of fuel and crashed short of the airport because nobody wanted to question the captain's ability or authority.

Even the cockpit of a general-aviation (GA) aircraft offers the opportunity for group decision-making between two pilots

The best remedy for this hazard is always to express any doubts or concerns you have if you think the aircraft is in danger, no matter how inexperienced you are compared with the other pilot. Student pilots sometimes think of instructors in particular as infallible. Clearly they are not, and any good instructor will accept constructive comments or questions in the right way. Indeed, your instructor may even be setting up a situation to see if you are alert enough to spot it (or so he will claim afterwards anyway). In any event, if you come across an intolerant or domineering pilot who simply refuses to hear your concerns or over-rides your comments without a good explanation, find somebody else to fly with. Such pilots are usually only fit to fly solo; they probably suffer from one or more of the hazardous attitudes of macho, anti-authority and complacency and are never as perfect as they think they are. Their agitated reaction to reasonable criticism or comment may well betray a deep insecurity that makes them a risk to themselves and others.

▶ Judgment and Risk Assessment

How nice it would be if good pilot judgment could be summed up in just a few words. Then we could all learn the right formula and *hey presto*, better flight safety in one easy lesson.

It isn't that simple, of course. The development of good judgment goes hand-in-hand with the development of good piloting skills, sound knowledge and a store of experience. Having the best aircraft-handling skills in the world is of little use if you do not have the judgment to go with them. An autopilot can fly an aircraft very accurately. But having no judgment, it can fly the aircraft into the side of a mountain on a perfectly clear day. It's probably no consolation that it will do so at exactly the speed, altitude and heading to which it was set.

Some believe that good judgment is part of a person's personality and something you either have or you don't. More commonly, it is presumed that good judgment comes with experience and knowledge. Since the advent of human-factors training, it is now more widely accepted that good judgment *can* be taught – something that enlightened flying instructors have been doing for years. This is all the more important when you consider that a significant proportion of aviation accidents (maybe up to 75% in general aviation, depending on which studies you read) are caused as a direct result of poor pilot judgment.

Human Factors

You may be surprised to learn that it is extremely rare for an aircraft accident to occur as the result of one single cause. It is much more common for there to be a chain of events. Taken individually, each event might be relatively insignificant. However, when taken together, the cumulative effect of all the factors can increase risk to such an extent as to make an accident or an incident a very real possibility. As a pilot, your aim should be to avoid and reduce risk where reasonably possible. As far as aviation is concerned, 'good' judgment has to mean that safe decisions are taken and reasonable actions ensue. It follows that to exercise good judgment, a pilot must be able to appreciate risk, because by definition reducing risk increases safety. Accident and incident reports normally concentrate on events directly related to the episode in question. It sometimes takes a more in-depth appreciation of the situation to understand exactly how the sequence of events was influenced by other factors.

It is no great surprise to find that accidents often occur where pilots are flying an aircraft they do not know well, or are in a situation they are unfamiliar with. For instance, a pilot used to flying a particular aircraft type from long tarmac runways in good weather is increasing risk if he flies a new type to a short grass runway in a gusty crosswind. Any single factor on its own – new aircraft type, a short grass runway or a gusty crosswind – might be quite manageable on its own. Taken together, these factors increase risk significantly and lead the pilot along a chain of events that can lead to an accident. If the pilot is actively assessing risk, he should recognise this and break the chain (e.g. by landing on a longer and into-wind runway) before a problem arises.

The second part of this book deals more with the concept of risk management and reduction. However, before leaving the subject we can take an educated guess at some of the factors that often crop up in aircraft accidents. This is not a list to be learnt, rather some food for thought.

Factors increasing risk

- Inadequate pre-flight planning
- Poor checks and in-flight procedures
- Breaking or ignoring (deliberately or otherwise) established rules and procedures
- Bad weather, or weather significantly worse than forecast or expected
- General inexperience
- Inexperience on aircraft type
- Inexperience of a particular situation or environment
- Exceeding the aircraft's limits
- Flying to the limits (or beyond) of the licence or ratings held
- Lack of currency (i.e. little recent flying experience)
- Hazardous attitudes
- Poor physical or mental condition
- Badly equipped or maintained aircraft

It should be no great revelation that the opposite factors to those above actively reduce risk!

▶Revision

37 How could you describe a personality which is motivated to achieve a goal or target, but which is uninterested in the welfare or feelings of others?

38 How could you describe the hazardous attitude of a pilot who regularly breaks rules and procedures, misses medicals and fails to maintain licence and aircraft documentation correctly?

39 You are sharing a flight with a pilot much less experienced than yourself. How should you advise this pilot to act if he has any doubts or misgivings over a decision you make?

Answers at page HF117

Cockpit Design and Procedures

Human Factors

*Cockpit
Design and
Procedures*

▶ Eye Datum

▶ Flight Instrument Displays

▶ Controls

▶ Warnings

▶ Checklists and Manuals

▶ Revision

Human Factors

*Cockpit
Design and
Procedures*

▶ Eye Datum

The cockpit of a modern aircraft will be designed around the *eye datum*, also known as the *design eye position* or *eye line reference*. If the pilot's eyes are at this level, his view both inside and outside the cockpit will be optimised. Where the cockpit has indicators to allow you to line yourself up with the design eye position, the seat height adjustment should be done (as you would expect) prior to flight.

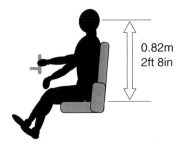

The 'average' shaped pilot with an average eye height

0.82m
2ft 8in

Unfortunately, general-aviation aircraft do not tend to have such indicators, so we have to assume that the position is at around the level where the eyes of a pilot of average height would be. For reference, we can take 'average' height to be about 1·77m or 5ft 10in. This leads to an average eye height when sitting (distance from seat to eyes) of around 0·82m or 2ft 8in. So where the seat can be adjusted for height, it makes sense to aim to place your eyes somewhere close to this ideal.

If for any reason the pilot's eyes are below the eye datum, he will be able to see significantly less ground ahead of the aircraft than if his eyes are at or above it. Given the amount of aircraft ahead of the cockpit in a conventional single-engine aircraft, which already reduces the vision forward and down, this can be a problem – especially for lookout when descending and during the final stages of the approach and landing. Eye height can be varied by adjusting the seat for reach, height, rake and lumbar support. If all else fails, a cushion behind the back can be useful, as can a cushion or two on the seat proper.

When the eyes are below the design eye position, less of the approach path and runway is visible on landing

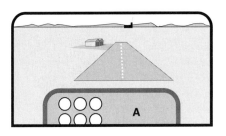

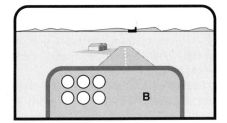

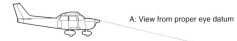

A: View from proper eye datum

B: View if below eye datum

All this stresses the point that next time you come to the checklist item "Seats...Adjusted" you might want to give a little extra thought to how the seat position affects your view of both the cockpit and the world outside.

▶ Flight Instrument Displays

When the non-aviator first enters the cockpit, the overwhelming impression is of the number of instruments, dials, lights, gauges and switches scattered around the cockpit. The common question from novice to pilot is "Do you know what all these mean?". Leaving aside the tempting response of "No, actually I was hoping that you might", it's actually not such a silly question.

The 'Technical' part of the PPL course deals with the mechanics of how the instruments work. But the way in which that information is displayed, and how it is interpreted by the pilot, puts us right back into human-factors territory. One of the more common pitfalls is the airspeed indicator, which may read in miles per hour, knots or kilometres per hour. The colour coding of the airspeed indicator is a considerable aid to its use, as long as you remember what the colours mean and assuming the thing is colour-coded in the first place (not all are). But what about the ASI which has an outer 'low speed' scale, and an inner 'high speed' scale? Or one which shows two units, but no clear indication of which is which? We can think about the VSI in the same way. Is it fitted with 'stops' or not? If not, an extreme rate of climb or descent will indicate in the opposite sense. What about the altimeter? The sub-scale can be calibrated in

The approach speed is 85kts. At a quick glance, do you have that airspeed now?

millibars/hectopascals, inches of mercury or millimetres of mercury. It usually reads feet but it *might* read metres, especially if it's in an ex-Eastern Bloc aeroplane. And of course the three-pointer display common in general-aviation aircraft can also be confusing. At a glance, exactly what altitude is indicated on the altimeter below? The instrument is accurate and reliable enough, but its display is open to misinterpretation. In a three-pointer display, the third needle indicates tens of thousands of feet. As the level rises above 10,000ft the striped area is covered up by the central disc. It will become visible again as the aircraft descends below 10,000ft.

If the VSI has no stops, an extreme rate of descent may indicate in the opposite sense as the needle just moves further round the dial

LEFT>
A three-pointer altimeter, indicating 10,600ft

And that's just three primary instruments. Ever seen an ex-Soviet 'roller blind' attitude indicator?

Do you *still* think you know what all these instrument readings mean?

The watchword is *preparation*. Before flight, especially if the aircraft is new to you, take some time to look at each instrument and check that you really do understand its display. If not, ask someone!

In terms of the instrument displays themselves, there are several common peculiarities to catch out the unwary aviator in addition to those described above. For instance, the sub-scale window of the altimeter is often rather small and contains even smaller numbers. In flight, especially if the pilot is overloaded (or "on the excessive side of the arousal curve") it is frightfully easy to mis-set this. It's not uncommon to set 1020 instead of 1030, for example, hence the importance of proper checks. Also, which way does the setting knob turn to increase the sub-scale value? There is no 'correct' answer here; it could turn either way depending on the make of altimeter. Moreover, if you spend some time exploring the cockpit (preferably on the ground) you will probably find that the direction of rotation of a setting knob and whether that rotation increases or decreases the associated setting varies between instruments.

You will no doubt have noticed that most flight instruments have an 'analogue' display, with a pointer (or pointers) sweeping around the instrument face. Although a digital display gives a more precise reading, it is not as easy to appreciate trends on a digital readout. On an analogue display it is easier to assess the approximate reading at a glance, and also judge quickly from the movement of the pointer how the value is changing.

Although many instruments appear to be randomly scattered around the cockpit (and in general, the older the aircraft, the more scattered the instruments), the six basic flight instruments should be arranged in a pattern known as the 'Basic T', which is illustrated below. This standardisation is most important for instrument flying, which involves 'scanning' the flight instruments from the attitude indicator (AI) outwards. By using the 'Basic T' pattern, life is made that much easier for the pilot even when flying a totally different aircraft type. To a certain extent, even the most advanced 'glass' cockpits have flight displays based on the 'T'.

The 'basic T' flight instrument pattern

▶Controls

The design of the principal flying controls is unlikely to vary greatly between aircraft. Rudder pedals are rudder pedals, and there will be a control wheel or control column (stick) to operate the elevators and ailerons. The only exceptions are those few aircraft which have a 'side-stick', although this still operates in the same sense as a control column.

The design of the secondary controls is more varied. The throttle and associated controls may be of the 'push-pull' type or the 'quadrant' type. Now variances begin to creep in. In most aircraft, the mixture control goes fully *forward* for fully *rich*, fully *back* for fully *lean*. However, if you are lucky enough to get your hands on a Chipmunk, be aware that the mixture control sense is reversed (fully back is fully rich). And it is not just older aircraft that can catch out the unwary. The Cessna 182 has cowl flaps, which are generally open for take-off and landing. To most pilots it might seem logical that the lever should move down to open (lower) the cowl flaps just as a lever usually goes down to lower flaps or undercarriage. You've guessed it; in the C182 the cowl flap lever has to be moved up to open (lower) the flaps and moved down to close (raise) them. Hands up all Cessna 182 pilots who have landed with the cowl flaps firmly closed but the cockpit lever reassuringly down…

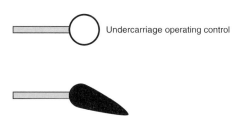

Undercarriage operating control

Flaps operating control

The undercarriage and flap controls are often shaped to represent the item they operate

The ideal is that cockpit controls which operate different systems should look and feel different from each other. In the case of flap and undercarriage controls, one really useful innovation is to shape the cockpit controls to resemble the item they operate; the undercarriage control looks like a wheel, the flap control resembles a flap. This helps to stop a pilot operating the wrong control. However, note the choice of words; it *helps*, but it does not *prevent*. It didn't prevent the mishap of the pilot who had just converted from one type of popular twin to another. It just so happens that the positions of the flap and undercarriage levers were directly transposed between the two. Immediately after landing, the pilot reached for what he thought was the flap lever, and up came the wheels…

On a more trivial note, the operation of the radios – and particularly the audio controller where one is fitted – often causes confusion.

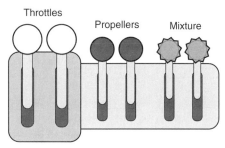

Throttles   Propellers   Mixture

Conventional engine control layout

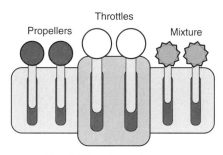

Propellers   Throttles   Mixture

Aircraft 'B' engine control layout

Virtually all GA multi-engine aircraft have the same engine control layout (top) except one (bottom) – with predictable results

All in all, preparation and training is the only answer. Otherwise you might find yourself trying to figure out how to operate some control or system at a very inopportune moment.

▶Warnings

Ideally, a warning system should perform three functions. It should:

- **Alert**: get the attention of the pilot;
- **Report**: tell the pilot what is wrong;
- **Guide**: steer the pilot to the remedy.

The warning systems found in most light aircraft can alert and report to the pilot, but few will guide him directly towards the remedy.

The most common warning system in a light aircraft is the stall warner, and arguably the worse type (other than none at all) is a simple light. Placed out of direct vision of the pilot, this is highly unlikely to have the attention-grabbing nature that such a device really needs. More common, and more useful, is a horn that sounds as the stall is approached. This is difficult to ignore, and being the only aural warning in many light aircraft, also has the effect of reporting the problem. The only other aural warning regularly found in light aircraft is an undercarriage warning for aircraft with retractable gear. This is normally triggered if the power is reduced below a certain value without the undercarriage locked down, and some will also activate if the flaps are lowered without the undercarriage down. It is worth remembering that many aural warning systems are electrically operated. In the event of an electrical problem, these warning systems cannot operate.

Lights are often used in small aeroplanes to warn of electrical problems such as low voltage or starter energised. They can also be used to tell the pilot about a suction-system failure or low oil pressure. In daylight conditions these lights tend not to be very obvious, and are only effective if they are regularly monitored as part of the pre-flight and in-flight checks.

The annunciator panel of a Piper Warrior with warning lights for vacuum, alternator and oil pressure

In more sophisticated aircraft and almost all helicopters, a 'warning' or 'annunciator' panel may be used. This is a panel of lights covering various aircraft systems and specific failures. If there is a problem, a master warning light or master caution light illuminates in direct sight of the pilot. This alerts the pilot and reports that there is a really-not-your-day problem (warning, usually red) or a rather less serious something-you-should-know problem (caution, usually orange). The pilot then refers to the warning panel for specific information.

▶ Checklists and Manuals

This is a book aimed at pilots, so the question of checklist and manual design can largely be left to those who write, design and publish these items. That said, it is an undeniable fact that the quality of checklists, manuals and other documentation used by the pilot varies enormously, from the very clear to the virtually unintelligible. If the pilot does not have control over the layout of the documentation he has to work with, he can only be aware of the dangers of poorly designed and incomplete material and proceed cautiously.

The use of checklists is a proven safety aid. In some ways, the operation of a light aircraft is more complex than that of a modern airliner. No pilot would dream of taking-off in an airliner without completing a proper checklist. Yet a significant number of PPLs are quite happy to do the starting, taxying, power and pre-take-off checks largely from memory, if at all, and without reference to a checklist or *aide-memoire*. However simple the aircraft, this is just plain foolish. When using a checklist, care must be taken to complete it methodically and carefully. It is easy to miss an item if you are interrupted (for example by an ATC message or a passenger query), so take care to ensure you continue where you left off. It is also all too easy to reply to the checklist items automatically, responding to an item in the way that you *expect* it to be. Pointing at the item being checked, and being sure to read individual instrument and gauge indications rather than just glancing at them, will help in this respect.

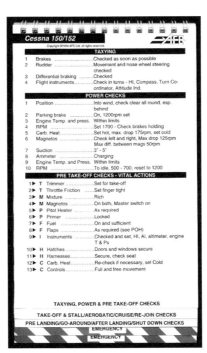

If you have a checklist: use it...

... or you never know what you might miss (such as closing and locking the door before take-off)

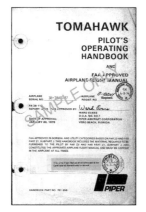

If you haven't read this document (or equivalent) for the aircraft you are flying, now is the time!

Specifically with regard to manuals, the most important advice in respect of the Pilot's Operating Handbook/Flight Manual (POH/FM) is **read them!** Too many pilots believe that they have 'checked out' on an aircraft type, and yet have never read the POH/FM (and don't even know where to find it). This is an obvious precursor to accidents such as running out of fuel. The pilot will mutter "I was told it uses 30 litres an hour". The insurance company man or accident investigator might reply, "Yes, but what does the POH/FM say for your chosen power setting and mixture leaning method?" Alternatively, the pilot is told by some well-meaning soul that the aircraft can operate from a 500m runway. This counts for little if the figures in the POH/FM say it cannot. The status of the POH/FM or equivalent is often under-appreciated by light-aircraft pilots, and unnecessary accidents are the result.

Other documentation to consider are the placards adorning most cockpits. These are placed there to inform or warn the pilots of specific items relating to the operation of that particular aircraft, and normally refer to a section of that particular aircraft's POH/FM. A good rainy-day exercise is to spend some time in the aircraft reading these placards and referring back to the relevant section of the POH/FM. You may well learn something interesting!

▶Revision

40 When should the pilot's seat height be adjusted for design eye position?

41 What is the altitude shown by the altimeter below?

42 In the 'Basic T' flight-instrument layout, name the instrument in the shaded position on the diagram below:

43 Which of the controls below is most likely to be an undercarriage control, and which the flap control?

A

B

Answers at page HF117

Safety and Survival Equipment

Human Factors

Safety and Survival Equipment

▶ **Passenger Briefing and the Pilot's Responsibilities**

▶ **Motion Sickness**

▶ **Seat Belts and Harnesses**

▶ **The First-Aid Kit and First Aid**

▶ **Fire Extinguishers**

▶ **Common Survival Equipment**

▶ **Flares, Lights, Strobes and Heliographs**

▶ **Transceivers & GPS**

▶ **Head Protection**

▶ **Flying Suit**

▶ **Basics of Survival**

▶ **Revision**

Human Factors

▶Passenger Briefing and the Pilot's Responsibilities

One of the principal privileges of obtaining your PPL is the right to carry passengers with you. Indeed, many pilots' first flights after receipt of the piece of paper are taken up with showing off their flying skills to a wide range of relatives, friends and colleagues. With this privilege comes accountability. Your non-pilot passengers are, in every sense, your responsibility. You are charged with their well-being and safekeeping; they will look to you not to put them at unnecessary risk and as pilot in command you are obliged – legally as well as morally – to consider and actively protect their safety.

Firstly, you may need to check whether the passenger has any susceptibility which could be a problem in the air. A passenger who is nervous, a first-time flyer in a small aircraft or perhaps a sufferer from a fear of heights will need careful handling and more than average attention throughout the flight. Any illness that would affect a pilot's flying abilities – such as a cold or flu, gastric problems or taking medication – is also going to be problematic in a passenger. Equally, a passenger might also have a condition such as epilepsy which bars him or her from being a pilot, and this might present problems in flight. In the case of epilepsy, this has been known to be set off by sunlight 'flickering' through a propeller or helicopter rotor blades. In such circumstances anybody who complains of discomfort or unease caused by such flicker should be advised to shield the eyes in some way, even if the person is not known to be susceptible.

An important element in passenger safety is to ensure that a proper safety briefing is given before the flight. As part of this briefing, you must ensure that all passengers know where the main exits are and how to open and close them. They must also know where to find and how to use any emergency exits, and where the fire extinguisher and first-aid kit are located. Passengers must be shown how to use the safety belts and/or harnesses, and they must be able to undo and fasten these unaided. If the seat is adjustable, or if a seat back needs to be moved to give access to rear seats, the passengers must be capable of doing this for themselves. If you will be carrying any specialist emergency equipment (life-jackets, dinghies, etc.) their use needs to be explained too. You may need to decide whether to permit smoking, although as a rule smoking is not encouraged in a light aircraft. All of this will take no more than a few moments, but in an emergency could save lives.

If your passengers are new to flying in light aircraft, they will need to be told not to touch any of the controls or switches without your permission, and to tell you right away if they move something accidentally. It might be worth showing the passengers the fresh-air vents and how to use them, particularly if these are well away from the main flying controls and instrument panel. Passengers also must appreciate that at certain times (especially around take-off and landing) they should not distract you from your primary task of flying the aeroplane; "What does this button do?" is the last thing you want to deal with in the middle of a gusty crosswind landing! If the aircraft is fitted with an intercom and the passengers are wearing headsets, ensure that they are adjusted for comfort. The operation of the intercom needs to be explained, and passengers must realise that they should not talk over any messages the pilot is listening to.

Your passengers must also be briefed as to what to do in the event of an emergency. If such a thing should arise, the pilot is likely to have his hands full and have little spare time or mental capacity to talk to the passengers too. Probably the most crucial point for passengers to appreciate is that in an emergency they will be expected to fasten and tighten-up their own seat-belts or harness as far as possible, and make sure that their seat is secure with the seat back upright. Headsets should be removed (they can get tangled up with seat belts as the wearer tries to leave the cabin) and sharp objects (such as keys and pens) emptied from the pockets. A recommended bracing position has been developed as a result of studies and accident investigations. The lap strap should be fastened tightly and then the upper body bent forward as far as possible to put the

The recommended brace position

chest close to the knees, probably with the head touching the seat back ahead (if there is one). The hands should be placed one above the other on top of the head (i.e. not with interlaced fingers) and the forearms tucked in each side of the face. The lower legs should be pulled back so that they are aft of the vertical, with feet flat on the floor. A jacket or sweater rolled up and placed in front of the face and head might also help. How closely this position can be adopted will largely depend on seating position and individual aircraft design. Nevertheless this 'brace for impact' posture is believed to significantly reduced the risk of injury compared to sitting in an upright position. If the aircraft has rearward-facing passenger seats, those seated in them are also less likely to be injured compared with forward-facing passengers.

Your passengers should realise that they must comply quickly with any instructions that you give, as there might not be time to repeat yourself. A call from you of "brace, brace" or something similar will at least give your passengers a chance to protect themselves (they may not realise there's a problem) but don't call for this too soon. Human nature being what it is, during a long wait someone is certain to be tempted to look up, probably just at the wrong moment.

Before committing yourself to carrying passengers, you should assess how they will affect the safe conduct of the flight. Passengers under the influence of alcohol or drugs should not be allowed anywhere near an aircraft. The disruption and danger they can cause is simply not worth the risk. As already discussed, a particularly nervous or reluctant passenger is going to need considerable reassurance and attention from the pilot. In these circumstances, if the conditions are not especially favourable (e.g. gusty winds or turbulence), you might consider whether to postpone the flight for another time. Many pilots have had the depressing experience of meeting somebody who, as a result of one bad experience as a passenger, has been put off flying in light aircraft for life. Young passengers may also demand a lot of attention from the pilot. Anybody who has travelled in a vehicle in the company of small children will know just how distracting they can be. In the confined space of a light aircraft the effect is impressively magnified. Where possible, it is prudent to take with you an adult specifically charged with keeping the minors under control by whatever means necessary!

You won't be thanked by your passengers for taking them flying in poor weather…

"If I'd wanted turbulence I'd have written it into your contract."

In summary, check the health and disposition of your passengers *before* you commit yourself to flight, and *before* flying with passengers you should ensure that, with the exception of young children, each of them will be able to:

■ open the doors or exits unaided and operate any folding seat backs;

■ fasten and release their seat belts or safety harnesses unaided;

■ know the location of the fire extinguisher and first-aid kit;

■ know how to use any specialist equipment carried (oxygen, life-jackets, dinghies, ELT's, etc.).

Finally, you should show your passengers where to find the sickbags (you have checked that some are on board, haven't you?) Few things are more distracting for a pilot than desperately hunting around the cockpit for an urgently needed sickbag!

▶ Motion Sickness

The true misery of motion sickness is probably a mystery to those few lucky people who have genuinely never experienced it. More commonly, most of us will have suffered at some time or another, either in an aircraft or in some other context (usually on a boat or in a car). Some people are more susceptible than others, and evidently somebody not used to the sensations of flying in a light aircraft is more likely to suffer than a pilot.

Motion sickness occurs because of conflicting information being received from eyes, the vestibular apparatus of the ears and other sensory organs. The sufferer will probably first experience a general queasiness. This is followed by sweating, increased saliva, dizziness, hot flushes, nausea, and eventually vomiting. The general malaise, misery and apathy accompanying motion sickness is every bit as debilitating as the physical symptoms.

As with many facets of safety, prevention is a lot better than cure. It is known that even a small amount of alcohol in the system increases susceptibility to motion sickness. On a brighter note, a person actively involved in some way in the conduct of a flight is far less likely to suffer than somebody who is (or feels like) merely a passenger. So, if possible, give a susceptible person some task to do – perhaps helping to fly the aircraft straight and level with reference to the horizon, or looking ahead for a landmark to assist visual navigation. Being occupied in this way may reduce the chances of someone developing motion sickness; hardly anyone is afflicted when they are the one doing the flying. Movement of the head aggravates motion sickness, so keeping still and focusing on a distant horizon is useful, as is a supply of cool air. Your own flying should be as smooth as possible. Abrupt manoeuvres, steep climbs or descents and steep angles of bank should be avoided and – a much under-appreciated point – the aircraft should be flown in balance.

If a person is susceptible to motion sickness, keep an unobtrusive check on their behaviour. Going quiet, developing a greyish pallor or beginning to sweat are all indications that something may be a trifle amiss. Check on how they are feeling, and act early to relieve the symptoms. There are a number of medications on the market to combat the problem. Anything that might work is worth trying for a passenger, but a pilot should never use any of these medicines without first taking proper medical advice because drowsiness and reduced reaction times are common side-effects of such drugs. Other common treatments for motion sickness are wrist bands and herbal remedies. If you are a sufferer, these are well worth a try. They don't work for everybody, but some people claim great things for them.

▶ Seat Belts and Harnesses

The first piece of advice about safety belts and/or harnesses is simple – use them! Whilst some older light aircraft may have seats fitted with a simple lap strap, the majority now have at least a diagonal shoulder strap too. Wherever these are fitted, they should be worn at all times. Experience has shown that 'upper torso restraint', meaning a single or double shoulder strap, is a major factor in reducing upper body, face and head injuries in the event of an accident. There have been a significant number of accidents where fatal injuries could have been avoided if the full safety belt fitted in the aircraft had been properly worn. Without upper torso restraint, the seated person is at much greater risk in the event of severe

If the aircraft has shoulder straps – wear them

deceleration. If this occurs, the upper body will tend to 'jack-knife' forwards and down around the lap strap. This means that the upper body, or more commonly the head and face, are at risk of violently striking whatever is directly ahead. For a rear-seat passenger, this may be the seat ahead together with whatever happens to be sticking out of the seat back pockets. For front-seat occupants there will be a coaming, an assortment of instruments with glass faces, protruding switches and levers and so on. Added to a painful coming together with any such item is the danger of 'whiplash' as the head and neck recoil back after impact.

Not all seat-belt systems work in the same way, so it pays to check that you understand how the belt should fasten. It is not uncommon for a belt to get twisted, and the attachment of a diagonal shoulder strap to lap strap may be of a type which displays a disturbing tendency to slip free in flight – especially if the shoulder strap is too loose. Although the belts do not have to be breathtakingly tight, they should be kept reasonably snug and secure, and should also be kept fastened throughout the flight. An encounter with turbulence or wake vortices is disturbing enough without also being bounced around the cockpit!

If you are intending to fly aerobatics, pay particular attention to the harnesses. Few things make a pilot less secure than a feeling of falling out of the seat whilst the aircraft is inverted or pushing negative *g*. Aerobatic harnesses often have five straps and a specialised 'quick-release' buckle. Make sure you fully understand how this works because they are not all the same, especially on older aircraft. The general condition and security of the seat belts or harnesses also needs to be assessed before flight. As with any other part of the aircraft they can become worn, damaged or broken with age and usage. Not the sort of thing you want to discover by accident.

On the subject of flying vintage (or open-cockpit or aerobatic) aircraft, you should also consider the question of head protection. There has been a growing trend for the pilots of such aircraft to wear a full safety helmet, or 'bonedome ' as military pilots call it. It has been proved that wearing such a helmet has saved lives in a number of aircraft accidents, and the point is discussed in more detail shortly.

▶ The First-Aid Kit and First Aid

The recommended contents of the first-aid kit are laid out in the Air Navigation Order. Those contents do not need to be memorised, and are not worth listing here. However, in essence if you open an aircraft's first-aid kit you should find at least bandages, plasters, wound and burn dressings, scissors, antiseptics and pain relief drugs. You should also find a handbook on first aid.

Safety and Survival Equipment

The principles of first aid are almost impossible to teach purely from a book, and a detailed knowledge is not required to pass any pilot exams. Nevertheless, the first-aid kit is part of the aircraft equipment, and a pilot does have an overall responsibility to his passengers including their care and safety in the event of an accident. All things considered, it is worth knowing a few fundamentals of good first-aid practice. The following is very general advice only; it certainly does not overrule any proper first aid instructions, and assumes access to a first-aid kit.

A standard aircraft first-aid kit with contents

The over-riding philosophy of first aid, especially relevant to an unqualified person is:

First do no harm!

It might look very dramatic to dive straight into the wreckage and drag out any person you find in there. But, if in doing so you cause further and possibly permanent injury to somebody who was in no immediate danger, you are not doing any good at all.

So, first of all assess the situation. Is anyone in immediate danger? Is anybody trapped or unconscious? Can the 'walking wounded' be aided or directed to a safer place up-wind from the incident? Are there uninjured people, bystanders maybe, who can aid or be sent to find help? Your actions will depend very much on the circumstances, and potentially how long it will take for aid to arrive. If for any reason help might not be on the way already, decide how you will call in assistance. A large airfield will have its own emergency services, which can usually be summoned via the internal telephone system (if you can't find the number, call ATC). Even on a smaller airfield there is a reasonable chance that an airfield employee, or someone else working on the airfield, will be a qualified first-aider.

If you absolutely do have to move somebody in order to remove them from immediate danger, work gently and smoothly, with the express aim of minimising movement of the neck and spine.

With any casualties out of immediate danger, check first for anyone who is unconscious. Do this by looking for a response from the subject using simple questions or instructions such as "What happened?", "What is your name?" or "Open your eyes". If there is any doubt about consciousness, check ABC:

A Airway   Remove any obvious obstruction from the mouth.
The airway can be opened by tilting the head back
if it is safe to do so.

B Breathing   Check whether the subject is breathing freely.

C Circulation Check for a pulse, or listen for a heartbeat.

If there is a lack or breathing or circulation, resuscitation in the form of artificial ventilation (breathing) or chest compression (circulation) is required. If the ABC check reveals no obvious problems, carefully place the subject in the recovery position to await qualified medical personnel.

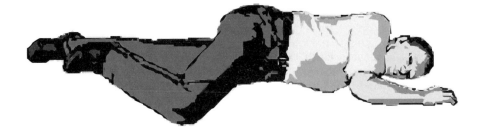

The recovery position

When assessing a casualty, bleeding will probably be the most obvious injury. Serious bleeding should be controlled by applying direct pressure to the wound, preferably using a sterile dressing or pad from a first-aid kit. If the bleeding is coming from a limb, raising and supporting it above the level of the heart may help. Laying the casualty down will also reduce blood flow to the injury and you can press on the bleeding vessel. Resist the temptation to apply a tourniquet. Modern thinking is that this will do more harm than good.

Burns should be first treated, if at all possible, by pouring cold water over the affected area for at least ten minutes. Remove watches, jewellery, belts and so on from near the burn before swelling starts, and cover the burn with a sterile dressing. Do not use an adhesive dressing or adhesive tape. Also do not touch the burned area or burst any blisters.

In the case of a broken bone, establish first whether it is an open fracture (i.e. the broken bone has penetrated the skin) and if so treat the area first to control the bleeding. If the broken bone is in a limb, secure and support the limb whilst keeping the casualty as still as possible. In the absence of splints, a broken leg can be bandaged to an unbroken one for support. An arm injury should be supported with a sling. Do not let the casualty eat or drink.

Shock may occur as the result of a heart attack, or as a consequence of blood loss or serious burns. What we are talking about here is not 'shock' in the form of distress or hysteria as an emotional response to an incident, but a serious circulation problem. Symptoms of circulation shock include sweating, weakness and dizziness, nausea, rapid breathing and eventual loss of consciousness. Circulation shock is treated by laying the casualty down, raising and supporting the legs, loosening anything constricting the neck, chest or waist and keeping the casualty warm with coats and/or blankets.

If you decide to make use of any pain-relief drugs, read the instructions on the packet carefully and adhere to them. Check with the subject first that they are not allergic to the type of drug, and do not exceed the stated dose. When qualified medical assistance does arrive, be sure to brief them carefully on the symptoms and signs you have noted and how they have been treated.

It must be emphasised that if you have no proper knowledge of first aid, it is especially important to do no harm. Above all stay calm, use your common sense, and summon assistance as quickly as possible. Once the immediate dangers have been addressed, it is the rapid intervention of qualified medical and rescue staff that is the most important factor in maximising survival and recovery.

▶ Fire Extinguishers

A fire in or around an aircraft is obviously a very serious situation, and one that needs to be prevented if at all possible, and fought by all means available if prevention fails.

Let's start with the basics. A fire needs three constituents to start and continue:

■ Oxygen

■ Fuel

■ Heat source

In the aviation environment, oxygen is present in quantity other than very high altitudes so we are stuck with that. The aviation environment also provides no shortage of flammable materials to act as fuel. Aviation fuel itself – be it AVGAS, Jet A-1 AVTUR, MOGAS or indeed anything else – is the most obvious fuel for a fire. Other less evident fuels include oil, the plastics, rubber and fabrics found in aircraft (and wood too in some types), paper and suchlike.

The heat source can be a variety of things: lighting a cigarette or performing a maintenance operation; sparks from an ignition system; a defective electrical circuit; a static electricity discharge or friction between metals or other materials; or simply a hot material such as a bright lamp or polished metal on a sunny day. Any of these may act to start a fire.

As always in safety terms, prevention is better than cure. As the pilot can do little about the amount of oxygen around, or the various fuels, controlling the possible heat sources is the key to fire prevention. An obvious danger point is during aircraft refuelling. Any naked flames (including lit cigarettes, cigars, pipes, etc.) should be kept well away from the refuelling area, and before starting refuelling the aircraft should be 'grounded' to the refuelling installation to prevent static discharges. And, just out of interest, the next time you are refuelling an aircraft, see if you know where the nearest fire extinguisher is – the one in the aircraft does not count. The refuelling installation should have its own fire extinguishers, but these are not going to be much use if you don't know where to find them in an emergency!

Aircraft hangars also contain plenty of opportunities for fire, especially if there are maintenance operations going on inside. Again the emphasis is on keeping fuels and heat sources well apart, and having plenty of serviceable fire extinguishers on hand. Hangers and associated buildings may also have fire blankets to smother a fire, and buckets of sand or similar to deal with flammable liquid spillages too. Within the aircraft cabin, the furnishings of the seats and insulation, the various papers carried around in aircraft and items of baggage or cargo are the most obvious fuels. The most obvious heat source other than a naked flame caused by smoking is the electrical system, concentrated in the instrument panel. The engine compartment is another matter, but of course any problems here in a single-engine aircraft should be capable of being isolated from the cabin by the firewall.

Fires can be classified as being of one of four types. These classifications do not have to be memorised but are listed here for reference:

■ Class A fire: involving ordinary combustible materials – wood, paper, fabric

■ Class B fire: involving flammable liquids – petroleum, solvents etc.

■ Class C fire: involving electrical equipment

■ Class D fire: involving flammable metals – for example a wheel-brake fire

Fire extinguishers are designed to put out the fire by removing one of its three constituents, and all contain some type of 'agent' to deal with a fire. Water can be used to cool the fire below its combustion temperature. Foam cools a fire and also prevents oxygen from reaching it. Gases dissipate or eliminate oxygen from the area around the fire, and certain types also interfere chemically with the combustion process. Dry powder smothers a fire, preventing oxygen from reaching it.

The different properties of each extinguishing agent make them suitable for certain types of fire, but sometimes unsuitable in particular circumstances. For example, water should never be used on fires involving flammable liquids or metals, and water or foam should not be used on electrical fires. The recommended uses for each type of extinguisher are as below:

Water extinguishers are only really effective for use on fires involving wood, paper or cloth (class A fires).

Foam extinguishers can be used on fires involving wood, paper, cloth, and flammable liquids (Class A & B fires). It is for the latter that they are particularly effective.

Carbon Dioxide extinguishers can be used on fires involving flammable liquids and electrical fires (Class B & C fires).

Dry Powder extinguishers can be used on fires involving flammable liquids and electrical fires (Class B & C fires). Certain types of dry-powder extinguisher, known as 'ABC' extinguishers, can be used for fires involving wood, paper or cloth (i.e. Class A, B & C fires). Wheel-brake fires (usually classified as class D) are also best tackled using a dry powder extinguisher.

BCF extinguishers can be used for virtually all types of fire (A, B & C fires). BCF is an abbreviation for bromochlorodifluoromethane, better known by its more snappy title of 'Halon 1211'. This type of extinguisher is generally regarded as being the most effective in the aviation environment, which is why it is the most common type found inside an aircraft although ABC dry-powder extinguishers have also been used. Unfortunately, Halon 1211 is no longer produced commercially; it's good on fires but bad for the ozone layer. However, the existing stocks mean that Halon 1211 fire extinguishers are expected to be available for the foreseeable future according to those in the know. There's also some dispute about whether using a BCF extinguisher in the confines of an aircraft cabin containing passengers and crew is wholly a Good Idea.

It is worth noting that many fire extinguishers are colour-coded, the colour of the extinguisher relating to the agent inside. However, this coding is no longer universally used and many extinguishers now being produced are red overall, although they may have a coloured patch to signify the extinguishing agent. This ambiguity is another reason why it is especially important to read the extinguisher information *before* use.

As far as a pilot is concerned there are two categories of fire; those on the ground and those in the air.

On discovering a fire on the ground, the first priority is to evacuate the immediate area whether it is an aircraft, a hangar, an office or whatever. Then alert somebody to the fire and make sure professional help is on its way. Only then should you think about whether to tackle the fire yourself, and you should only consider doing this if it is possible **without placing yourself in danger**. If in any doubt, *get out*. If you do decide to tackle the fire, try to assess what type it is. Does it involve wood or paper, or flammable liquid, or is it electrical? Then, before loosing off with the first fire extinguisher that comes to hand, check to see what type it is. The appropriate information should be clearly stated on the extinguisher, together with what types of fire it is suitable for and instructions for use. Taking a few moments to read this information could save serious problems.

A fire in the air is a rather different proposition, mainly because in most circumstances it is not an option to evacuate the aircraft. Unless you have any good reason to suspect otherwise, smoke in the cockpit is most likely to come from an electrical fire and may have a distinctive acrid smell. In these circumstances, your first action should be to try to isolate the exact source of the problem. Did the smoke start after turning on a particular service, for example? If so, try turning it off and pulling the relevant circuit breaker if possible, to see if the smoke ceases. Otherwise, close down the whole electrical system by turning the master switch off. If you are faced with a continuing fire, you will have to use the fire extinguisher in the aircraft – you do know where it is, don't you? . As discussed, it is likely to be either a dry powder or Halon type. In either case, take a moment to check the information on the side of the extinguisher and then use it in accordance with those instructions. After the fire is out, it will probably be necessary to ventilate the cockpit to clear any residual powder or mist in the air, as well as clearing any remaining smoke or fumes (which may be toxic). It goes without saying that by this stage a diversion or forced landing with power should be uppermost in your thoughts, although your actions should be dictated by a rational assessment of the actual situation. Although most pilots have an understandable fear of an airborne fire, smoke in the cockpit which clears when the offending electrical service is switched off is more likely to suggest a diversion to the nearest airfield than a desperate dive for the ground.

Although pilots do not need to become directly involved in the care and feeding of fire extinguishers, they should certainly be inspected as part of the pre-flight checks – not least because they tend to be hidden away. Indeed, they may even be missing altogether and nobody has noticed! Most gas-type extinguishers will have a small contents gauge near the handle. If the needle is in the green arc, the extinguisher is properly charged. The extinguisher may also have a label giving the date of the last inspection. If this date is more than a year or two

Refuelling an aircraft: where's the nearest fire extinguisher?

ago, you should start asking awkward questions. It is also important to check that the extinguisher is properly secured and not likely to come loose at an inopportune moment – such as during aerobatics, for example. And if you haven't tried it before, take a moment one non-flying day to remove a cockpit fire extinguisher from its cradle (assuming it isn't wire-locked for some reason) to find out how easy or otherwise this is from the pilot's seat.

The fire extinguisher, rather like other pieces of safety equipment, is one of those items you might never use in anger in a life-time of flying. Nevertheless, good safety practice is all about preparing for worst-case scenarios, no matter how remote or unlikely they might seem. Taking a few moments every so often to prepare for such an event is never time wasted and might one day pay dividends.

▶ Common Survival Equipment

The survival equipment most often found in the average light aircraft are life-jackets and life-rafts for flight over water. It is essential that the pilot has at least a basic knowledge of their features and correct use. Otherwise they are just wasted weight (or should that be mass?) and hardly worth carrying at all. It is also important to recognise the limitations of these items of equipment and what they can and cannot do. It is fair to say that some of these limitations might come as an unpleasant surprise. So if, for example, you think a life-jacket will guarantee your survival in the event of a controlled ditching, think again.

The basic principle of the life-jacket is that it is an inflatable bag, worn in such a way that when inflated it will keep the wearer afloat in a face-up position. Most life-jackets will have one or two inflatable chambers, which are connected to a pressurised bottle containing carbon dioxide (CO_2). The inflation sequence is activated by pulling a red toggle, and there is often a mouthpiece so that the chambers can be 'topped-up' if they are under-inflated. The jacket should also have a whistle attached, to be used for attracting attention. Many designs have a light, which helps the life-jacket (and wearer) to be located in the dark, and there may also be a spray hood. This is a particularly good feature because it will help protect the wearer from exposure and water ingestion, especially in rough seas.

An inflated aviation life-jacket: do not do this until you are outside the aircraft

Although these features of life-jackets are fairly standard, the exact design – in particular, how the jacket is packed or stored – varies from type to type. The traditional aviation life-jacket is packed is a type of casing known as a *valise* which can be soft fabric or a hard shell. This is the design you will find under the passenger seat of most airliners. The main point to remember about this type of design is that it is only intended to be taken out of the valise

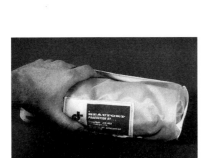

The 'valise'-type life-jacket: not well suited to being repeatedly unpacked, worn and then repacked

once, when it is about to be used for real. Constantly taking the life-jacket out of the valise and attempting to repack it after wearing will greatly increase wear and tear unless exceptional care is taken. This is a problem because in a single-engine aircraft, life-jackets *must* be worn for flight overwater. Merely having the life-jackets onboard is not good enough; there will simply not be time to unpack one and put it on in the event of an imminent ditching.

A better life-jacket design for light aircraft is a constant-wear type. This may consist of a belt with a pouch containing the life-jacket. For flight over water the belt is worn; in the event of ditching the pouch is opened and the life-jacket pulled over the head. Unfortunately this does mean undoing your seat belts, taking off your headset and so on. So this design is also not entirely practical for use in a light aircraft.

The 'constant wear' aviation lifejacket

The best form of GA life-jacket is probably the modern constant-wear 'collar' type. This looks rather like a waistcoat, being worn over the shoulders and fastening around the waist with some sort of clip. One of the prime features of this design is that it is specifically intended to be worn many times and so is better able to withstand a degree of wear. For this reason it is rapidly becoming the most popular type for light-aircraft use.

A life-jacket is an item of life-saving equipment, and it should be treated with as much care and respect as you might treat a parachute just before making a jump. A life-jacket stuffed in the bottom drawer of a filing cabinet under a pile of junk, heaped in a corner or discarded on the floor of the aircraft's baggage compartment could well be nothing more than a waste of space. It should not need to be stressed that life-jackets should be kept away from sharp edges and heavy objects, but real-life experience has proved that not all pilots treat them with any degree of respect. Furthermore, life-jackets need regular servicing to keep them in good condition. Once a year is the normal recommended service frequency. If you think this is excessive, consider the experience of life-jacket servicing organisations who find that on average around 40% of the jackets presented to them – most of which had not been serviced regularly – fail to inflate properly when activated.

So, you have a modern life-jacket, which has been properly cared for and regularly serviced. What else do you need to do? Simple – put it on! If you plan any flight in a single-engine aircraft that will take you out of gliding distance of dry land, put on a life-jacket *before* you get into the aeroplane. A life-jacket stored in the baggage compartment is of precious little use if you are in a hurry to get out of a sinking aircraft. Alternatively, trying to put a life-jacket on whilst flying an aeroplane is at best hazardous and at worst impossible. It also vastly increases the risk of the getting tangled up with the seat belts or headset leads.

Now that you are wearing your life-jacket and flying over the water, the only other major factor to consider is when to inflate it. In short, the life-jacket should *never* be inflated whilst you are still inside the aircraft. The bulk of the jacket will make it difficult to move around, and of course there is a vastly increased risk of puncturing an inflation chamber. In a recent airliner ditching, a number of passengers were lost simply because they ignored the crew's instructions and inflated their life-jackets whilst still in the aircraft. As sections of the cabin flooded, these passengers were unable to escape. This type of panic-driven reaction can be avoided if you have properly prepared for such an eventuality and fully briefed your passengers likewise.

For flight over water, wearing a properly functioning life-jacket is only half the story because the jacket may keep you afloat, but it won't keep you warm. This is a vital point, often not fully appreciated. In the seas around western Europe, the sea temperatures ensure that survival times may be as little as *twenty minutes* when

Likely survival time for a relatively thin person in calm water with no liferaft

Likely survival times in the sea

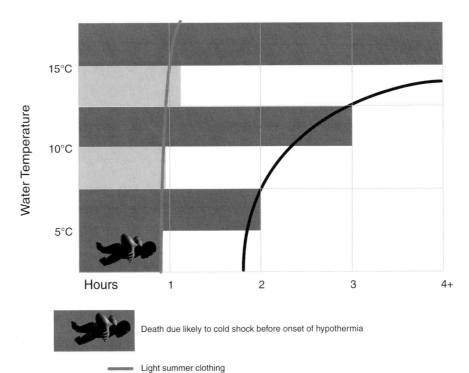

Death due likely to cold shock before onset of hypothermia

Light summer clothing

Survival suit, with long cotton underwear, trousers, shirt and heavy pullover

INABILITY TO PERFORM SIMPLE TASKS WILL OCCUR LONG BEFORE DEATH

the water is at its coldest in the late winter. Even in the late summer, survival time in the sea can be no more than a couple of hours and in bad conditions it may be as little as 40 minutes. Now consider this sobering fact. Even if you ditch in the English Channel less than ten miles from land, get out a Mayday call which is noted

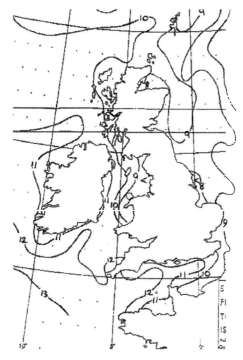

Average late autumn/early winter sea temperatures around the British Isles

and give an accurate location, an SAR helicopter is not guaranteed to reach your location in anything much less than one hour. It will then have to start searching for you once on scene. Next, consider how difficult it is to spot a single life-jacket from a few thousand feet when surveying many square miles of water. The answer is that it's exceedingly difficult.

Even in mid-summer, and even if an SAR crew is scrambled immediately and has a reasonably accurate location, you can expect to be floating in the water for *well over an hour* before that lovely yellow rescue helicopter is hovering over you. And in the cold waters around Europe, that short 60 minutes or more could be – in every sense – a lifetime.

There is a simple solution – a life-raft. A life-raft will keep you afloat and, more importantly, keep you out of the water. It may not feel that warm, but survival time is now a matter of days as opposed to minutes. The comments about the care and servicing of life-jackets apply equally to life-rafts, with the added *caveat* that because life-rafts tend to be quite heavy, it is even more important not to place them on sharp objects. As with life-jackets, life-rafts should be serviced every twelve months. There is the story of the pilot who took his life-raft to a 'dinghy practice drill' held by his flying club at a local swimming pool. The pilot pulled the inflation cord, threw the life-raft into the pool, and looked on in dismay as it sank like a stone to the bottom. It is not

Wear a life-jacket, carry a life-raft

recorded when the life-raft had last been serviced, nor what the unfortunate owner said as his life-raft sank from sight.

If you accept that a life-raft is an essential for overwater flight, the next step is to make sure that is accessible. A life-raft may look nice on the rear parcel shelf, but in such an inaccessible location it is worse than useless. If you are flying solo, place the life-raft on the seat next to you if at all possible. If you have company, make sure that one person is nominated as responsible for getting the raft out of the aircraft and has proper access to it. Also ensure that the responsible person knows how to inflate the life-raft, and knows not to attach it to the aircraft, lest the sinking aircraft take the raft with it. However, do keep hold of the inflation line after activating the life-raft so that it does not blow or float away.

If you are lucky, you may be able to step from a low-wing aircraft into the life-raft. If not, you may have to climb into it from the sea. This is far easier said than done, as anybody who has tried will tell you. The raft should have grab lines, which will help, but practical advice is difficult to give although no doubt the incentive to get out of the sea and into the dinghy will be fairly strong. Practice in the local swimming pool beforehand is probably a good thing.

Once in the life-raft you should find certain standard items of equipment, and these will be discussed later in respect of survival techniques. One item of sea survival equipment which is rarely found in civilian flying but deemed essential to military pilots is the *survival suit.* This is essentially a waterproof garment, which vastly increases survival times for a person in the water by giving protection from the cold. However, survival suits are also bulky, uncomfortable, time-consuming to put on and expensive. Many civilian pilots would consider a survival suit excessive for a short over-water flight, but for a longer sea crossing they are well worth considering.

Having survived a ditching, or a forced landing on land, your next priority is to be rescued. In terms of being located by the rescue services, undoubtedly the most effective piece of survival equipment is an Electronic Locator Transmitter (ELT). An ELT is essentially a radio transmitter that when activated emits a distinctive tone on one or more of the emergency radio frequencies. Handheld ELTs often transmit on 121·5MHz (the international aeronautical VHF emergency frequency) and 243MHz

An ELT

(the NATO combined distress and emergency frequency) and their transmissions can be received by suitably equipped vehicles such as rescue helicopters, maritime patrol aircraft and lifeboats. All can then 'home' on to the location of the ELT. In Sea King SAR helicopters, this homing facility is so good that the aircraft can come into the hover directly above your ELT in IMC without having to locate you visually.

As transmissions on 121·5 and 243MHz are essentially 'line-of-sight', the range at which the ELT can be received is dependent on the height of the receiver. If the ELT is at sea level, an aircraft at 30,000ft should theoretically be able to detect its signals from just over 200nm. A helicopter at 1000ft should detect an ELT on the surface at around 40nm. Even a lifeboat should be able to home to an ELT from around 5nm. Of course these are theoretical maximum figures. High seas, a damaged antenna or a mountain between yourself and a SAR unit might all conspire to reduce the ELT's actual range to something less than these ideal figures.

Some ELTs also transmit on 406MHz, which means that the transmissions can be detected by one of the COSPAS/SARSAT satellites. Once detected, the approximate location of the ELT is transmitted to a ground station which will alert SAR services in the appropriate region. In some areas over-flying aircraft also listen out on 121·5MHz routinely. So even if an ELT is activated in a particularly remote area, its transmissions should not go undetected. As a matter of fact, if you're undertaking a long trip over what might be considered hostile terrain such as mountains or water, it's good airmanship to listen out on 121·5MHz if you have a spare radio available.

ELTs come in several forms. Aircraft flying over particularly remote areas might have a fixed ELT, usually on or near the tail. Normally this is automatically activated by a *g*-switch, which operates in the event of excessive forces such as those produced by a crash landing or ditching. ELTs are also available as portable 'hand-held' models, activated by a simple on/off switch.

ELTs are normally sealed and self-contained units. They don't require any regular checking by the pilot although they will need to be serviced at a stated interval, normally to replace the batteries. If you are buying a portable ELT, check that it floats upright; if its antenna is under water, nobody is going to receive its transmissions. In use, try to attach the ELT to your life-jacket in some way (some jackets have a pocket for this purpose). It should then stay more or less upright, and bring the SAR services straight to you. Finally, when flying with an ELT, make it part of your shutdown checks to tune to 121·5MHz and listen out. If your ELT has activated for whatever reason, a distinctive 'whoop-whoop' tone will be audible. Another give-away is a big yellow SAR helicopter hovering over the aircraft (or building, or vehicle) containing the ELT. This has happened more than once, and if nothing else it proved the system works.

▶ Flares, Lights, Strobes and Heliographs

Aside from the ELT, there are several other aids to location in widespread use. Self-propelled flares or rockets are common in the marine world, and may be found associated with an aircraft or in its life-raft. Although not particularly visible in bright conditions, a flare can be seen from a considerable distance in dull weather or at night. Flares should be used in accordance with the manufacturer's instructions (one for the lawyers!) and only when you can see a rescue vessel close enough and in a position to spot the flare. The normal procedure is to fire one flare, look for a sign that the searching vessel has spotted it and turned towards it. Then fire a second to allow the searchers to line up towards you. Lights can help rescuers locate you, but only at night or in very dull weather conditions.

The light on your life-jacket (which normally activates on contact with the water) will help you to be located in the water at night. Flashing a torch may also help, but more conspicuous than a torch is a high-intensity strobe light. Hand-held battery-powered strobes are widely available.

A set of self-propelled flares

All the above items are only really effective at night or in very dull lighting, and have the drawback that they do not last forever. Once you have used up your flares or exhausted the batteries on your light, torch or strobe (a hand-held strobe will last up to twelve hours on average) these items are regrettably of no further use. One piece of equipment that does not suffer these problems is the *heliograph*. If this sounds like some hi-tech piece of intricate electronics, prepare yourself for a shock – it's a mirror. A heliograph can be any piece of material such as a proper mirror or a section of glass or polished metal that reflects sunlight. The 'flash' thus produced can be aimed towards searchers, and may be visible for a great distance. So it achieves the primary purpose of attracting attention. Purpose-made heliographs (sometime called signalling mirrors) can be bought for under £5, although the inside of an aeroplane and its luggage contents could well offer up a suitable substitute. A heliograph is sometimes found in a standard survival kit such as that within a life-raft, but is generally a much overlooked piece of survival equipment. Given its utter simplicity, and the fact that in trials a detection range of up to 100 miles (in ideal conditions, presumably) has been claimed, perhaps more pilots should be keeping hand-held mirrors as part of their flying equipment.

▶ Transceivers & GPS

The advent of the hand-held VHF air-band *transceiver* was widely welcomed in general aviation. Flying machines that might not normally carry a radio (microlights, vintage aircraft, homebuilts, balloons and so on) now have access to radio communications if they wish, and pilots flying in IMC have a back-up radio. This last has been a lifesaver to more than one pilot after suffering an electrical failure whilst in IMC. A hand-held transceiver also gives the pilot an additional means of calling for help or talking to SAR services which is independent of the aircraft's systems. As such, it should be seriously considered for anyone planning to fly over the sea or other hostile terrain. The only problem is in always ensuring that adequate battery power is available, and some personal discipline is necessary here. Most hand-helds use rechargeable nickel-cadmium batteries, which are notoriously susceptible to mismanagement or misuse. Like fuel in the bowser and runway behind you, there is nothing quite so useless as a fully functional hand-held VHF transceiver with a flat battery…

The advent of the hand-held Global Positioning System (GPS) receiver has caused nothing less than a revolution: a package no bigger than a mobile telephone can give the pilot the sort of navigational accuracy and flexibility that used to be the preserve of airliners and military machinery. In the context of survival, the use of GPS to provide an accurate location can offer great benefits. In the middle of the sea, one wave looks pretty much like another; one patch of moorland can be surprisingly similar to one several miles away. Even the sort of location report that dead reckoning or other radionavigation equipment might give you (e.g. "about 10 miles north-west of Toytown VOR") still leaves the SAR service with a lot of square mileage to cover. But with a functioning GPS and a radio for relaying its information to the outside world, you can give a position accurate to a few hundred metres at worst. *In extremis* the time saved in rescuing you could make all the difference.

One development in this line is a combined transceiver and GPS unit, which makes life even easier. That said, all GPS receivers demolish batteries at a rate which leaves one suspecting that the receiver manufacturers are in league with the battery makers to maximise profits. The combination of a GPS receiver with a hand-held sounds likely to display an impressive thirst for battery power. So your battery management will have to be extremely good if you go down this route. But of course we always carry spare batteries, don't we?

▶Head Protection

In the same way that you rarely see a car driver wearing a crash helmet, the use of head protection is rare in everyday touring aircraft. However, the protection offered by a helmet can be crucial in certain situations. Because of the risks attached to the type of flying they do, military pilots wear 'bonedomes' as a matter of course even in light aircraft. For civilian pilots, the use of a helmet becomes a serious consideration when flying open-cockpit or vintage aircraft, or when performing aerobatics or display flying. Crash helmet-type headgear is also used by 'flexwing' microlight pilots. Where accidents have occurred in these aircraft or situations, head protection has proved to be a lifesaver on several occasions – especially if an open-cockpit aircraft finishes a flight upside-down on the ground. In this case a flying helmet might be the only thing between your head and a very unyielding piece of *terra firma*.

Flying whilst wearing a bonedome can be a little disconcerting if you are not used to the sensations. The extra weight makes head movements more cumbersome, which can affect your lookout. Additionally, the sound-deadening qualities of the helmet will reduce or completely remove audio cues such as engine note and airflow noise. If you have not previously worn head protection in an aircraft, the moral is not to plan anything too exciting until you have got used to the associated sensations. The leads connecting the helmet to the aircraft's radio systems can present a danger of their own, unless they are designed to pull out or break under a certain amount of strain (it's better to break the leads than your neck). A lot will depend on the position of the aircraft's radio lead sockets in relation to the flying helmet, and you should seek expert advice if in any doubt.

A final point concerning headgear is that if you are going to buy some, get the best you can afford. Military bonedomes can run into several hundred pounds. However, as motorbike riders say, "if you have a £30 head, buy a £30 helmet!"

For an open-cockpit aircraft, head protection is pretty much essential

▶Flying Suit

Although not strictly speaking a piece of survival equipment, an all-in-one flying suit is almost essential for flying certain vintage, homebuilt and 'sports' aircraft. If the cockpit has little or no provision for storing charts, flight equipment and the like, the pockets of a flying suit might be the only option. Also, if the flying control runs are visible in the cockpit, a flying suit will allow pens and so on to be kept sealed up, and reduce the risk of such items finding their way into a control-cable pulley or something else important. Wearing a flying suit if you fly aerobatics also reduces the risk of finding assorted pieces of flight equipment floating around the cockpit at inopportune moments. Flying suits are available in flame-resistant materials such as Nomex, the advantages of which are obvious. Some types of suit (although not the ordinary ex-RAF variety) can also provide extra warmth and protection when flying an unheated aircraft, especially an open-cockpit type – although few 'proper' flying suits are especially flattering to the wearer!

If flying an open-cockpit aircraft, flying gloves of some description are also a must. This might sound excessive, but even on a day with a surface temperature of +20°C the temperature at 5000ft could be close to freezing, and with an impressive wind-chill factor too as all that cold air rushes past. Gloves of the right kind can also help protect your hands in the event of a fire.

Before closing this section, a further thought about flying clothing. An enclosed-cockpit aircraft with a proper heater allows you to fly in the clothes you were wearing when you arrived at the airfield. And why not? There's nothing wrong with travelling in comfort. However, a sensible pilot will also consider the surface conditions along the planned route and prepare accordingly. So if it's not your day and you find yourself making an unexpected landing, you're reasonably equipped to face the elements. This may amount to no more than carrying a coat or jacket in the aircraft if you are flying over high ground, or may mean acquiring dedicated sea-survival equipment for an over-water flight. The important point is the *preparation*, even for an extremely unlikely event such as a forced landing or ditching. Never was the old adage "to fail to prepare is to prepare to fail" more applicable. In terms of survival, the ultimate cost of failure is very high indeed.

▶Basics of Survival

Here we will consider the basic rules of survival following a successful forced landing or ditching in or around Europe. Specialist survival skills, such as those needed for arctic, jungle or desert conditions will not be covered. Moreover we will assume that the survivors can reasonably expect to be rescued within a matter of hours or a couple of days at most. So don't look for useful tips on trapping unsuspecting wildlife for food, or how to skin and gut a polar bear armed only with a paperclip. There's an abundance of literature on this sort of thing if you really feel the need to learn all about it.

Safety and Survival Equipment

Whatever the circumstances that lead you into a survival situation and wherever you are, the four essential survival principles remain the same. They are, in order of importance:

- Protection
- Location
- Water
- Food

In outline, these principles are applied as follows:

Protection   Get the occupants clear of the aircraft, attend to any injuries, get the survivors protected against the elements and local conditions.

Location   Ensure that rescuers know where to look for you, and can find you easily once they arrive on the scene.

Water   The need for drinking water should not become a problem until more than 24 hours have passed.

Food   A reasonably healthy individual should be able to survive comfortably, if not entirely happily, for many days or weeks without food.

The two survival situations most likely to be faced by a GA pilot are those following a forced landing in hostile terrain such as mountains or moorland, or a ditching in the water. We will look at each in turn.

▲ Survival on land: protection.

As with so many other aspects of good airmanship, in survival terms proper preparation is vital. Before flight, check that you have a fire extinguisher and a first-aid kit on board and ensure that the seat belts are secure and worn properly.

"Twenty-three doctors, thirty-eight scientists and forty-one technologists. Can't anyone cook?"

Consider what items of clothing you might want to take with you. In general, as we mentioned earlier, you should carry clothing appropriate to the terrain you will be flying over. Think of it as carrying with you the clothes you could walk home in! A simple piece of protective clothing, often overlooked, is a woolly hat or similar. It costs next to nothing and can stay hidden in the bottom of your flight bag if you are worried about your street cred. However, whilst sitting on a cold mountainside waiting for rescue, a distinctly unfashionable woolly hat will retain far more heat than you might realise; ask any experienced walker or climber.

With the appropriate equipment on board, make sure that your passengers receive a proper safety briefing before flight. Pay special attention to seat belts and how to exit the aircraft unaided. There won't be time to do this in an emergency.

Protection means first of all vacating the aircraft without delay. Following an unplanned arrival on dry land, the greatest danger is fire caused by fuel spilling and igniting. If you hadn't shut down the electrical, fuel and engine systems before landing, do so straight away to minimise the risk of fire. Evacuate the aircraft and get everybody well away, preferably upwind of it so that if it does decide to burn they will not be harmed. If anybody is unable to leave the aircraft unaided, assist them as best you can without putting yourself in danger. If they are unconscious or trapped in some way, and possibly hurt, you will have to weigh up the risk that you may injure them further by moving them against the risk of fire. Once clear of the aircraft, check everyone for injuries and administer first aid as needed. Don't go back to the aircraft until you are absolutely sure that it will not catch fire.

With any injuries attended to, consider your protection against the prevailing conditions. The most important problem is likely to be that of cold, possibly exacerbated by wind, rain or snow. Unless there is particularly good shelter nearby, the aircraft itself will probably provide the best protection from the elements. It is especially important to keep as dry as possible and out of cold winds. At this time, having dealt with the immediate dangers, take stock and think about what you are going to do whilst awaiting rescue.

Having considered the situation and the available options and decided on a course of action, resolve to stick with it unless there is some drastic change of circumstances. Decisions made now are likely to be better than those made once cold, shock or hunger have reduced your mental reasoning abilities.

"Damn! There goes my chance of getting through 'War and Peace' without interruption."

Safety and Survival Equipment

Now that your flying machine has become a shelter, start to salvage the aircraft and its contents for anything likely to help you. Baggage may yield up extra clothing, and laminated maps and charts are often virtually waterproof and can act as an extra layer of clothing or headgear. They can also help to seal and insulate your shelter. Books and other paper documentation can be used to start a fire (well away from the aircraft) as can as any remaining fuel or oil. Remember that the first-aid kit should have a pair of scissors, which will be a useful tool. If you have marine survival equipment on board you can use this: life-rafts can give you an extra shelter, a first-aid kit and possibly a knife. Keep your fellow survivors involved and occupied with any task, no matter how minor. Generally the human spirit copes a lot better if it has something to do, no matter how trivial, rather than being left to dwell on circumstances.

▲ Survival on land: location.

Again, this element of survival starts at the planning stage. Before you jump into your aircraft, ask yourself whether somebody knows where you are going, your routing and when you should arrive. Is somebody likely to raise the alarm if you fail to reach your destination? If you will be flying over a particularly remote area (and even the apparently crowded islands of the British Isles have plenty of these), consider filing a full flight plan. In any case, make sure that you book out properly before departure.

Once airborne, talk to ATSUs *en route* and use the transponder if you have one, even if only on the conspicuity squawk. In effect you are leaving a trail that can be followed later by somebody telephoning ATSUs or replaying radar images (most modern radar systems have this latter capability) to look for you. If you are faced with a forced landing, try to tell somebody about it. Without distracting yourself from your primary role of flying the aircraft, making a Pan Pan or Mayday call sooner rather than later increases the chances of it being heard and responded to. If you have a transponder,

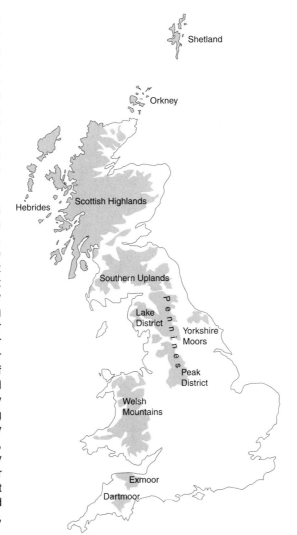

The more remote areas of the mainland UK

setting the emergency squawk of 7700 should have alarm bells ringing all over the place and guarantee you a very attentive audience. Any of these actions will make a major difference in the time it takes rescuers to find you, and the knowledge that someone somewhere has a good idea of where to come looking for you (even if you don't know exactly where you are yourself) will be particularly comforting. There are plenty of instances where a failure to take these basic precautions has led to survivors enduring a long and uncomfortable wait for rescuers to even begin looking for a downed aircraft, let alone locate it.

Once on the ground, and after the risk of fire has passed, see whether the aircraft's radio is still working. If so, you may be able to raise a passing aircraft either on the frequency you were using or on the distress frequency (121·5MHz). Seek to make your aeroplane as conspicuous as possible. Oil painted on snow or brightly coloured material may help by day, especially if you lay it out to form the internationally recognised letters SOS. If you want to be pedantic, a large 'V' also indicates that you require assistance and an 'X' means that you need medical help: think of the 'X' as two pieces of sticking plaster over a cut. Bits of glass, shiny metal or at best a mirror can be used as a heliograph, as already described. A fire or torch can be visible for some distance in low light or darkness, but it is best not to wear out batteries by signalling unless you know rescue services are nearby. Short blasts of a whistle will also attract attention to searchers in the vicinity. If you have marine survival equipment on board, life-jackets will supply bright material, a whistle and possibly a light. As well as shelter and a first-aid kit, a life-raft can provide acres of brightly coloured material and possibly flares too. It goes without saying that if you have an ELT with you, now is the time to use it.

Except in exceptional circumstances, it makes sense to stay with the aircraft. It's a bigger target for rescuers to spot, and the information the SAR service have will usually direct them to the likely location of the aircraft rather than whatever direction the survivors may have wandered off in. If you absolutely have to leave the aircraft,

"No, Angela dear, it isn't a bunch of drunks at the bar."

be sure to mark an arrow in your direction of travel and leave details of when you left the aircraft, how many are in your party and where you are trying to reach.

▲ Survival on land: water and food

Unless you have the misfortune to make a forced landing in some very remote spot many tens or hundreds of miles from human habitation, shortages of food or drink are unlikely to become serious considerations. You may be able to salvage food and drink from your baggage or a rations kit in a life-raft, but a reasonably healthy human can survive for several days without water outside the desert environment and several weeks without food. With the exception of a desert, most terrain will have some source of water. High ground and mountains normally have lying snow, streams, rivers or ponds, and regular precipitation (which can be caught and drunk) is a feature of these regions. However, treat all of these sources with caution and only use them if you have no other water to drink. If you are planning to fly over particularly remote or hostile terrain, simply carrying some drinking water may be worthwhile.

Opinions vary about the advisability of rationing of water. Modern thinking seems to be that you should drink just enough to quench serious thirst, as often as required. The benefit of carrying some sort of snack food with you whenever flying, be it a couple of chocolate bars or whatever, has already been discussed. In the aftermath of a forced landing, the wait for rescue will be made more pleasant if you have something to eat. In extreme situations, however, food should not be eaten in the absence of drinkable liquid because eating increases the demand for water.

▲ Survival at sea: Protection

Only the most foolhardy pilots will approach a flight over water without some consideration of the survival aspects of a ditching. The range of marine survival equipment available, and the importance of proper care and maintenance of this equipment, has already been covered in some detail. Nevertheless, the basics are so important that at the risk of becoming boring, it is worth reiterating them:

■ Don't accept survival equipment which hasn't been properly cared for and maintained.

■ Life-jackets must be worn (but not inflated) for any over-water flight.

■ The life-raft must be properly accessible.

■ All crew and passengers must be briefed about their actions in the event of a ditching.

The aircraft's POH/FM may contain advice about ditching, and if so read this fully – ditching cannot be practised. And if you are unlucky enough to be faced with a real one, you will have only one chance to get it right. A common point of debate is whether or not to unlatch and open a door before touchdown, to avoid the door being becoming jammed by distortion of the airframe during the ditching. Some pilots even advocate holding the door open with a shoe or similar. It's a nice theory, although whether it's possible in practice to remove your shoe, jam it into the doorway and then make sure it doesn't fall overboard whilst also flying down to a ditching is open to question. The general principle of the ditching is to aim to alight along the direction of the swell (i.e. parallel with the swell ridges) even if that involves touching down with a crosswind. Touchdown should be tail-low and as slow as possible while maintaining full control. Avoid heading straight into the face

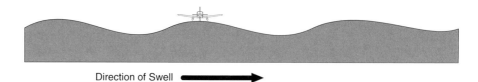

Direction of Swell ➡

In a strong swell and light wind, ditch along the swell. Only land into the swell if ditching into a very strong headwind

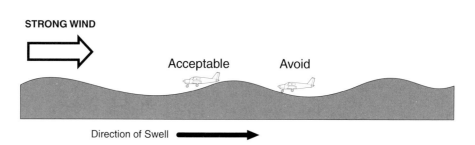

STRONG WIND

Acceptable   Avoid

Direction of Swell ➡

of the swell or waves; ideally the touchdown should be on the crest of a swell. In very strong winds (say above 30kts, evidenced by streaks of spray blown across the sea) it might be better to touch down into wind on the crest of a swell or wave, but again trying to avoid nosing straight into a wave.

*"Hurry up, sir—I'll **tell** you how the film ends."*

Exact touchdown techniques vary between types: again the aircraft's POH/FM is the best source of information and advice. In general high-wing aircraft should touch down using full flap for the lowest airspeed whereas in low-wing aircraft it may be better to leave the flaps up to avoid the aircraft nosing down on arrival on the water. Retractable-undercarriage aircraft are best ditched with the gear up. Warn your passengers to brace just before touchdown and expect more than one impact. Keep the control column hard back once the aircraft has stopped flying to avoid nosing over, and do not be too surprised if the windscreen breaks at some point.

Once the aircraft has stopped, there is a fundamental difference between high-wing and low-wing designs. In a low-wing aircraft it should be possible to open the doors straight away; in a high-wing aircraft you may have to wait for the cabin to start filling with water before it is possible to open the doors. In either case, the cold water rushing in is bound to cause an involuntary gasping reaction from the shock of the cold. Try to avoid swallowing water at this time and do not allow panic to set in. Experience suggests that a light aircraft will usually float long enough (a few minutes) for an orderly evacuation to be made, although in some cases the cockpit will flood quite quickly. Indeed, even if the foregoing seems rather daunting, it should be some comfort to know that the vast majority of ditchings by light aircraft have been survivable.

Back to the aircraft floating in the water. This is when the pre-flight preparation and crew/passenger briefing will come into its own. Everybody should know how to undo their safety belts and how to exit the aircraft, and somebody should have specific responsibility for getting the life-raft, ELT and similar items out of the aircraft. Evacuation will be easier if everyone has removed their headsets. Remember that it's vital not to inflate life-jackets until out of the aircraft, so try to remind your passengers about this. The life-raft should be inflated once clear of any pieces of aircraft that might damage it, and little incentive will be needed to board it. This might be a simple as stepping off the wing into the life-raft, or might be as difficult as trying to right the life-raft and then climb into it. There is little practical advice to offer here, but a pilot who has practised in the calm of a swimming pool is going to have a clear advantage over someone who has never even thought about it.

Your chances of getting into a life-raft are vastly improved if you've had some practice

Once safely into the life-raft, it is time to take stock and decide on your actions. If the raft has a canopy this should be put up quickly. Then first aid should be administered where needed and any water in the raft should be bailed out. As with a forced landing on land, decisions made in the first hour or two are likely to be more rational than decisions made once cold or shock have taken hold. Many life-rafts have sea anchors which should stop them floating too far from their present position. This is usually a good thing if your approximate ditching position was known to the outside world, because this is where the SAR services will come looking for you. Of course, for somebody to come looking for you they need to know that you need rescuing, and have some idea of where to start...see below.

▲ Survival at sea: Location

Mid-channel. If this aircraft's engine stops now, it can't glide to land, nobody will hear its Mayday and it won't appear on any radar screen

Assuming you've equipped yourself with the essentials of a life-jacket and life-raft, the most vital element of survival at sea, in terms of getting rescued, is *location*.

You can start by filing a full flight plan before making an over-water flight, maintaining contact with an ATC unit (preferably with a radar service), knowing where you are yourself and making regular position reports. Routing by the shortest crossing and flying as high as practical will keep you out of gliding distance of land for the shortest time. These precautions will also make it easier to maintain contact with ATC and radio navigation aids, and be seen on radar.

If something does go drastically wrong with the engine, the normal forced-landing procedure calls for the Mayday call to be some way down the list of priorities. In the case of an overwater flight, the Mayday call assumes much greater importance and should be made as soon as you realise you have a serious problem. Give the best position report you can, and set the emergency squawk (7700) on the transponder if you are not already using a squawk allocated by an ATSU. Remember that the sooner you make the call, the sooner help can be on its way. Update your position if time permits. Information such as a range and bearing from a specific point (such as a VOR/DME) and the current heading is going to be much more use than a vague "10 miles out from the coast" or thereabouts. This naturally emphasises the importance of knowing where you are and keeping your awareness of your position updated constantly. Some years ago a light aircraft ditched in the Irish Sea, having given a position report that was in error by approximately 20 miles. The aircraft ditched *only five miles* from the coast and the full emergency resources of lifeboats, coastguards, police, helicopters and shipping broadcasts were deployed – but to the wrong location. The (wooden) aircraft stayed afloat, the mid-summer weather was good and there was plenty of daylight remaining. However, it was no less than *ten hours* before the aircraft and survivor were located, when a fishing boat came across them by chance. The sea is a vast and empty expanse, and the few vessels crossing it are infrequent and widely spread. Even supposedly crowded waterways such as the English Channel, filled with traffic of every description, have claimed their fair share of victims lost without trace.

Once you are adrift on the sea, and having given the best position reports you were able before ditching, any further aid you can give your rescuers will depend on what equipment you have with you. An ELT should be activated straight away, taking care to keep the antenna upright and out of the water to ensure the best transmission. A transceiver can be used to try to make contact with an aircraft but it is unlikely to reach an ATC unit. Bearing in mind the limited battery life, the best strategy might be to listen out on 121·5MHz but transmit as little as possible, conserving power for when SAR units are close enough to talk to. Other aids to location, such as flares, need to be used when you can actually see a potential rescuer nearby. Firing flares in the hope that somebody *might* be close enough to spot them is a triumph of self-deception over reality.

Cold is likely to be a problem even if you are in a life-raft, and will probably be the deciding factor in survival time if you are not. Any extra clothing you can salvage will increase survival time; as mentioned earlier, even the humble woolly hat will make a real difference in retaining body heat. Thrashing around in the water will *not* keep you warm and it's much better to adopt a foetal position: chin against the life-jacket, arms folded across your chest, legs drawn up. A group of survivors in the water should huddle together, not only for warmth and morale but to present a bigger target for searchers. These simple measures can double survival time compared with trying to stay afloat by treading water without the benefit of a life-jacket.

As before, apart from proper preparation in terms of planning and equipment, the will to survive may be the deciding factor. Take heart that even in some apparently hopeless situations, such as a ditching in mid-winter without a life-jacket or life-raft, the pilot has survived to tell the tale.

▲ Survival at sea: water

Ironic, isn't it, to have to think about the provision of water when floating around surrounded by the stuff! Drinking sea water is an absolute non-starter so that only leaves any water you have actually brought onboard with you (or any in a rations kit) and the remote chance of capturing enough rainfall to collect a decent drink. How you decide to use any water that you have is one of those decisions best taken at early stage, and will be influenced by your assessment of how long you expect to wait for rescue. The previous comments on the rationing of water apply, with one additional proviso; given that it's unlikely you'll be able to collect additional supplies, great care must be taken not to waste any water through spillage, leakage, contamination or non-essential use.

▲ Survival at sea: food

As with a forced landing on land, unless you end up somewhere very remote, lack of food is unlikely to become a deciding factor in survival at sea. The life-raft may contain food rations and even fishing equipment and instructions. And even if you don't catch anything, the activity might give you something to do and thereby keep morale going.

All in all, it is abundantly clear that preparation for survival is more than just carrying the right equipment and supplies. It is a matter of adopting the right state of mind, having a sensible plan of action and seeing it through. Time and again, human endurance, tenacity and resourcefulness has triumphed over mechanical misfortunes, the forces of nature or even just pure bad luck.

▶Revision

44 Who is responsible for making sure that a passenger safety briefing is completed before flight?

45 What causes motion sickness?

46 When should 'upper torso restraint', i.e. a single or double shoulder strap, be used?

47 What is the first principle of first aid?

48 What class of fire is one involving flammable liquids such as petroleum, solvents etc., and what sort of extinguishing agent should *not* be used on such a fire?

49 For an over-water flight in a single engine aircraft out of gliding range of land, how should life-jackets be carried and when should they be inflated in the event of a ditching?

50 In order of priority, what are the four essential survival principles?

Answers at page HF117

Revision Answers

The Functions of the Body (Basic Physiology)

1   21%; the proportion of gases in the atmosphere remains largely unchanged with increasing altitude.

2   Carbon dioxide (CO_2)

3   Any six from:
Personality changes and impaired judgment
Confusion and difficulty concentrating
Loss of co-ordination
Drowsiness
Headaches
Blue/grey skin colour
Hyperventilation
Loss of basic senses
Unconsciousness

4   30-45 seconds.

5   Any three from:
Time at altitude
Exercise
Stress/workload
Cold, Illness, Fatigue
Alcohol
Smoking

6   Hyperventilation.

7   Nitrogen; decompression sickness (DCS or 'The Bends'); 24 hours.

8   The Eustachian tube.

9   None at all!

10   In short and regular eye movements, with a definite pause in between to focus.

11   Because the light of the object is now falling on an area of the retina with more rods than cones (rods work better in poor light).

12   Increased *g*.

Health and Flying

13   One unit of alcohol is equivalent to half a pint of beer, or a standard (small) glass of wine or single measure of a spirit.

14   14-21 units per week for a woman and 21-28 units per week for a man.

15   By 1300

16   Carbon monoxide

17   The smoker will experience the onset of hypoxia at a lower altitude than the smoker.

18   Gastroenteritis (associated with viral infections of the stomach and intestines or food poisoning).

19   A 24 hours, B 48 hours, C 24 hours.

20   You must inform the authority, in writing, as soon as possible.

21   You should close the heater controls, ventilate the cabin with the maximum fresh air, divert to the nearest airfield and seek urgent medical advice on landing because of the risk of carbon monoxide (CO) poisoning.

The Functions of the Mind (Basic Psychology)

22 Seven

23 By rehearsal, i.e. regular practice of a procedure.

24 Spatial disorientation.

25 The acceleration might be perceived as a pitch-up, but in IMC the pilot should trust the instruments and not conflicting balance or sensory sensations.

26 The pilot might believe that his approach is too low.

27 The approach may well be flown too 'shallow', by descending too early and continuing below the safe approach angle.

28 No! In hazy condition objects appear to be further away than they really are.

29 Constant bearing = constant danger. An object that does not move relative to you is one that is most likely on a collision course.

30 20 seconds (closing speed = 540 knots divided by 60. i.e. nine miles per minute. Therefore three miles will be covered in 20 seconds).

31 About a metre ahead of the eyes.

32 By knowing what is happening in the aircraft and around it, making safe and accurate decisions and having good judgment based on all available facts.

Stress and Managing Stress

33

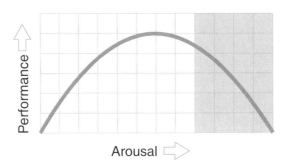

34 20°C (68°F)

35 divorce, new family member, change in home

36 Action coping

Personalities and Cockpit Resource Management

37 P-G+

38 Anti-authority

39 The other pilot should be encouraged to always openly express any doubts or misgivings.

Cockpit Design and Procedures

40 Before flight

41 15,800ft

42 Altimeter

43 A= undercarriage control lever, B= flaps control lever

Safety and Survival Equipment

44 The Pilot in Command (PIC)

45 Conflicting information received from the eyes, vestibular apparatus of the ears and other sensory organs.

46 Whenever available in the aircraft.

47 First do no harm!

48 A class B fire; water should not be used on such a fire.

49 Life-jackets should be worn, and only inflated once outside the aircraft.

50 Protection, Location, Water, Food

Prologue

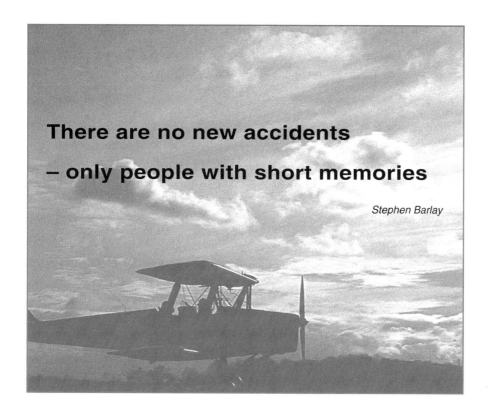

There are no new accidents

– only people with short memories

Stephen Barlay

Flight Safety

It's a bright and sunny Sunday afternoon at a small airfield. A light wind is tugging at the windsock, the spring colours on the distant hills are bright and vivid in the clear air. Some scattered clumps of cumulus drift by at 3000ft or so: it's probably the best flying day of the year so far. Where else would a pilot be on a day like this?

This pretty airfield has no controlled airspace, no air traffic control and no landing fees. In the clubhouse the local pilots are watching the coming and goings, whilst the radio in the corner crackles with position reports and passing traffic. A visiting aircraft is parked on the grass; its three occupants are drinking coffee in the clubhouse and passing the time of day. Their aeroplane, a reasonably sophisticated touring type, has caught my eye because I have recently been flying a similar model; I am interested to see how it copes with the airfield's fairly short runway. In just a few minutes I will know a little more about the aeroplane but much, much more about the pilot. However, for now, with the quiet drone of circuiting aircraft drifting on the breeze, the scene is about as peaceful as an active airfield can get.

The visitors say their goodbyes and start to leave. A club member has to follow them out to ask if they wouldn't mind booking in and booking out on the movements sheet. The obvious reluctance with which the pilot complies with this simple request seems a little out of place.

Warning sign number one, and the first link in an accident chain.

Out at their aircraft, the visitors stand for a while to watch the aircraft landing and taking off on the adjacent runway. I turn to greet a newly arrived regular and we talk for maybe two minutes. When I turn back, I am surprised to see that all three have boarded their aircraft and the doors are closed. If any of them did do a pre-flight check, it must have been conducted at an impressive sprint.

Warning sign number two.

Within seconds the engine is running (did the pilot call "Clear prop"? I didn't hear it). The radio crackles into life for the briefest of calls, and the aircraft taxies straight onto the runway. With no further trivial formalities the pilot lines up on the centreline, the throttle is slammed open and the aircraft accelerates down the runway. No more than 90 seconds can have elapsed since the engine was started. I heard no power checks, there could have been no proper pre-take-off checks.

Warning sign number three.

Events are snowballing fast now. What if the control lock is still in, or the trimmer set full-up, or the fuel selected to an empty tank or the mixture not fully rich? Also, I can see that the pilot is not using the POH/FM-recommended short-field technique, despite the fact that the runway length is close to the minimum for the aircraft type.

The warning signs are accumulating fast and events are snowballing. An accident chain is nearly complete. But the pilot has committed the aircraft to its course and it lifts off...

There is an awful inevitability about what happens next. As the aircraft gets airborne, the pilot holds it down close to the ground. The undercarriage starts to come up and, as it crosses the end of the runway, the aeroplane abruptly banks steeply to the left. Arcing across the airfield, its upper surfaces are clearly visible to those of us watching from the ground.

All very impressive of course (if you're easily impressed, that is) except for the minor detail that the circuit direction on that runway is *right-hand.* One reason for the right-hand circuit is so that traffic departing the main runway doesn't cut across traffic using the parallel grass strip to the left of it. Which is what our dashing pilot has just done. At less than 100ft, the aircraft crosses the airfield boundary, flashes across the road bordering the airfield and roars directly over two houses that are the airfield's nearest neighbours. The field has a public enquiry pending into its future. When the time comes will the operators have the support of those house owners?

Still only about 300ft high, the aircraft straightens out in the general direction of its home base. The radio comes alive briefly with a cheery, self-satisfied, goodbye and is silent again. Meanwhile, back in the clubhouse there is a collective sigh – a mixture of relief and despair – and a weary shrug of the shoulders amongst those of us who have witnessed this sorry spectacle.

It is all too easy to dismiss the pilot as simply an idiot, totally unfit to be put in charge of an aeroplane. Yet, the fact remains that he must have completed a course of training, passed a number of theoretical examinations of his knowledge and practical tests of his flying skills. There is no reason to believe that he is any less intelligent, or any less skilful, than any other pilot. Foolish, reckless, selfish and careless? On the evidence of this performance, yes. Stupid? Probably not.

I am left wondering whether this pilot would have acted any differently if he really understood the many fundamental safety rules and procedures that were breached in such a short space of time? Would he be more interested if he knew how many fatal accidents have been caused in the last 20 years by any one of those lapses? Would his behaviour have been any different if he knew how many lives his oh-so-dazzling departure steep turn has claimed in the past decade alone?

Perhaps I am being naive, but maybe if he knew – if he really understood – the lethal risks he was taking with his own life and those of his unfortunate passengers, he might hesitate. And in hesitating, he might just decide to get his thrills in some other more constructive way. Would it be possible to persuade that aviator to be better educated, safer and more professional? Is it possible for a pilot to improve his or her standards without losing the fun of flying? I think it is. I have seen the consequences of a serious accident, and it's not something I want to see again. If I could do something practical to prevent an accident, shouldn't I do it?

Now I am thinking that a Flight Safety section to the PPL course could detail what lies behind general-aviation accidents, why they happen and how most of these accidents might be avoided. This section would not form part of the official syllabus for the PPL course. It can not have an exam, because there can be no question papers and no pass mark. What's more, if you – the reader – decide that you don't have the time or the inclination to read it, that won't stop you acquiring a PPL. I don't generally have a lot of spare time myself; why write something that people might not even bother to read?

But perhaps something I could write in this section might – just might – make you pause and think one day. I'm sure you're not a reckless and negligent individual; very few pilots are. More likely you're someone who is normally careful and cautious, but who could be caught out by an unexpected turn of events – it's happened to all of us at one time or another. And perhaps on that day you will remember something you read here, and then you will choose a safer course of action and avoid a needless risk. Maybe you will then at the end of the day find yourself filling in your logbook, not an accident report.

And while my coffee goes cold in front of me and the engine note of departing aircraft recedes into the distance, I have already decided: that's good enough for me.

Accidents Will Happen

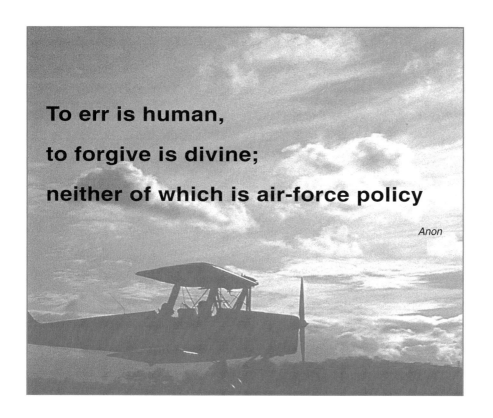

To err is human,

to forgive is divine;

neither of which is air-force policy

Anon

Flight Safety

Imagine the scene. Laden down with a plate-full of food, knife & fork, condiments, a mug of tea and a newspaper or magazine, you steer an uncertain course from the kitchen to the lounge. You're intending to hit the comfy chair just in time for the start of your favourite TV programme. The hallway is dark, but you have no spare hand to turn the lights on and no time to search for the light switch in any case. The door to the lounge is closed, so you rearrange your burden in an effort to get just one finger to the door handle to pull it open. At that exact moment, someone bursts through the door from the other side, totally unaware of your presence. Food, drink and assorted accessories are flung all over you, the walls and the floor. Dinner is lost, the programme is missed, and your evening is blighted.

Despite the inevitable recriminations and counter-accusations that accompany this little vista, the only real culprit is apparently the invisible hand of fate that led the two of you to the same spot at exactly the same moment. Rather like the aftermath of any trivial accident, when the debris has been cleared away and the damage repaired, the most fitting epitaph seems to be that accidents will happen.

In this way we deal with the unknown forces that often seem to determine our destiny. It is generally accepted that in any field of human activity, there is the potential for things to go wrong. In the multitude of decisions and physical actions accompanying every human task of any significance, there lie dangers and endless possibilities for misunderstandings, mistakes and errors. This is an undeniable fact but it does not mean that all accidents are a matter of chance, as likely to happen to any one person as to another. The dictionary defines an accident as an "event that is without apparent cause or unexpected", but in reality very few accidents, especially flying accidents, can be truthfully described as being without apparent cause or even unexpected. It's true that genuine accidents happen from time to time, but there is no inevitability about them; in fact, the vast majority of accidents are avoidable. Rather than saying accidents *will* happen, we should say that accidents *do* happen.

It is only very occasionally that a pilot is the victim of an event which appears to be a true 'accident' in the sense of being totally unforeseeable, or what the insurance companies call an "Act of God". When such a sporadic episode happens, it could be indeed said that the pilot was simply unlucky and happened to be in the wrong place at the wrong time. Such an accident can be viewed as the workings of chance or fate, and part of the risk we must accept if we are to leave the safety of the ground. Harsh as it is to those who provide the raw material that becomes an accident report, however, such an event is rare indeed. In truth the vast majority of flying accidents are *not* caused by chance or random factors. It is much more commonly the case that a surprisingly predictable course of incidents led to an entirely predictable outcome – a damaged or destroyed aircraft and/or damaged or destroyed human beings. What is more, in most cases the pilot in command almost always had the means – even up until the last few moments of flight – to avert the accident. So in the sense that insurers and the authors of Greek tragedy meant it, the word "accident" very rarely applies to aviation. Indeed, it very rarely applies anywhere else.

The root causes of most accidents have been well understood and widely reported for decades, and any investigator will tell you that there are almost no new accidents. The first recorded crash in aviation history befell Icarus, who (according to Greek legend) flew with wings held together by wax. Despite the warnings of his father, he flew too high and too close to the sun. The heat melted the wax, the wings fell apart, and thus Icarus featured in aviation's first accident report – written by an unknown Greek author in about 700BC. And this simple pattern has been repeated by non-mythical pilots ever since. Despite rules or advice to the contrary and despite being aware of a known hazard, a pilot decides (or 'elects', as the accident reports put it) to do something dangerous or unsafe – with inconvenient, expensive and sometimes tragic results. And the verdict, all too often true, is pilot error.

To some of us, Icarus was merely a fool who got what he deserved. To others, perhaps he was just unlucky. Scholars and philosophers have argued through the ages as to how much a man's destiny is shaped by his own actions and how much by fate – by forces completely beyond the control of mere mortals. I wouldn't wish to get too tied up in this age-old debate. But I would argue that in the narrow field of flight safety, everyone involved must accept that they do have control of their destiny as far as the safety of each flight is concerned. The purpose of all the systems and checks and double-checks that contribute to flight safety is to deny the hand of fate a chance to strike a mortal blow to man and machine. Fate (or chance or luck, depending on your world-view) is always waiting in the background. If we leave too much to chance, we are in effect relinquishing the command of our own destiny.

The concept of 'luck' is one that surfaces again and again if you read the accounts of pilots who have defied the odds in some way or another. Those pilots who have flown aircraft as instruments of war often have an intimate understanding of the part played by luck in their survival. One such pilot, Patrick Gibbs, wrote "*Luck could be courted; it would never deputise for skill, but it might be persuaded to walk hand in hand with it through danger. It seemed to me that careful attention to the detail of individual operations not only improved* [the pilot's] *chances of success, but also the pilot's chances of survival... Luck flew with those who, before embarking on even the most hazardous flight, were confident of landing safely at its end. Such confidence could only be obtained from careful preparation before take-off...*" This attitude is not unique to the flying business. A self-made billionaire was once asked if luck had played a major role in his achievements. After due consideration he replied caustically that strangely enough, the harder he worked, the luckier he became.

So let's accept that to ensure flight safety, we as pilots must be prepared to take charge of our own destinies. One of the columns in a pilot's logbook is headed 'Pilot In Command' and it's filled in by the captain irrespective of the size of aeroplane being flown, be it ever so small and simple. The term 'Pilot In Command' implies authority and power: it also denotes *responsibility*.

At this point I wouldn't want you to start thinking that I am going off on some judgmental head-trip, but the concept of responsibility is in real danger of becoming an old-fashioned and redundant notion in modern society. Bear with me – this isn't a political judgment, but a pragmatic one. When things go awry it's a natural human reaction to want to avoid admitting being in the wrong, especially if some error or omission on our own part might be the cause. Through anger, pride, shame or just embarrassment, there is a natural temptation to present ourselves as a victim of unforeseen circumstances rather than the author of our own misfortune. We look for an alternative explanation, passing culpability to somebody else or even a higher authority such as 'fate' in an attempt to pass the blame. Our 'modern' society encourages this natural response; rare is the politician who will state "I made a serious mistake and it's all my own fault".

Harsh experience has taught the providers of goods and services to surround their products with an ever-increasing array of warnings and advice to protect them from the complaints of those unable to exercise common sense in everyday life. There's the case of the iron sold with the stern warning "Do not iron clothes whilst wearing them". Or the bags of nuts provided by a certain airline which carry the solemn instructions "Open packet, eat contents". As I write this I have a jar of peanut butter in front of me. The label clearly states 'Peanut Butter'. In slightly smaller writing the contents are marked as 'Peanuts and salt'. Yet, the manufacturer still feels obliged to add an extra caution; "Warning, this product should not be eaten by those with a known peanut allergy". This is not to trivialise the problem of nut allergy but to illustrate how much the manufacturer must consider the user incapable of independent thought; clearly the public at large have to be protected and cautioned from every eventually. Not long ago a motorist was stopped by the police after attaining a speed of over 150mph in a brand new £100,000 sports car. When questioned about this turn of speed our hero claimed "I really did not realise how fast the car would go. It wasn't explained to me when I bought it". I wonder, should such a fact really have to be explained to somebody capable of attaining a driving licence?

This is all very entertaining but it sits uneasily with the business of piloting aircraft. A pilot simply cannot – indeed must not – assume for one second that he will be cautioned, warned and protected from every eventuality. A fully developed cumulo-nimbus containing a violent thunderstorm does not display big neon signs stating 'Flight into this cloud might prove fatal'. If a pilot tries to enter an impossible aerobatic manoeuvre from 10ft above the runway, no automatic limiting device will intervene on the controls. Weather, aerodynamics and the laws of physics do not come with legal indemnity notices. It is the pilot's responsibility to use knowledge, experience and skill to avoid dangerous situations.

You might think that an instinct for self-preservation would lead any reasonable pilot to accept responsibility for his own safety. Nevertheless, it is surprising how many light aircraft apparently encounter sudden and inexplicable windshear on

"Why does it always have to be me that is wrong?"

crossing the runway threshold, in conditions which would not normally give rise to this occurrence. The pilot insists that this must be what happened; how else to explain the subsequent heavy landing and damaged aircraft? Never mind the dozens of pilots who managed to land similar aircraft safely that day on the very same runway in the very same conditions without encountering the mysterious windshear? Then there was the pilot who over-ran the end of a short runway, claiming that the brakes had failed (an explanation heard many times before and since). A witness to the incident, a person of no little mechanical knowledge, observed dryly that brakes can't do much to slow an aircraft while it is still airborne more than half-way down the runway.

The real problem is that once individuals try to persuade others of their own lack of responsibility for safety, they can also begin to persuade themselves. This becomes an abdication of responsibility; a reluctance or even refusal to accept the consequences of their own actions. For example, instead of keeping in current practice at landings, some pilots will instead blame bad arrivals on a range of factors from mysterious weather phenomena to undetectable mechanical failures and thus feel better about themselves. (At least, they may in the short term; there's a body of knowledge that describes what happens when this sort of self-deception is forced into the unconscious – the technical term is 'repressed' – and operates from there. However, that's perhaps something for another book). Instead of making a proper pre-flight check, such an aviator might reason that it is the engineer's job to look after the aeroplane. If something goes wrong, it's clearly not the pilot's fault. Instead of being the perpetrator of an incident, this pilot becomes the victim deserving of our sympathy – a role much easier to bear for the average human being.

A proper pre-flight check

This is all well and good but it ignores the unfortunate fact that when things do go wrong – for whatever reason – it is the Pilot in Command who must sort out the consequences. Regardless of who is 'to blame' or the legal niceties of the situation, pilots have to take responsibility for solving aviation-related problems if only to ensure that after the event they are actually around to argue their case. As the person most likely to be first on the scene of an accident, the Pilot In Command needs to have a strong vested interest in the safety of the flight, as a simple matter of self-preservation if nothing else. This is why a pass-the-buck attitude is so out of place in the aviation world. If the crash or incident is of a fairly minor nature, the pilot's attitude might be of little more than academic interest except perhaps to his insurers. However, once people start getting hurt or worse, the 'somebody else's responsibility' approach is shown up for what it is – a dangerous and potentially fatal self-delusion.

Holding a pilot's licence of any description means accepting the obligations that come with the freedom of flight. Every pilot's seat could come with a sign repeating the clichéd words of the executive desk plaque: "The buck stops here". If you can accept the fact that on each flight you are quite literally taking your life in your hands, you are thinking along the right lines. A pilot is in many ways the first and also last line of defence in the flight-safety battlefront, and in the very worst cases it is left to the pilot to make the final stand for safety versus danger. Thus it is that pilots have sometimes performed almost miraculous feats of courage and skill to rescue their aircraft and themselves from apparently hopeless situations. More mundanely, a simple query of a strange ATC instruction, a return to base because of an unknown noise or vibration or simply the self-discipline to listen to a nagging doubt that seems out of place has averted many an accident. In every way pilots are at the top of the food chain of the aviation world; the vast supporting network of airfields, ATC services, meteorologists, engineers and even the regulatory authorities exist primarily to provide a service to us lucky aviators. When everything is going right it is the pilot who enjoys the spoils, revelling in his ascendancy over mere earth-bound mortals. When things start going wrong, however, it is often the pilot who has to find the solution. And it is nearly always the pilot who will suffer the most serious consequences if he cannot.

The pilot in command – the top of the aviation food-chain

If all this seems a bit portentous and tiresome, consider the medium in which a pilot operates. With the possible exception of deep-sea divers and astronauts, pilots ply their skills in the most unforgiving environment humans can enter. Although all humans have a life-long affinity with life on solid ground, even the most experienced aviators can claim no more than about 5% of their life has been spent airborne. Whilst 30,000 flying hours might rate as more than a passing acquaintance with the art of aeronautical travel, they do not alter the fact that aircraft operate in utterly merciless surroundings. When things start to go wrong in the air, the one thing you *can't* do is probably the one thing you would most like to do – stop everything, freeze the moment and think things over before deciding what to do next. Or even better, stop the aeroplane and step out on to solid ground. At its heart, the whole concept of heavier-than-air flight means keeping the aeroplane moving through the medium at a safe attitude and airspeed, and thereby maintaining a mastery of aerodynamics over gravity. It is no coincidence that the single most common cause of serious accidents is that of a pilot (maybe one of considerable experience) upsetting this fundamental balance. Usually he was in an aeroplane that was complete and fully functioning until it hit the ground.

I have a plaque on my office wall. It shows an old biplane perched in a tree, comical and embarrassed. How it got there can only be imagined, but next to the picture are printed these sage words:

Aviation in itself is not inherently dangerous. But to an even greater degree than the sea it is terribly unforgiving of any carelessness, incapacity or neglect.

I am not seeking to frighten or depress anyone, but by now you might be beginning to feel rather vulnerable. If so, something worthwhile has been achieved already. When pilots feel too safe, they tend to become over-confident and complacent and the seeds of calamity are sown. Indeed, the majority of serious accidents can be traced back, in part at least, to an overconfident – even reckless – pilot. Conversely if a pilot feels just a little vulnerable, he tends to be more careful and cautious. This needn't mean that this person is destined for a career of boring and pointless flying. It just means that he or she takes care to assess risks, minimises them where possible and stays within his or her own limitations. Aviation has many sayings – proverbs, if you like. Some will be referred to later, but to here is one that could usefully be carved into the psyche of every pilot:

There are old pilots and there are bold pilots,
but there aren't any old, bold pilots.

Yes, accidents do happen. Above all, they happen to those who through overconfidence, ignorance or misjudgment lead themselves into dangerous but often entirely avoidable situations. Pilots have an impressive network of support personnel, information systems and regulation to keep them safe. But pilots also have the autonomy to step outside this safety net if they choose to do so. The ultimate accountability and the final decision always rests with the pilot, and the first step towards safer flying is to recognise and accept this in full for what it is. This responsibility is the price of our freedom of flight.

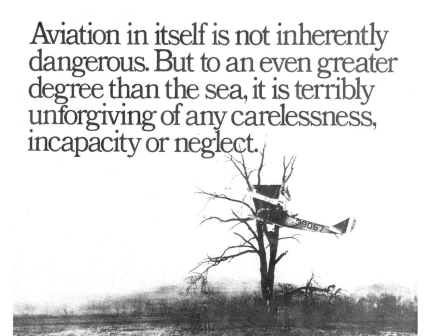

Aviation in itself is not inherently dangerous. But to an even greater degree than the sea, it is terribly unforgiving of any carelessness, incapacity or neglect.

Lies, Damned Lies and Statistics

"There are lies, there are damned lies and there are statistics"

Disraeli

Flight Safety

Whenever dealing with statistics, it is first necessary to sound a note of caution, which is that statistics can be used to prove almost anything if you want to. As far as I know, no aviation accident has ever been caused by massed formations of passenger-laden airliners flying under the bridges of the Thames in fog. This does not mean that such an activity is safe – common sense alone would suggest that it's a rather dangerous thing to do, and the lack of fatal accidents from this cause means that most pilots recognise the fact. More realistically, there have been a mere handful of fatal accidents in the last 20 years directly attributable to flight in thunderstorms. Again, this doesn't mean that flying in thunderstorms is safe. You could interpret such a statistic to mean that the hazards of thunderstorms and the importance of avoiding them has been appreciated by all but a handful of bold (and destined not to be old) pilots. So to get the best out of any statistical study, it is necessary to approach the subject with a fair dose of common sense.

It stands to reason that if you know more about accidents that have occurred, you are in a much better position to avoid repeating the errors and misjudgments often involved. With this purpose in mind I went to Aviation House, the headquarters of the UK's Civil Aviation Authority, close to the bustling south terminal at London Gatwick airport. The main hall of this magnificent glass and steel edifice is a bright and airy atrium and off to one side you will find a fountain of knowledge – the CAA library. On these shelves, amongst other worthy tomes, reside the records of aviation accident reports stretching back as far as most of us can remember. To appear within one of the reports is to achieve a lasting fame of sorts, but it is difficult to read through these catalogues of disaster without pausing to reflect on the human tragedy that lies behind the stark report "Aircraft: Destroyed. Injuries: 2 fatal".

In this library I researched the Air Accident Investigation Branch (AAIB) reports of fatal accidents to general aviation (GA) aircraft for the 20 years from 1977 to 1997. These reports cover accidents in and around the UK to both UK-registered and overseas-registered aircraft. Where reliable information has been published, I also included in my survey accidents to UK-registered aircraft that occurred outside the UK and accidents to military aircraft comparable with GA types. My endeavours produced a database of around 300 fatal accidents, an average of 15 per year. This is not a huge number, and in what follows it must be remembered that in such a small sample it is easy for random variation to create undue distortion. For example, in 1986 there were 14 fatal GA accidents but in 1987 there were 25, a number so shocking that a special report was commissioned to look into the causes. The report could draw few conclusions as to why this particular year should have produced so many fatal accidents, but the following year the number of fatal accidents fell to 11. This only seems to confirm that when dealing with such a small sample, apparently inexplicable peaks and troughs will occur from time to time.

The number of accidents on its own means little until you can compare it with some measure of how much flying is actually taking place. This presents something of a problem because nobody really knows exactly how much GA flying goes on each year. The best guess the authorities can come up with is based on estimated hours flown, which reveals (as you might expect) a considerable increase in GA activity over the last 20 years. Using this measure, the message regarding the accident rate (hours flown versus accidents) in recent years is mixed. It's not getting worse, but it's not getting markedly better either.

In researching these accidents, I looked not just for a primary cause such as loss of control or controlled flight into terrain but also for other patterns or common features. It is fair to say that accident reports have become a lot more comprehensive over the years, and I was therefore able to categorise not just the 'primary' cause of all but about a dozen mysterious accidents but also classify any obvious contributory factors. Many of these contributory factors, often known in the business as 'causal factors' appeared frequently. One way or another they usually amount to poor pre-flight planning, a lack of qualification for the flight or operating the aircraft outside its limits.

I don't pretend to be a statistician, so my conclusions must not be seen as a definitive work of reference. I have sometimes taken it upon myself to read between the lines of the accident report, and reach my own conclusion as to the probable causes. All that said, over the sample of 300 reports I like to think that any errors or assumptions on my part should have been largely evened out.

Before continuing, ask yourself what you think is likely to be the most common causes of fatal accidents, and in what phase of flight they are most likely to occur. Write down your answers so that there will be no cheating later. Now read on, and see how close you are.

Fatal GA accidents 1977-1997

Primary Cause

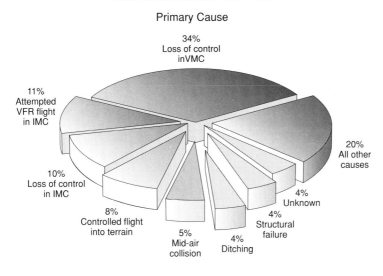

Phase of Flight

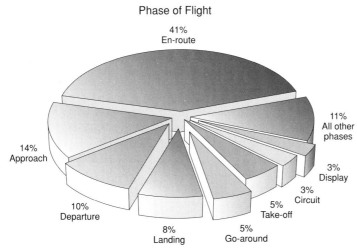

A more detailed study of the statistics also reveals some other interesting facts. Less than 5% of the fatalities were student pilots; far more instructors and professional pilots than students were involved in fatal accidents. In fact, pilots with more than 1,000 hours were involved in three times more fatal accidents than pilots with less than 100 hours. More than half the fatal accidents involved PPL holders without any additional licence or rating and nearly 60% of fatal accident pilots had less than 100 hours on the aircraft type they were flying.

The most common contributory (causal) factors were, in order:

- Pilot not legally qualified for the flight attempted (i.e. a non-instrument qualified pilot flying in IMC)

- Poor pre-flight planning and preparation

- Engine failure

- Incorrect operating procedures

In the following chapters we will look more closely at these statistics and what they can tell us about avoiding accidents. However, before getting carried away with the notion that aviation is an incredibly risky undertaking, let's put these figures into some perspective.

"UP ABOVE THE WORLD SO HIGH"
Housebreaker. "Well, that don't look to me 'ardly safe some'ow."

We can assume that an average of 15 fatal accidents a year means around 18 deceased pilots (discounting for a moment their unfortunate passengers). This is not a huge number given a UK pilot population estimated at 30,000 or so. Moreover, an average of 26 fatalities per year in general aviation seems rather small compared with the annual carnage of over 3,500 killed on the roads of the UK every year. This means that more people die on the roads in an average four-day period than die in small aeroplanes in a whole year. Put another way, in less than two months more people will die in road accidents than have been lost in GA accidents in a 20 year period. Of course road accidents generally receive little national attention, whereas the perceived glamour of aviation means that few serious aviation crashes escape the attention of the press.

There are many other less publicised dangers to life and limb. In an average year in the UK, up to 50 people die in frying-pan fires and a further 4000 are injured. Around 40 people die after falling from open doors on trains. Each year around 75 hunters in France are accidentally shot dead by other hunters, and an average of 140 people die after swallowing pen tops. The list goes on. Every year 20 people are electrocuted by their alarm clock and a further 60 are seriously injured whilst putting on their socks. I kid you not. So statistically, a pen top or a sock is far more dangerous than an aircraft in flight.

We said earlier that "Aviation in itself is not inherently dangerous..." It is easy to forget that the vast majority of flights are undertaken and completed safely. "Aeroplane lands safely, nobody hurt, nothing damaged" may not be the stuff of tabloid headlines, but it is how must of us would like to see our flights reported.

Let us leave abstract numbers and concepts for now and look at some real-life examples of what can go wrong in the everyday business of flying aeroplanes. However, before moving on I must repeat the opening caution – we must not place too much trust in the bare numbers thrown up by statistics. The trends and probabilities must be treated with caution and examined in the light of common sense. In the real world, the underlying problem with flight-safety statistics was summed up by a former wartime pilot who had witnessed many accidents and tragedies. He observed sadly that a rare or unusual accident hurt just as much as one with what he called a "seen it a hundred times" cause.

"…they didn't crash-land – they crashed elbows at the bar talking hairy manoeuvres…"

The Accident Chain

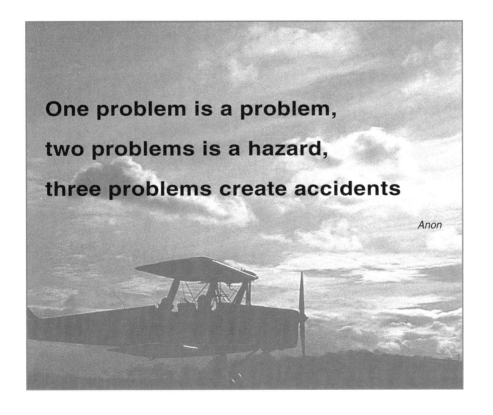

One problem is a problem,

two problems is a hazard,

three problems create accidents

Anon

The Accident Chain

When most think people think of an aircraft crash, the mental picture summoned up is usually one of a sudden catastrophe in which the pilot is overwhelmed by an unexpected and abrupt disaster. Occasionally this is a fair reflection of the last few moments of flight but more often the truth is somewhat different. The majority of serious accidents can be attributed to a number of factors. Rather than being pole-axed by a mighty blow from the fickle hand of fate, what usually seems to happen is that the usual safety margins of a safe flight were gradually eroded, nibbled away by a series of small cuts that chipped away at the bedrock of flight safety.

I don't want to get too metaphysical about this, but just as a mature tree is unlikely to be felled by a single blow from an axe, so a serious crash is unlikely to be precipitated by a single error or mischance. It is a series of blows, a sequence of cuts into the solid trunk, that bring the tree crashing down. A single blow is highly unlikely to fell the tree: it is the constant chipping away of the axe which brings down the mighty oak.

In much the same way, an accident is normally preceded by a series of mishaps or errors. Each on its own may not be enough to endanger a flight. But as the sequence progresses and mishap builds upon mischance, so the outlook darkens and the vultures gather. At almost any stage in a typical accident chain, the pilot has the means and the opportunity to avert disaster. More often than not, right up until the final moments, the pilot could have chosen a different course of action that would have led the flight to safety. Instead the pilot failed to break the links in the accident chain. And with each new link forged, the chain became strong enough to bring the flight to a disastrous conclusion.

Troubles never come singly

Proverb

To put this proposition to the test, we need to look at some real-life instances. In doing so, let's remember that it's all too easy to sit in wise judgment with the inestimable benefit of hindsight. Additionally, because the pilots in question are unfortunately not available to give their viewpoints, we have to make certain assumptions about what motivated them to carry out or omit certain actions. In doing this we should be neither too harsh nor judgmental, but instead try to make an impartial assessment of the pilot's motivation.

The Piper Cherokee has been a stalwart of the general-aviation movement since the 1970s, and even now almost any GA airfield will be able to boast a number of examples. It is reasonably reliable, docile and largely devoid of nasty surprises; anybody who has practised stalling in one will probably agree that for the most part a stall in a Cherokee is a non-event. Provided, of course, that you are doing your stalling with a sensible amount of space between yourself and the ground. On the negative side the Cherokee – and in particular the 140 version – is no great load-carrier. You can fill the tanks with fuel, you can fill the baggage compartment with suitcases or you can put an

The Piper PA-28 Cherokee

adult in each of the four seats. However, you can't do all at the same time without overloading the aircraft. Additionally, the Cherokee 140 is not renowned for its turn of speed, a sedate 90kts or 100mph being typical in the cruise.

It may have been this latter characteristic that was in the mind of one Cherokee 140 owner when he decided to fit a drag-reduction kit to his aircraft. This was essentially a set of aluminium strips covering the gaps between wing surfaces and each flap and aileron, with additional fairings covering the flap hinges. The kit is designed to reduce drag and so increase cruise speed by a few knots. A Supplemental Type Certificate (STC) covers its use for American-registered aircraft, but this has no status for a UK-registered aircraft. Whether the owner was legally entitled to fit the kit himself is open to question. Certainly the work should have been signed off by a licensed engineer, but there is no evidence that this was done. Maybe the owner was planning to get the necessary paperwork done later. Maybe the owner thought that what he did with his aeroplane was his business. Whatever his intention an unapproved modification was now illegally fitted to his aircraft and the first link in the accident chain was created.

That evening the pilot made a short flight, perhaps to see what improvement had been gained. If the pilot practised any slow flight or stalling in the new configuration, he might have noticed that the stall warner was intermittent. The significance of this mechanical failure is not clear. The stall warner in this particular aircraft was merely a red light – not a warning horn or klaxon – located outside the normal field of vision. Few pilots would spot the light unless they were looking almost straight at it. On the other hand, the Cherokee 140 can be very docile in the approach to the stall, so any extra warning is useful. Of course, we don't know whether the pilot considered stalling, although it is almost certainly the first thing that a test pilot would have considered after fitting a modification to the aircraft. However, as the sortie only lasted for 25 minutes that evening, it is unlikely. Maybe he was thinking about the next day, when he planned to visit a major light-aircraft 'fly-in'.

The next day dawned sunny, if a little windy. As he prepared to depart his home airfield, the pilot was approached by an acquaintance who was hoping for a lift to another airfield to collect an aeroplane. Despite the fact that he had to reach the fly-in by 1230 before it closed for an airshow, and although the other airfield was somewhat out of his way, the pilot agreed. In itself this was a kind gesture of the sort we're all sometimes very grateful for, but it would leave our man with much less time than he might have wanted. The pilot dropped off his acquaintance at the first airfield just after 1100 and departed within 15 minutes bound for a second airfield where he had agreed to collect two friends and take them to the fly-in. There can be little doubt that by now he knew that he could not afford any further delay if he was to reach the fly-in before 1230.

By 1150 the pilot was approaching the second airfield to collect his friends. He experienced some difficulty in locating it, initially confusing it with a nearby military airfield. This must have entailed a further delay the pilot could do without. Nevertheless he was guided to his true destination where he touched down just before 1200. After touchdown he was given parking instructions. Instead he stopped on the taxiway, collected his friends without shutting down the engine and immediately requested clearance back to the holding point for departure. The aircraft was now close to its maximum weight, and within seven minutes of landing it was airborne again, heading towards the fly-in.

With less than 30 minutes to cover the 50 or so nautical miles to his destination and with no help from a tailwind, the pilot must have been hoping for some speed gain from the new drag-reduction kit. It is not difficult to imagine his mind-set. With the clock ticking and every chance of arriving at the fly-in too late to be accepted, it would be a very disciplined pilot who could avoid checking his watch every few minutes and inching the throttle forward to seek a few more knots airspeed. What would the passengers say if they were turned away from the airfield for arriving too late? Few humans work well under time pressure or close scrutiny; for most of us these are sources of unwelcome stress. We have no way of knowing this pilot's disposition, but his situation was certainly one that most aviators would find stressful.

We can only wonder whether an alternative plan of action was considered, perhaps a diversion or return to base if he arrived too late. Did he weigh-up the possibility of landing elsewhere and waiting until after that day's air display had finished? Or even returning the next day, since the fly-in was to last two days? Or did he focus solely on arriving before 1230 as matter of pride, convenience or simply a failure to plan an alternative course of action? Such single-mindedness has been a feature of many an accident, with pilots turning down or refusing to consider options other than their pre-decided goal. It is this sort of narrow thinking that has led more than one aviator into a dead-end.

Just three minutes before the 1230 cut-off time, radio contact was made with the destination airfield. There was no ATC in force, merely an AFIS. So the pilot would have sole responsibility for integrating safely with the 20 or so other aircraft already in the circuit, of which up to half were established on finals. Sitting safely in our favourite armchair, most of us can probably dredge from our memories the rules of the air now required to avoid other traffic. But how many of us in that pilot's position – perhaps stressed and flustered from the rush to arrive on time – could instantly recall the necessary information whilst looking-out for and tracking up to 20 aircraft all approaching the same airfield? Of course it might have been better to arrive earlier and beat the rush, but that was no longer an option. In addition the weather was not perfect. The visibility was a hazy 8-10km, meaning that the horizon was probably indistinct, and the surface wind was blowing at 15kts and gusting up to 25kts.

The pilot reported downwind, his last radio call, and must have thought he was nearly home and dry with the landing runway so close to hand. In actual fact, more links in the accident chain were developing. The pilot turned on to base leg and descended towards 500ft, although the flaps remained retracted. He was now on a collision course with an aircraft already established on finals. Just as the other aircraft was about to take avoiding action, the Cherokee pilot turned steeply to his right to pass behind the other aircraft. Having cleared it he was now facing into a stream of oncoming aeroplanes. His reaction was to reverse the bank into a steep turn (at least 60° Angle Of Bank) to the left, back towards the runway in an attempt to regain the centreline. We can probably all imagine the swiftly applied aileron, the urgent pull on the control column and

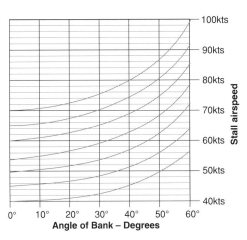

The increase in stalling airspeed with increasing angle of bank

Angle of Bank – Degrees

Stall airspeed

perhaps a bootful of left rudder as the pilot tried to get the runway threshold back in sight. The aircraft was now only about 200ft above the ground.

Most of us would, after due consideration, agree that a stabilised approach is a key element to making a safe landing. Most of us would also accept that a 60° AOB turn at 200ft in an aeroplane close to gross weight, with a gusty wind and an indistinct horizon and with up to 20 aircraft close by, is not at all a good idea. And as a precursor to a safe landing, such a manoeuvre does not sound like a particularly promising plan. Taken in isolation this seems patently obvious. However, in the situation the pilot had led himself into, the steep turn so close to the ground might have seemed necessary, if rather dramatic. And indeed it was this manoeuvre that nearly completed the accident chain. As the wings rolled level, the nose was seen to rise. Maybe the pilot was still holding the back pressure on the control column and the left rudder he'd presumably applied for the steep left turn. Did he know that crossing the controls (in this case probable left rudder and right aileron) is a time-honoured instructor's technique to get a reluctant aircraft to spin? We will never know.

What we sadly do know is that at about 200ft the Cherokee entered an incipient spin to the left and crashed into the back garden of a house about a mile from the runway threshold. Thankfully nobody on the ground was injured, but it was in the impact that the final link of the accident chain was added. The pilot and the front-seat passenger were probably wearing lap straps with diagonal shoulder straps attached. However, deterioration of the seat-belt attachments meant that the diagonal shoulder straps probably disengaged from the lap belts prior to the crash. The rear-seat passenger was wearing a lap strap of a type prohibited by the CAA several years earlier. Whether the owner should have known about this is not clear because the aircraft's logbooks were never found. In any event, all three occupants of the aircraft were killed. According to the autopsy report, they would probably have survived if their seat belts had worked properly. The accident chain had run its full course.

In common with most people at the fly-in that day, the first I knew of these events was when the wailing of alarms and sirens began to echo across the airfield. Within the hour, the usual rumours and second-hand eye-witness accounts of the accident were in circulation. Six months later, when the full accident report was published, all could read a full and impartial account of the crash and the events that led to it.

The accident chain had run its full course

We could then shake our heads sadly and wisely, and maybe resolve not to allow ourselves to be led into the same situation. Then the report would be filed away in a far corner of the flying-school briefing room, later to be stored or thrown away with the passage of time. Today, the report of the crash that claimed three lives gathers dust on a shelf in a quiet corner of a library in a big glass building near Gatwick airport, as jets roar overhead on their final approach to land.

The point of this story is not that it is exceptional and extraordinary, but that it is not; I could have chosen *any number* of reports to illustrate the theme of the accident chain. There is no doubt that the reading and relating of these accounts can easily be seen as a depressing and off-putting business. I like to think differently. The harsh truth is that nothing can be done to bring back those who are the subject of a fatal-accident report. Once the accident has happened, the damage cannot be undone – the clock cannot be turned back. However, if lessons can be learnt and lives saved in the future by understanding something of the circumstances of the accident, at least something useful has been achieved.

The associations which have responsibility for investigating aviation accidents are usually fiercely independent of the national aviation authorities, as is the case for the Air Accident Investigation Branch (AAIB) in the UK. Their work is best summed up in their own words:

> "*The fundamental purpose of investigating accidents is to determine the circumstances and causes of the accident with a view to the preservation of life and the avoidance of accidents in the future; it is not the purpose to apportion blame or liability.*"

In that frame of mind, let's look at a summary of other accident chains. The more we know about these and the better we understand them, the better our prospect as individual pilots of recognising the onset of an accident chain. Remember that what we're trying to learn to do as a matter of course is to break the links before a routine flight becomes an incident, or an incident becomes an accident.

Experience is the knowledge that enables you to recognise a mistake when you make it again

Anon

A pilot with 150 hours experience planned a VFR flight one winter's morning to another airfield about 80 miles away. If he had used the weather briefing facilities at the departure airfield, he would have learnt that the route was covered by a slow-moving warm front bringing a general cloud base of 1200ft and poor visibility, and that severe airframe icing in cloud was a distinct possibility. Further research would have shown that at an airfield on high ground (850ft) along the route, the weather was 500m visibility in freezing drizzle, the temperature was 0°C and there was a stratus overcast with a base lower than 150ft. Although he had done some instrument-flying training, the pilot had no instrument qualification. In any event, the POH/FM for his aircraft stated that flight in icing conditions was prohibited. Indeed, the aeroplane lacked even a pitot heater. Nonetheless, the pilot departed with two unwitting passengers aboard, apparently intending to fly the route VFR at 1500ft.

Half an hour later the aircraft passed over an airport *en route* where the weather was 3000m visibility with broken cloud at 700ft and 1200ft. For most of us it

Should you press on? If there's doubt, there's no doubt. Turn back.

would have been a very tempting option to land here, have some coffee, check the Met again and think about what to do next. But instead the decision was presumably taken to press on. Shortly afterwards, the pilot reported that he was IMC at 1300ft. So now he was flying well below the minimum safety altitude, approaching high ground in conditions for which he was most certainly not qualified. *But still he did not turn back.*

Twenty minutes later the pilot contacted his destination to say that he was IMC at 1500ft and unsure of his position. ATC advised the aircraft to climb to the minimum safety altitude of 2600ft, but on reaching this level the pilot reported icing. The controller gave the aircraft a new heading to avoid a TV mast and clearance to descend to 2000ft, but during this the pilot reported that the controls were freezing over and that he was unable to stop the descent. The last radio call from the pilot was a brief Mayday, cut short as the aircraft crashed and caught fire 10 miles short of its destination.

Portrayed like this, the accident chain is evident:

- VFR flight was not possible in the prevailing weather;
- The pilot exceeded his licence limitations;
- The pilot exceeded the aircraft's limitations;
- The pilot did not divert or turn back while he still could have done so.

What on earth could have been so important about making that flight that the pilot was prepared to go to such lengths and take such risks to get to the destination? We can only guess at his motivation, but his decision to attempt that flight in those conditions is even more mysterious when you know that the departure and destination airfields are connected by motorway. The distance could have been covered by car in around two hours...

Some people are natural risk-takers, and might fly in unsuitable conditions in an attempt to 'prove' their skills to themselves or others. Some pilots are more mature but susceptible to pressure from others – so-called peer pressure – to make flights that they might not otherwise attempt. Consider this accident chain:

■ A young pilot had just begun glider-towing and had just a few days experience of the operation, the airfield and the local area.

■ The pilot had complained of being unwell, and had also mentioned difficulty orientating in the local area.

■ The pilot's towing abilities had allegedly been criticised, in particular the caution and time taken to complete each tow.

■ Before the final flight the pilot expressed concern over the low fuel state, but was apparently treated unsympathetically and admonished for wasting time.

■ The pilot became lost after releasing the glider on the next tow and was seen to make a low pass over the runway at a nearby disused airfield, but did not land.

■ A short time later the aircraft is believed to have suffered an engine failure due to fuel starvation (about 1 imperial gallon was on board at this time).

■ Control of the aircraft was lost at about 50ft AGL and it crashed. The pilot was killed.

This accident chain clearly started well before the aircraft got airborne for its final flight, and we are left with many 'what-ifs'. *What if* the pilot had decided that he was too unwell to fly? *What if* the pilot had resisted the pressure to fly against his better judgment? *What if* the pilot had insisted on uplifting more fuel? *What if* the pilot had landed at the disused airfield? *What if* the pilot had kept control of the aircraft during the forced landing? There is no evidence that there was any defect in the airframe or the flying controls. It is most likely that the aircraft stalled and spun while trying to stretch the glide, or perhaps as the pilot tried to turn off the fuel tap which was difficult to move.

Air Traffic Controllers, in their various guises, can be a pilot's best friend

Sometimes the problem is not that pilots are too easily influenced by others but that they seem completely impervious to what others are trying to tell them. Air Traffic Controllers, in their many guises, can be a pilot's best friend – especially if you deal with them respectfully and do not spring nasty surprises on them too often. The folks in ATC, AFIS and other sorts of ATSU have access to all sorts of information, and a great deal of local knowledge that can be invaluable to a pilot. It makes sense that all help and assistance should be gratefully received. But sometimes it seems that the pilot just doesn't want to listen.

Late one summer afternoon, ATC at Land's End airport took a phone call from a pilot intending to arrive that evening. The controller advised that the weather was poor and that no lighting or ATC service would be available at the expected arrival time. It is not known whether the pilot checked any other weather information, but he certainly did decide to make a VFR flight from the Midlands to Land's End. His first recorded contact with an ATC unit was as he passed Bristol at 1500ft, following the M5 motorway southbound. The concern of ATC was obvious:

> Bristol ATC: "...*my suggestion is that you keep an eye on the weather as you proceed southbound...I've just spoken to Exeter and their weather is deteriorating quite quickly...they have 3000 metres in rain, one okta at 700 feet and six oktas at 1000 feet.*"

This is as broad a hint as an ATC unit is likely to give a pilot. Attempting visual navigation in a visibility of 3000m and a cloud ceiling below 1000ft is a marginal activity, to say the least. And with high ground rising to around 1000ft ahead of him, the pilot must surely have thought about the advisability of continuing. If he did, he kept such thoughts to himself. The ATC controller at Bristol then obtained the weather for an RAF station close to Land's End. He tried to pass this information to the pilot but could not contact him; it seems that he had already changed frequency to Exeter. The Bristol controller was concerned enough to contact Exeter ATC on the telephone. By now the pilot was talking to Exeter, to whom he said that the weather was "*fairly thick in front but it's quite clear here*". The controller passed the Exeter weather and then relayed the following message,

> Exeter ATC: "*Bristol tried to pass you the St Mawgan weather...obviously you did not get it. St Mawgan weather is...visibility 2000 metres in mist, two oktas at 200 feet, five oktas at 300 feet, eight oktas at 4000 feet. St Mawgan think that Land's End weather will be at least as bad as that.*"

VFR flight was clearly not a realistic option in this weather. Indeed, the weather was actually below licence minima for a non-instrument pilot and marginal for a IMC-rated pilot. In the circumstances, the pilot's response was remarkable:

> Pilot: "*...I have that, I can just about climb in under that I think*".

Minutes later the aircraft passed within a couple of miles of Exeter airport, but still the pilot ploughed on. What could have him so determined to continue towards Land's End in the face of all available evidence that the weather was simply too bad for VFR flight? We simply don't know.

Shortly after the aircraft had passed Exeter, the seriousness of the situation must have finally come home to the pilot,

> Pilot: "*It's getting a bit thick here, I'm down to 500 feet*"

> Exeter ATC: "*...well the ground three miles ahead of you rises to over 800 feet.*"

> Pilot: "*That is understood, but the motorway goes straight through I believe.*"

> Exeter ATC: "*Well, it goes over the top of it.*"

> Pilot: "*I'll see how it goes on. I'll come back to you if I get into trouble.*"

In the safety and comfort of our favourite armchair, the situation is clear enough. The weather at the destination makes a VFR arrival impossible for all practical purposes; cloud has forced us down to 500ft in visibility of around 3000m with hills just ahead rising to 800ft. Just a few miles behind us lies lower ground and a fully equipped airport, with which we are already in contact. They have radar, long runways and hot coffee on offer. From the safety of our armchair it's clearly what the Americans call a "no-brainer" – it takes no thought to see the correct course of action. But the man in the hot seat clearly didn't see it that way. Four minutes after his last radio transmission, his aircraft crashed into the ground at an elevation of 760ft AMSL. The AAIB concluded that the aircraft had hit the ground in a stalled or semi-stalled condition. Including the advice from RAF St Mawgan, four separate ATC controllers went out of their way to advise the pilot that his planned flight could not be completed safely. With the benefit of hindsight, it seems he went out of his way to prove them right.

For the most part, we assume that pilots whose flights end in an accident are rational human beings who did not set out with the deliberate intention to have an accident. Sometimes their conduct seems foolhardy to the extent of being reckless. However, on occasion the accident chain is a very short one by choice.

On rare occasions a pilot deliberately decides to end his life in an aeroplane. With roughly the same rarity but exactly the same results, a pilot will get drunk and then take an aircraft into the air. The verdict in either case is often that the pilot's balance of mind was temporarily disturbed. There are also a very small number of accidents caused by pilots who seems to be harbouring a genuine death-wish, with perhaps a more long-term disturbance of their balance of mind as the root cause. What else to make of the pilot who crashed a mile short of the runway whilst trying to make an instrument approach in dense fog? In the wreckage the accident investigators found no instrument approach charts for the airport. There was only a military document, which was four years out of date. They also found the pilot's licence and instrument rating, which proved to be forgeries. What can we learn from the pilot who attempted to loop a cabin-class twin that was most definitely not cleared for aerobatics? At best, we know the aircraft endured determined mis-handling before it broke up.

To most of us, the demons that must plague these poor souls and drive them to their apparent self-destruction are unimaginable. Maybe the only rational conclusion is that in the final analysis, the aircraft was only an incidental instrument in that person's demise and they might just as easily have met their end in some other form of Russian roulette.

You've got to ask yourself a question – do I feel lucky?

Dirty Harry aka Clint Eastwood.

Film buffs will remember that the person in question turned out to be very unlucky just a few moments later.

We are back with the concepts of luck and chance. Already we can see that many accidents involve pilots getting airborne when the weather or other circumstances make a safe conclusion of the flight much less likely. Perhaps these pilots persuade themselves that somehow the weather will be better than forecast, or that "it's bound to be OK".

This is trusting an awful lot to luck. It also rather misses the point that if you leave too much to chance, bad luck is just as likely as good luck. In the face of this, and despite the hostile environment awaiting them, these pilots choose to commit themselves to the air. I say 'choose', because in all of this we must remember that general-aviation pilots, flying for their own benefit, are not obliged to get airborne to get paid. Neither do they take to the air as part of some life-or-death struggle.

Pilots may have come to grief because of a decision to fly, but I don't know of one that suffered a flying accident as a result of staying on the ground. Once committed to the air, once the wheels have left the ground and the runway is behind us, we are irretrievably consigned to making an arrival at some later point. Getting airborne, even for a single circuit, is an absolute commitment to making a safe landing at some later point, and this is why a minimum amount of planning and preparation must precede any flight. The principle is very simple:

Take-offs are optional, landings are mandatory.

Now we know a little more about accident chains and about how minor and sometimes apparently inconsequential incidents and occurrences can come together to bring about a much larger hazard. Let's not forget that we are working with the benefit of hindsight here. Rather than being wise after the event, which is as easy as it is futile, we need to develop the skill to recognise the accident chain as it is developing, and break the links whilst the chain is still weak and incomplete.

The fact is that if things start to go wrong, there is every chance that more misfortune will follow. The proverb 'troubles never come singly' is all too true. And as we've seen before, it is the pilot's responsibility to make a positive intervention to rectify the situation. It's all too easy to operate in denial, believing that as long as we continue as if everything is normal, 'something will turn up'. Wanting to complete the flight as planned is a natural inclination, but there have to be some reasonable alternatives available too. All too often it seems that an aviator flies himself straight up a one-way street into an all too dead end simply for want of having an alternative course of action prepared.

At all times we should only consider our present course of action or intentions as 'Plan A'. There must be at least a Plan B (and preferably some Plans C and D as well) to hand. Plan B might be a diversion airfield or a return to base. Plan C might be a go-around instead of landing in unsuitable conditions and so on. The important thing is that in the words of another proverb, you must not put all your eggs in one basket. You must always have other options available. This thinking is also known as "belt and braces". By all means wear a belt to hold your trousers up, but use braces too in case the belt fails.

Your alternative plans of action should be constantly reviewed and updated in the light of the unfolding situation. The actual physical work of flying an aeroplane should not unduly tax the cerebral capacity in normal circumstances, and what's left over should be devoted to *thinking.* Even the most relaxing flight should involve concentration on the part of the pilot. So, next time you are cruising along with the aeroplane trimmed to fly hands-off and happy with your lot, ask yourself whether you are thinking. Because if you are not thinking you are not concentrating, and if you are not concentrating you are missing something for sure. And maybe the links of an accident chain are being formed right beneath your nose.

Common Causes of Serious Accidents (and how not to have one)

▶ Loss of Control in VMC

▶ Loss of Control in IMC

▶ Attempted VFR Flight in IMC

▶ Controlled Flight Into Terrain

▶ Mid-Air Collision

▶ Other Causes of Serious Accidents

Flying is not dangerous;

crashing is

Anon

Flight Safety

▶Loss of Control in VMC

We have already established that the biggest single cause of fatal GA accidents is that of pilots losing control of their aircraft in reasonable weather conditions (i.e. VMC) and the aircraft consequently hitting solid ground or water very hard indeed. 'Loss of control' in VMC conditions invariably means a stall or spin condition. For the purposes of my survey I have included in this category accidents occurring during low-level aerobatics. It might be argued that in some such cases the aircraft was actually under control when it hit the ground. This is possible, but my view is that the pilot clearly did not intend his manoeuvre to end in a ground impact, and that most often something went wrong in the course of it. Whether the aircraft was fully out of control when it hit the ground seems an academic distinction.

The probability of survival is equal to the angle of arrival

Anon

Virtually all loss-of-control-in-VMC accidents fall into one of three categories:

- Low-level aerobatics
- Extreme attitudes and manoeuvres at low level
  (i.e. a steep turn and/or steep climb)
- Low-level stall/spin probably caused by distraction

A properly flown sequence of aerobatics can be both a pleasure and a thrill to watch. A badly flown set of aerobatic manoeuvres can be frightening, especially when conducted close to the ground. Aerobatics take both the aircraft and the pilot closer to the limits than 'ordinary' flight manoeuvres. If an aerobatic manoeuvre goes

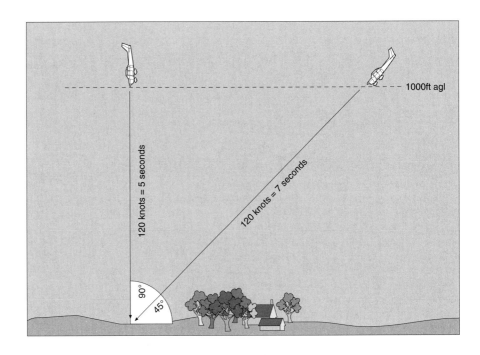

1000ft agl

120 knots = 5 seconds

120 knots = 7 seconds

90°
45°

wrong, for whatever reason, it will require an awful lot of airspace to recover to controlled flight. Imagine that an aircraft exits a manoeuvre in a vertical dive at an average speed of 120kts. In this situation, the aircraft will consume 1000ft of altitude every five seconds. Think about that for a moment (say five seconds or so) and imagine orientating yourself from an out-of-control situation, recognising your current circumstances, analysing the problem, deciding on recovery actions, taking those actions and the aircraft responding all the way back to at least level flight in this time. Five seconds: it will have taken longer than that to read the previous sentence.

Frightening isn't it? What's more, thanks to the wonders of trigonometry, even in a 45° dive at the same average airspeed it will take just 7 seconds to transition from fully functioning aeroplane at 1000ft AGL to crumpled wreckage at 0ft AGL. In reality, most low-level aerobatics accidents involve pilots who were manoeuvring well below 1000ft, so the already slim margin for error was so reduced as to be almost non-existent. In some cases the pilot was so low that the manoeuvre never had a realistic chance of success, especially in a relatively low-powered light aircraft. Pulling up to a stall turn from low speed at ground level or attempting a half-roll and pull-through from 300ft are good examples where disaster was inevitable.

A common feature of accidents during low-level aerobatic manoeuvres is that they happened to pilots of considerable experience. That said, it is often the case that although the pilot had a lot of flying hours overall, he had relatively little experience (or recent experience) on the aircraft type he was flying. Thus it can be imagined that a small error of skill, or a momentary lapse caused by unfamiliarity with the aircraft type, precipitated a problem which further above the ground would merely have been an embarrassment. Taking the case of accidents at air displays, while the average total flying experience of the pilot involved was some 6000 hours, in 60% of cases the pilot had less than 100 hours on type. The fact that no bystanders were lost in accidents at air shows is a tribute to the regulation of air displays and the discipline of pilots in observing these regulations. Even excluding displays, there is a similar pattern of pilot experience. Pilots involved in accidents occurring during low-level aerobatics outside air displays had an average total flying experience of almost 1500 hours, but an average time on type of just 40 hours.

Low-level aerobatics are for those pilots with the training and experience to stay out of trouble

Few of the aircraft involved in low-level aerobatic accidents were 'production' types, similar to those used for flying training; the majority were vintage, homebuilt or specialist aerobatic machines. This in itself is to be expected because the majority of aerobatic flying is probably done in such craft, but it does raise the question of differing stall/spin characteristics. By the nature of the airworthiness requirements, the vast majority of aircraft used for flying training (including those often used for initial aerobatic training) are relatively docile in the stalling and spinning regime. Vintage and homebuilt machines in particular are often considerably less forgiving and tolerant, and may give much less warning that they are about to depart from controlled flight. In particular the high control forces, the well-back control-column position and high nose attitude you recall from basic training may bear little resemblance to a stall in a less forgiving aircraft. If you cast your mind back to basic aerodynamics, you may recall that increased load factor, felt by the pilot as a so-called *g* force, increases the stall speed. Even a gentle aerobatic manoeuvre can involve a load factor of at least three and possibly more. At this, the stall speed increases by 71%. So an aircraft with a normal wings-level stall speed of 50kts would now stall at 85kts. In addition, a stall under increased load factor is more likely to involve a wing drop, especially if the aircraft is out of balance.

So before embarking on aerobatics in a new type, any pilot – no matter how experienced – should be prudent enough to spend some time thoroughly investigating its stall/spin behaviour at a safe height. Only then should he start exploring aerobatics, and again the pre-requisite should be a comfortable margin of airspace between the aircraft and the surface. As a good rule of thumb you should aim to be able to recover to controlled straight and level flight by *at least* 3000ft AGL, although even this margin may need to be increased in some cases. Most pilots who have undertaken aerobatic training have made errors whose result was either a spin (as might happen during a vertical manoeuvre) or a prolonged 'pull-through' as the aircraft falls out of a roll. In either case they are still around to relate the tale because they were astute enough to put a safe distance between themselves and the surface *before* attempting the manoeuvre. In aerobatics as in all flying, there's nothing quite so useless as the amount of airspace above you.

Practising aerobatics at a safe altitude (such as the 3,700ft this Chipmunk pilot has in hand as he completes a loop) is the way to a long and stress-free flying career

Talking of aerobatic training, the straightforward advice is not to attempt any aerobatics unless you have undergone proper training. If this seems to be stating the blindingly obvious, the accident reports appear to show that not all pilots appreciate this common-sense approach to aerobatics. Possibly the most poignant example I know of was the 18-year old pilot who came to grief whilst attempting aerobatics over his girlfriend's school. He was not known to have undertaken any formal aerobatic training, but an aerobatics textbook was found in his aircraft's wreckage. This is not an isolated incident, and the simple truth is

Common Causes of Serious Accidents
(and how not to have one)

that aerobatic flying is not a 'teach yourself' activity. It also illustrates another feature of low-level aerobatics accidents, namely that they often occur whilst the pilot is performing for an audience. This might be found at the home airfield, or the pilot may have chosen to perform over a relative's house or a gathering of friends. In all these instances there is an even greater perceived pressure on the aviator to show-off his or her piloting skills, and thus the temptation arises to fly just a bit lower, or try some new manoeuvre, or throw in a spectacular (and unrehearsed) flourish just for effect. All too often the effect is to leave a permanent and very lasting impression on both the audience and the ground.

LE BONJOUR AUX AMIS...
TROP SOUVENT
C'EST UN ADIEU !

Vols et virages à très basse altitude

"The hello to friends is too often a final goodbye. Flying and banking at very low level = danger of death"

The 'showing-off' phenomenon is also a common feature of accidents occurring when pilots indulge in extreme attitudes (such as steep turns and/or steep climbs) at low level. Often the crumpled result is attributed to 'low-level manoeuvring flight', and the line between this and a proper aerobatic manoeuvre can be a very fine one. So if we choose to beat-up a particular spot at low level and then throw in a steep turn just for good measure, we are in many ways exposing ourselves to just as much risk as if we perform a proper aerobatic manoeuvre. You will remember that increased load factor means increased stall airspeed. A properly flown 60° AOB turn will increase stall speed by 41%, so that a 'wings-level' stall speed of 50kts becomes 70kts. Again, stalling with increased load factor and with the aircraft possibly out of balance makes a wing drop and consequent spin more likely. The loss of airspeed in the turn (due to increased drag) and the higher stall airspeed can make the margin between stall and controlled flight very slim indeed. Moreover, it is easy to 'pull' increased load factor by trying to tighten the turn. Quite simply, the harder you haul back on the control column, the faster the stalling speed.

The harder you pull back on the control column, the faster the stalling speed

The fact that many accidents are precipitated by low-level manoeuvring also raises the question of windshear and visual illusions caused by turning at low level. The dangers of both, especially during the take-off and approach phase, are well publicised. Windshear is possible not just around thunderstorms, shower clouds and active cold fronts but at any time at low level when a strong wind is blowing. Local terrain effects such as hills, trees and buildings or even sea breezes all increase the risk of a significant wind shift at low level. This real effect can be exacerbated by the visual illusion of a change in speed as an aircraft turns in a strong wind. In turning so that a 20-knot wind on the nose (headwind) becomes a 20-knot tailwind, the pilot will see an acceleration in speed *over the ground* of 40 knots even though the airspeed remains constant. The lower you are, the more apparent is the change in groundspeed. Even an experienced pilot can be fooled into thinking that the aircraft's airspeed is increasing, and the natural reaction might be to reduce power, increase bank angle or pull back harder on the control column. Any of these will just bring the aircraft closer to a stall. This perhaps goes a long way towards explaining why many of the accidents caused by steep turns at low level seem to follow a stall/spin as the aircraft was passing through a downwind heading.

Speed is life,

altitude is life insurance

Anon

If we can make a conjecture about why an aeroplane departed from controlled flight, we still have to consider what motivated the pilot to take his or her aircraft into this dead end in the first place. Keeping your options open and always having alternative plans of action available is the basis of good airmanship. The problem with extreme manoeuvres at low level is that if they go wrong the pilot has nowhere to go but

Instructors prefer their students to have good judgment, because skills are easier to teach than judgment

"…how d'you know his name is 'Shortstraw'?"

Common Causes of Serious Accidents
(and how not to have one)

down. Gravity will take a hand very quickly if the pilot gives it the chance. And once Sir Isaac (Newton) has taken a hand, the only thing that will help the pilot is having enough height to rectify the problem. Fast reactions won't save him. As an experienced aerobatic display pilot once observed, if things do go wrong at low level, the fastest reactions in the world will not help; you have to avoid getting into the situation in the first place. This leads us to another favoured flying adage, namely:

A superior pilot is one who uses his superior judgment to avoid situations that might require the use of his superior skill.

It is lack of good judgment that leads pilots into the majority of accidents, not a lack of 'hands-on' flying skill. Ask any flying instructor to choose between their students having good judgment or good skills and they will probably choose good judgment. This is simply because pilots who have sound judgment will avoid risky situations and so not require finely honed flying skills to get them out of trouble.

Once outside the flying training system, it is largely left to the pilot's own discretion to keep developing and exercising good judgment. Like all other human beings, aviators are susceptible to a range of external pressures and influences that can lead them to make decisions that they might not otherwise make. The influence of other pilots – so-called peer pressure – can be very strong, leading the unwary to think "Well, he/she/they are doing it, so it must be OK". In an effort to prove their prowess or to be seen to be part of the crowd, humans can easily travel down paths they might never otherwise consider. The following accident-report extracts give a flavour of typical scenarios:

An accident may be nature's way of telling you to watch your airspeed

"A fly-in social event had been organised...after lift-off, the aircraft accelerated and the landing gear was retracted while still at low level...the aircraft was observed to pull up into what was described as a steep climbing attitude. The aircraft then entered a steep banked turn to the left, with some eyewitnesses estimating the bank angle to be approaching 90°. The aircraft then appeared to sideslip to the left and then yawed and rolled to the left, assuming a steep nose-down attitude..." (pilot 6 hours on type).

"...it appears that an impromptu air display had developed at the fly-in...[The accident aircraft] accelerated slowly at a height of less than 20 feet. When it reached a point abeam the aircraft parking area it commenced a steep climb with a pitch angle of at least 20° combined almost immediately with a steeply banked right turn. The bank achieved appears to have been at least 60° and possibly as much as 80°. By the time the aircraft had turned through 180° [on to a downwind heading] and reached a height of about 200 feet it appeared to have stalled...The aircraft hit the ground at a pitch angle of more than 45° nose-down..." (pilot 43 hours on type).

"[The accident pilot] *suggested to the pilot of* [another aircraft] *that they could practice formation flying. They agreed that they would fly down the strip 'a couple of times'. Witnesses on the ground saw* [the accident aircraft] *circling to the left at an estimated 3-400 feet…*[it] *was seen to be in a medium banked turn to the left with a nose-up attitude when the left wing dropped followed by the nose and the aircraft rotated to the left through approximately 90°…"* (pilot 1 hour 40 minutes on type).

Left>
Just how low…

Right>
…do you need to fly?

No matter how skilled the pilot, a fall is inevitable if he or she exceeds the aircraft's limits. Only a safety net in the form of altitude will offer a realistic chance of salvation. An aviator who chooses to take his aircraft right to the edge of its performance at low level is walking a very narrow tightrope, and to do so for no good reason (or without proper training and practice) is absolute folly.

So far we have looked at loss-of-control accidents caused when the manoeuvring of the aircraft was probably the pilot's principal concern. Such accidents also occur when for some reason the pilot's attention is directed away from the primary role of flying the aircraft. A significant percentage of loss-of-control accidents which were not precipitated by low-level aerobatics or manoeuvring happened following an engine failure. The exact causes of the engine failure varied (although fuel exhaustion and fuel starvation feature frequently). However, the simple fact is that even without engine power, the pilot was left with a functioning flying machine – albeit a glider rather than a powered aircraft. In these circumstances he had every expectation of reaching the ground under control. Having reached the ground in this way, the same pilot could also expect to walk away from the resulting arrival. The physics are quite simple; at average light-aircraft landing speeds, and assuming a landing into at least a 5-knot wind, most single-engined aircraft will arrive at the surface with a groundspeed of no more than 40-50kts. This speed will dissipate very quickly under braking, even on a rough surface, and so within 100 metres or so the aircraft should be travelling slowly enough for any collision with an obstruction to leave the occupants (if not the aircraft) undamaged. By comparison if an aircraft arrives at the surface with an uncontrolled flightpath, the chances of the occupants escaping harm are very slim indeed.

This is such a fundamental point that it needs stressing. **Keeping the aircraft under your control is your primary task as a pilot. Nothing, but nothing, should become more important than that over-riding priority.**

Of course, an engine failure is bound to be a major distraction to any pilot. Many of us start our flying careers by wondering if the engine really will keep running at all. "What do you do if the engine fails?" is probably the most common question asked during introductory flights. We practice various engine failure scenarios in training until we

Common Causes of Serious Accidents
(and how not to have one)

can satisfy an examiner of our ability to land the aircraft safely in this unlikely event. But once we have passed our tests and left the training system behind, how many of us will practice an engine-failure situation voluntarily? The unfortunate answer is very few. Instead, we go into a denial mode and convince ourselves that an engine failure is an almost unthinkable improbability. After flying behind reliable and apparently healthy engines for tens, hundreds or even thousands of hours, practising for an engine failure seems churlish. In the face of such complacency, many of the basic flying skills needed in an emergency are lost and forgotten. Most instructors will have had the depressing experience of presenting a PPL on a check-ride with a practice engine failure, only to watch

them fastidiously checking around the cockpit for the imagined cause of failure whilst the airspeed slips away unnoticed. Locating the exact cause of an engine failure is likely to be of little use if the aircraft enters a spin half-way through the checks. The mantra of 'Aviate, Navigate, Communicate' is constantly referred to in flying training manuals, but it is truly vital for the pilot to practice this discipline at all times – above all when everything seems to be going wrong and there is the distinct feeling of being over-loaded.

"Captain, excuse me for disturbing you but I have a little problem with the flushing of the toilets…"

Loss of control following an engine failure often occurs in the last few hundred feet, either as the pilot makes a desperate steep turn to find a landing site or attempts to 'stretch' the glide if the aircraft is undershooting the chosen landing area. The dangers of steep turns at low level have already been explored in some detail. The mechanics of trying to stretch the glide are also well known. Every aircraft has a best glide-range airspeed – know this speed and use it. Flying more slowly than this speed may reduce the *rate* of descent, but it will *steepen* the angle of descent. So the pilot gets into a vicious circle whereby the higher the nose is raised, the steeper the aircraft descends. Pull the control column back too far and the aircraft will stall. It is as simple as that.

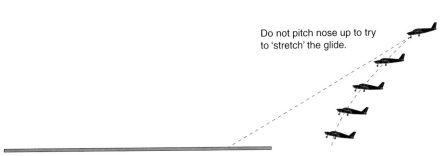

Do not pitch nose up to try to 'stretch' the glide.

Undershoot and possible stall.

Trying to 'stretch' the glide only makes the aircraft descend more steeply

An experienced flying instructor once related to me a simple set of flying instructions:

- Push forward, houses get bigger
- Pull back, houses get smaller
- Keep pulling back, houses get bigger again

Think about it…

Later we will look more closely at the common causes of engine failure, but in this context the essential point is the absolute necessity of avoiding a loss of control regardless of pressures or distractions. The pilot in command is only in command for as long as he is in control of the aircraft. If he loses control, he is demoted to the role of a mere passenger. It is gravity which will then determine his fate.

Loss of control following engine failure is not confined to single-engined aircraft. The fact that loss of control following the failure of one engine is one of the most common causes of accidents to multi-engine GA aircraft too may come as a surprise to those who think that twins offer extra safety in the engine-failure department. The reason is mostly that multi-engine aircraft offer a bigger range of options in the event that one engine fails. In theory the remaining good engine should not only keep the aircraft airborne but also allow it to climb, even if the failure occurs just after take-off. However, following an engine failure in a twin, a delicate balance of rudder and some aileron must be used to maintain direction. At the same time the loss of power means that in reality the aircraft may be able to achieve little or no climb performance (especially with flaps and undercarriage lowered or the propeller of the failed engine not feathered). What little climb performance is available will be achieved at a slower than normal climb airspeed (known as Vyse or 'blue line' airspeed). As the airspeed reduces below this figure, there comes a point where even full rudder will not stop the aircraft from yawing off heading as the live engine – usually throttled up to full power by the pilot – starts to roll the aircraft over. This will happen before the stall is reached, and if it is allowed to develop the logical conclusion is that the aircraft will roll on to its back. This is not an appealing prospect at a few hundred feet. Hence the cynical old adage that the second engine in a twin is there to take you to the scene of the accident after the first engine fails.

Keep thy airspeed up, lest the earth come up from below and smite thee

William Kershner

To successfully handle an engine failure in a heavily laden GA twin immediately after take-off, or during a go-around, requires skill and recency of practice. More than one instructor has speculated that if an out-of-practice pilot is faced with an engine failure in this situation, the safest option may be to simply close the throttle on the live engine and make a forced landing straight ahead. Arguably this entails less risk to life and limb than losing control of the aeroplane half a mile further on.

Flying twins is the sort of status symbol many aviators aspire to. Multi-engine aircraft tend to have more seats, more instruments and more controls to play with. They fly higher and faster than many single-engine types; they might have leather seats, coffee-cup holders and even switches on the ceiling. Nevertheless, they are as vulnerable to gravity and the laws of aerodynamics as any homebuilt creation put together in a garden shed. It is also only logical to assume that flying with two engines instead of one doubles your chances of experiencing an engine failure! Either way, remember that what keeps pilots alive whether they fly gleaming airliners, executive twins or humble trainers, is practising for emergencies and keeping the aircraft under control no matter what.

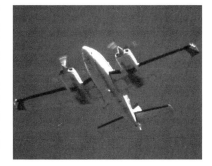

The real value of a twin-engine aircraft is that it will double your chances of having an engine failure

►Loss of Control in IMC

Although not strictly next in order of causes of fatal accidents, logically it makes sense to look at loss of control in IMC after having talked about loss of control in VMC. The end result is the same (i.e. aircraft hitting the ground very hard) but the causes are quite different. The majority of loss of control in IMC accidents can be traced to a single root cause, namely non-instrument qualified pilots trying to fly in IMC.

It's easy to get this far, but why somebody should want to fly deliberately in conditions for which they are not qualified might seem a bit of a mystery. Instrument flying is nowhere near as easy as experienced instrument pilots make it look. It requires both thorough training and regular practice to be competent to fly an aircraft by sole reference to the instruments. Of course, most pilots will have undergone

Accidents happen when you run out of experience

Anon

some limited instrument-flying training during their PPL course at least. They may even have done some further training without gaining any additional qualification. Neither alters the awkward fact that there is a world of difference between flying in smooth conditions under the guidance of a flying instructor and being pitched into cloud at low level, possibly in turbulent conditions, maybe years after last practising instrument flying. Indeed, there is also a major psychological difference between practising instrument flying 'under the hood' and flying in real IMC.

Clearly a pilot who is already operating under considerable stress and pressure (assuming that the flight was not started with the intention of deliberately flying in IMC) is hardly likely to be in the best frame of mind to cope with this new demand. The result is that very quickly the instruments seem to disagree with each other and the pilot's own sense of the aircraft's attitude. If it doesn't stall, the aircraft will probably fall into a spiral dive with increasing airspeed, increasing angle of bank and rapidly decreasing altitude. The apparently logical action – pulling back on the control column – merely makes matters worse. Unless proper recovery actions are taken, it is only a matter of distance above the ground that will determine whether the aircraft is overstressed by the pilot and breaks up or hits the ground first.

The fact is that many pilots involved in these accidents were not at all inexperienced, with an average total experience of nearly 1000 hours apiece, and average hours on type of nearly 100 hours. This only goes to emphasis that

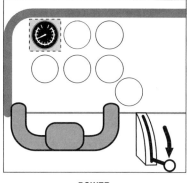

POWER
Check airspeed
Close the throttle

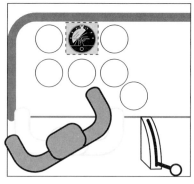

BANK
Check Attitude Indicator
Roll wings-level

*The proper actions to
recover from a spiral dive*

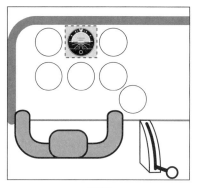

PITCH
Check Attitude Indicator
Pitch to level flight

In summary:
Check Airspeed
POWER
BANK
PITCH

hundreds or even thousands of hours of VFR flying does not guarantee that a pilot will be automatically capable of flying safely in IMC. Scenarios of a non-instrument pilot getting into IMC without having set out to do so have already been described elsewhere in this book, including cases where pilots struggled on trying to stay VMC until that became impossible and instrument flight was forced upon them. In many cases the pilot set out to fly in conditions that were, at best, marginal VMC. Although unforecast bad weather does occur from time to time, it is more common for the weather forecasts to have accurately predicted the conditions experienced by the accident pilot. What's more, checking the actual weather conditions would confirm what was actually happening. Maybe the pilot had flown under similar forecasts in the past, but found the weather better than expected. Maybe he had 'scraped home' a few times before, and come to believe that he could do so again indefinitely. Maybe the desire to reach his destination, a willingness to press on – a condition sometimes called 'press-on-itis'– over-ruled his better judgment and he merely carried on, hoping for the best. However he got himself into an attempt to fly in IMC, his touching faith in the laws of chance ultimately proved to be misplaced. In aviation, things are most certainly not guaranteed to be all right on the night.

The other category of pilots without instrument qualifications involved in these accidents are those who deliberately set out to fly in IMC, and indeed may have done so on a regular basis. In some cases these pilots were flying well-equipped and sophisticated aircraft, but for some reason they had chosen not to equip themselves with the skills to use the machinery to its full potential. By deliberately flouting aviation law, these folk are demonstrating a classic example of a law-breaking 'anti-authority' attitude. There's perhaps a touch of the macho "I'll show them who's ace of the base" thrown in for good measure. By featuring in accident reports, such pilots are also helpfully demonstrating exactly why the rules they chose to ignore are there in the first place.

When it comes to law-breaking, we have to remember that following the laid-down rules and procedures – especially those regarding pilot licensing – are largely matters for the individual. If an aviator approaches an airfield within controlled airspace in IMC, the controller will not quiz him about his training, qualifications and ratings. At best he might ask the pilot whether he can accept an IFR clearance. If the pilot says yes, that is the end of it as far as the controller is concerned.

Those new to the aviation business are often surprised to find that there are no aerial equivalents of police patrol cars lurking behind the clouds waiting for law-breaking pilots to fly past. Instead, abiding by the rules is first and foremost the responsibility of each individual

A fool and his money are soon flying in more aeroplane than he can handle

Anon

aviator. If a pilot transgresses the rules in a particularly blatant way, somebody may report the matter to the relevant authorities. However, in reality such an occurrence is rare. Maybe this should not be so. Maybe we should all be a bit more willing to do our bit in curbing the behaviour of those with a self-destructive streak, or those simply too foolish to see the error of their ways. All too often in the aftermath of an accident it emerges that the accident pilot was known locally to be a bit of a 'cowboy', prone to dangerous flying and rule-bending. Fellow pilots might have little sympathy for the miscreant, but what about the innocent passengers or bystanders that might also suffer from an accident? For many pilots flying is an escape from an over-regulated world, a chance to exercise a true freedom. But we've already seen that freedom comes at a price, which is a responsibility for our own actions. Pilots who reject that responsibility should not expect to be protected from their transgressions by some vow of silence amongst the flying fraternity. Making a genuine mistake or learning a lesson from a 'close shave' is one thing; setting out to deliberately break the law is another. The sad fact is that some personality types will continually flout the law purely for the sake of it, and each time they do so undetected they mentally notch up another victory. Very few pilots would call for more regulation in most areas of flying. But if the existing licensing rules were properly observed by all pilots in the area of IMC flight alone, at least 16 fatal accidents and 30 deaths would have been avoided over the 20 years studied.

Loss of control in IMC can have other causes. Some accidents seem to have at least a casual link to pilot fatigue. Instrument flying does demand a high degree of concentration – all the more so if flying without the benefit of an autopilot and picking your way through uncontrolled airspace where radar units and navaids are few and far between. Anything that reduces your concentration, such as a lack of sleep (perhaps due to an early-morning start) or the natural weariness that comes at the end of a long and busy day, will have an adverse effect on your piloting ability. Unexpected situations or complications become more difficult to deal with and a particularly complex task such as an IFR departure, go-around or approach can be enough to push the tired pilot beyond his limits.

When flying on instruments, make a regular check of the suction gauge

Apart from these situations, instrument failure, and in particular failure of the attitude indicator (artificial horizon) also features in IMC loss-of-control accidents. Flying safely in IMC following the failure of the AI is not easy and requires training and practice. What is more, the failure of an AI tends to be insidious. It usually becomes sluggish and 'winds down' over a period of several minutes if the gyro's power supply (usually a suction pump in the case of a GA aircraft) fails. A proper instrument scan and regular checks of the aircraft's systems are the best way to spot an instrument failure, and regular practice in instrument flying without the AI is the best way of ensuring that you can cope in this situation.

In summary, instrument flying is a discipline that does not come naturally to *any* pilot, no matter how many hours of VFR flying he or she has. It requires proper training and recurrent practice to maintain instrument-flying skills, and concentration and application to fly on instruments even if your skills are current. **To enter IMC deliberately without the proper skills to cope is exceptionally dangerous, regardless of how well equipped the aircraft is. Don't do it!**

▶ Attempted VFR Flight in IMC

Perhaps it is this category of accident more than any other that demonstrates how the accident chain can grow and strengthen, often starting with reckless or ill-informed decisions made before the pilot even entered the aircraft. In essence, such accidents are caused by pilots trying to fly and navigate by visual references when the weather was too bad to do so. Technically many 'VFR into IMC' accidents involve rule-breaking on the part of the pilot, because conditions were not VMC (remember that to fly VFR you must be in VMC) but let's not be over-pedantic here. Most of these pilots were not deliberately setting out to break the law, but by the same token there was usually ample warning that the forecast and actual weather conditions made safe VFR flight unlikely.

Flying is not Nintendo.

You can't push a button

and start again

Anon

A causal factor that crops up again and again in 'VFR into IMC' accidents is that of poor pre-flight planning, in that either pilots simply did not bother to make full

Common Causes of Serious Accidents
(and how not to have one)

use of the information available or they deliberately ignored what they did not want to hear. What else can we make of the pilot who set off in a single-engined non-deiced aircraft to fly in forecast icing conditions at night and in IMC, over mountains that were being battered by 70-knot gales and thunderstorms? We will never know whether the inevitable impact against an

High ground and low cloud: this is not a VFR proposition

unyielding mountainside was caused by downdraughts, rotor turbulence, icing, a navigational mistake or an attempt to fly visually in cloud and darkness. What we *do* know is that the pilot had no place being there at all. The investigators could not even reach the accident site for two days after the crash because weather conditions were so treacherous. This single fact speaks more eloquently than any dry account of the forces of nature he chose to confront.

It is worth noting that the pilot had especially requested a weather forecast for the route, which proved to be substantially accurate, and he was aware of a thunderstorm warning. He even expressed concern about the CBs in the area. Despite this, he chose (we must assume he had free choice in the matter) to attempt a flight in conditions that can at best be described as extremely dangerous. He must have felt a very pressing need to get to his destination. We do not know what this need could have been. We do not actually know whether he was returning to his home base; if he was, so-called 'get-home-itis' (a variation of press-on-itis) must have been a factor. 'Get-home-itis' is a non-medical expression for the desire to get back to base, be it for business, domestic, financial or simply personal reasons. It invokes that shadowy and fascinating portion of the human psyche called the ego; it clouds the judgment and makes pilots ignore (or repress) factors that greatly reduce the likelihood of their safe return. It causes them to take risks with their safety that on most occasions they would almost certainly think ludicrous. But don't start thinking in terms of 'us and them'. This syndrome could afflict you, or me. We are all terribly vulnerable to 'get-home-itis' at one time or another, and the only known antidotes are self-discipline and clear thinking.

TAF 301813Z 301904 16004KT 7000 SCT025 BECMG 1921 4000 BR BKN 008

METAR 302150 302150Z 01001KT 0100 FG SKC 11/11 Q0997

The importance of checking forecasts against recent actual weather reports

Thus a forecast minimum visibility of 4000m had become in reality a visibility of 100m less than three hours into the forecast period.

The inoculation process starts with proper pre-flight planning, because to fail to prepare is to prepare to fail. In the above example the pilot obtained accurate information but did not act on it. In another case, a pilot seems to have deliberately avoided (repressed?) information that might have indicated problems ahead. This pilot planned an IFR flight in controlled airspace, something for which he was not qualified. He was also expecting to arrive at his destination after both it and his nominated diversion were scheduled to be closed. The weather at both was forecast to be well below any realistic approach minima due to fog, something the pilot may or may not have known because apparently he *specifically refused a set of weather reports and forecasts at the departure airfield* [my italics]. After two approaches in darkness, the pilot found the destination airfield and tried to manoeuvre for a visual landing but crashed close to the runway threshold. The visibility at the time was estimated at 100m. Even after crashing, the pilot might have survived had he been wearing a seat belt. One can really only begin to glimpse the sort of motivation underlying this type of extreme behaviour by looking into some very murky parts of the unconscious.

The theme of the accident chain of 'VFR into IMC' accidents beginning even before the aircraft leaves the ground is also illustrated by the pilot who obtained a face-to-face Met briefing at the departure airfield (in the far-off days when such things were possible). Extensive low cloud and poor visibility was forecast along the route and the Met officer even told the pilot directly that the intended VFR flight was simply "not on". Within 90 minutes of this conversation, the pilot proved the Met man perfectly correct by killing himself and his passengers. His aircraft hit a ridge at 300ft AMSL in visibility estimated to be less than 1000m, whilst attempting VFR flight.

So the first conclusion to be drawn is that having obtained weather information for our planned flight, we have to act on it. The most sophisticated weather recording and forecasting equipment – billions of pounds-worth of computers and satellites and communications systems – are totally worthless if the person receiving the end result then ignores that information. Because take-offs are optional, the pilot must always have the prerogative to cancel or postpone the flight if the weather forecasts and reports indicate that it cannot be safely completed. "We'll just go and have a look" is high on the list of famous last words.

Of course, these precepts are easy to accept from the safety of your favourite armchair. They are rather less simple to apply when you are stranded at a strange airfield on a Sunday afternoon, many miles from your home base and faced with the prospect of not getting home that day. The pressure to return a rented aeroplane to its owner, to get back home or just to complete the return flight as planned can be very strong. Hence the phenomenon of 'get-home-itis'. In this case ask yourself a simple question. Faced with the forecast and reported conditions you now have in front of you, would you leave your home airfield to fly out to where you are now? If the answer is "no", an attempt to make the return flight is clearly against your better judgment. In this situation simple precautions such as carrying a small overnight bag and enough financial wherewithal to pay for a night stop will do a lot to ease the symptoms of the dreaded disease.

Forecasts and reports of CBs and thunderstorms are not to be taken lightly. Would you leave your home airfield to fly into this lot? Of course not. But might you be tempted if you were trying to get home…?

Common Causes of Serious Accidents
(and how not to have one)

The other pressing reason to make a flight might be a business meeting or other appointment whose timing has been predicated on arriving by air. In this case it helps to explain to all involved that your attendance is conditional on suitable weather. You should also have an alternative transportation plan to hand in case it is needed. Flying for business can be very effective, but it definitely adds to the demands on the pilot. There is never any cast-iron guarantee that a flight will proceed to destination, even in the best-equipped aircraft with a well-qualified crew. *In extremis* that applies to supersonic airliners as much as to little 152s. Flying to an appointment is very likely to be more interesting and more fun than driving there, but it is also more demanding and there will always be days when a safe flight is simply not possible. No business meeting in the world is worth risking your life for. If you are absolutely convinced that you must not under any circumstances fail to be at a certain place at a certain time, a light aircraft is probably not the best mode of transport.

Why is this microlight pilot so determined to land when the fog is so dense that the trees next to the runway are almost invisible?

Let's now imagine that we have made the decision to fly. We have done proper pre-flight planning (including calculation of minimum safety altitudes for each leg of the flight), and the latest weather forecasts *and* reports have been checked. Don't forget that the cloud bases given in regional forecasts (such as Airmet, Metforms etc.) are in feet Above Mean Sea Level (AMSL), *not* distance above the surface. On CAA 1:500,000 charts, terrain is not generally depicted below 500ft AMSL and obstructions are not generally depicted if their tops are less than 300ft above the ground. So, if you are flying at 1300ft QNH (to stay below a 1500ft cloudbase) you might well come across a hill with an obstruction on top rising to 798ft AMSL that is not shown on your chart. You will clear the said obstruction by just 500ft. So a cloud base of 1500ft AMSL is not as flyable as you might think. Of course, airfield forecasts and actual reports do give cloud bases in feet above airfield level. But these also need to be treated with caution. Imagine you're flying into a small airfield which does not issue forecasts or reports, but there is a nearby major airport which does. If the major airport gives a cloud base of 1200ft AGL, you might decide that is acceptable. However, if the reporting airport is at an elevation of 100ft and the nearby destination has an elevation of 900ft, the cloud base at the destination is likely to be no more than 400ft AGL – a rather more risky proposition.

Monitoring weather en-route: cloud and mist rolling in from the sea to cover high ground

Back to our flight. Part of our *en route* task is to monitor the weather as we proceed, and simply looking out of the windows at what is happening is part of this. Ask yourself if the weather is shaping up as per the forecasts. If not, is it still suitable for carrying on? You can also make use of an increasing number of Volmet and ATIS broadcasts to check the actual weather either at your planned destination itself or at airfields close to your route and destination airfield. Details of Volmet and ATIS can be found in the AIP and flight guides. Check these and you may be surprised how much weather information is being transmitted through the ether for your benefit. Moreover, you can ask an ATSU to obtain weather information for you (although they may or may not be able to get it) and ask for reports from other pilots who have perhaps flown from the area into which you are heading.

Now let's imagine that lowering cloud is forcing us to descend to maintain VMC. This is the time to refer to the Minimum Safety Altitude we so carefully worked out before the flight. Are we being forced to descend below this? If the answer is yes, we need to do some very careful thinking *right now* about whether to continue or divert. Safe

Monitoring weather en-route: a snow shower in the hills

flight below the MSA is possible, but **only if you have good in-flight visibility and know where you are and where you are going**. If you are not exactly sure where you are, or if the area is unfamiliar, flying below the MSA – especially in deteriorating visibility – becomes an exercise in Russian roulette. It is difficult to give hard and fast practical guidelines, but in general terms if you are forced to within 1000ft of the surface over an area with which you are not familiar, you should seriously consider turning back or diverting. Poor visibility, low-lying mist and fog, the onset of darkness or more low cloud and showers will all make the situation worse and increase your chances of getting lost or entering IMC inadvertently.

Now is the time to remember that keeping your options open is the basic safety rule of good flying. Can you still turn back into better weather? Are there nearby airfields where you could make a safe visual landing? Could you deviate to either side of track to reach better weather or avoid high ground? Should you be reducing speed to slow safe cruise to give more time to think and navigate? Above all, do not fly yourself into a dead-end situation where you either have to enter cloud at low-level to avoid the ground, or fly dangerously close to the ground to avoid cloud.

Judging the point beyond which not to go is not easy, and can only be decided by the pilot based on the individual circumstances – every situation is different.

Monitoring weather en-route: If I was over my home airfield now, in these weather conditions and with those ahead, would I land or would I carry on?"

However, here is a simple rule that should keep you out of trouble. If the weather does start to close in and is giving you concern, ask yourself a simple question:

"If I was over my home airfield now, in these weather conditions and with those ahead, would I land or would I carry on?"

Common Causes of Serious Accidents
(and how not to have one)

If the answer is that you would land, then it is time to turn back or divert without delay.

The locations of accidents caused by attempting VFR flight in IMC tell you a lot about the motivation of the pilot. More than half occurred within 10nm of the destination airfield. In some cases the pilot was trying to manoeuvre visually for landing following an instrument approach. In others the aircraft had descended below the approach decision height, having apparently seen some sort of ground contact. Most often the pilot was trying to find the airfield visually in totally unsuitable weather conditions. If the temptation to begin a flight can be very strong, imagine the almost overpowering temptation to complete your flight by reaching your destination airfield when you know you are only a few minutes' flying time from it. Having nearly finished your journey, after maybe a long and difficult flight, it is easy to persuade yourself that you can press on just a little bit further, find that welcoming runway and land safely. In these circumstances you might well fly on into conditions you would certainly not have deemed safe in the departure and *en route* phases of the flight.

It is at times such as this that the self-discipline to accept that the weather is too bad to continue is needed more than ever. In these last few minutes, it is all too easy to ignore the true facts. Having got this far, surely there is no need to turn back or divert when you are so close? The accident reports bear out the fatal flaw in this thinking. IMC weather is IMC weather; it doesn't matter if you are two miles or 200 miles from your destination.

Monitoring weather en-route: nearly home, but a layer of fog has rolled in. Time to divert elsewhere

'Continued VFR into IMC' accidents also tend to take place around high ground (more than about 900ft AMSL) or within 10nm of the coast. The real significance of this fact is that both localities are notorious for how quickly the local weather can change for the worse. Anybody who has lived near high ground or the sea knows how fog and low cloud can roll on to a hill or over the coastline almost without warning. Visibility goes from quite flyable to practically nil in a matter of minutes. To the pilot flying towards such an area, possibly already close to the cloud base and in poor visibility, there might be no warning that he is about to fly into low cloud or fog. In several accidents the aircraft was seen by witnesses to enter cloud or fog only moments before it crashed. We can assume that the stuff covered high ground, and the pilot could not see what he was flying towards. We can also assume that in such cases he did not know exactly where he was, since presumably one does not knowingly fly towards a 1000ft ridge at a steady 900ft. This scenario only highlights the importance of calculating an MSA (or minimum height for an instrument approach) and sticking to it – especially when the weather is poor and you do not know exactly where you are.

It is often thought that 'VFR into IMC' accidents tend to happen to relatively inexperienced pilots who perhaps do not have the option of flying IMC. Although this is true in a few isolated cases, the reality is that in these accidents the pilots had an *average* of around 2000 flying hours total and 300 hours on type, and most were qualified to fly on instruments. This is a high average level of experience for a GA pilot and only emphasises the fact that lots of flying hours are, on their own, no guarantee of an accident-free flight. No matter how many flying hours you have recorded in your logbook(s), you are only as good as your next hour. Bad decisions and risky flying are dangerous whether you have 10 hours or 10,000. We must also remember that few, if any, of these pilots were caught out by an unforecast change in the weather. In most cases the pilots were well aware of the conditions they were flying into, and indeed were being accurately updated on conditions by ATC right up to the last. These extracts from accident reports stress the point:

[ATC] *"...then warned that a helicopter pilot had reported that the cloud base further north was down to 3-400 feet. This information was acknowledged by the pilots and this was the last transmission to be received from them."* [CPL/instructor, almost 9000 hours]

"...the controller informed [the accident pilot] *that the control tower was in fog, with visibility 500 metres, and this was acknowledged. The aircraft requested the QFE, asked for it to be repeated, and then acknowledged it. Subsequent calls from ATC were not answered..."* [PPL, approx. 6000 hours]

"Declining the offer of a meteorological information folder from the ATC assistant on duty at the time, the pilot booked out for his return flight. [En-route ATC to accident pilot, destination weather report] *'...it's raining, the unofficial visibility 4000 metres and the cloud base is between 800 feet and 1,200 feet...do you intend to continue to* [destination]*?' The pilot replied in the affirmative.* [Pilot to destination ATC]*...the pilot advised that he thought that he had 'about two miles to run'.* [Two minutes later] *the pilot transmitted that he was reasonably confident where he was but that he could not actually see the runway lights or airfield beacon. Seconds later the controller asked 'Are you actually following the motorway?'. The pilot replied 'No, I'm coming on to I hope on to* [runway] *07'. This was the last transmission recorded from the aircraft."* [PPL, almost 1000 hours]

[The accident aircraft had called the destination airfield to check to weather]. *ATC: "...the visibility is 2000 metres in drizzle the cloud broken at 400 feet overcast at 700 feet...'. Pilot: '...I have the cloud base copied where you've obviously got 400 feet it doesn't sound too good, you've got drizzle. We're going back to* [en-route ATC] *and when we get there we'll have a look and see what it's like'. The pilot re-contacted the en-route ATC unit, discussed the destination weather and said '...I'm not even sure it's safe to come in on that but we'll wait until we get over the sea and then get down – see what we can see'. The controller obtained weather reports for two possible diversions which the pilot acknowledged, adding '... it looks as though it'll be* [diversion] *but I'll just see what I can see at* [destination] *first then I'll come back to you'. This was the last recorded transmission from the aircraft. It flew past the destination and struck trees five miles beyond it at 440ft AMSL."* [PPL with no instrument qualifications, over 400 hours].

In the last three instances it seems that the pilots were attempting to reach their home airfields, and so were presumably quite familiar with the area. The fact that they crashed is proof that no amount of flying experience or local knowledge gives a pilot some sort of x-ray vision to see through clouds and fog or darkness. The rules regarding minimum visibility and distance from cloud required to permit VFR flight are perhaps not as clear as they could be, but nevertheless most pilots know when conditions are simply too bad for visual navigation. Deliberately flying into such conditions is simply inviting trouble. A turn-back to better weather, a diversion or a forced landing with power are all options that allow the pilot to walk away from the end of the flight and be around to fly another day.

Common Causes of Serious Accidents
(and how not to have one)

The impatience or impetuousness that leads pilots into attempting VFR flight in IMC is all the more pointless and poignant when the accident site is bathed in the sunlight of a weather clearance that came perhaps just hours after the accident. Irksome as delay or diversion can be, it really has to be better to arrive at your destination in this world a few hours late rather than arrive at another destination in the next world many years too early.

▶ Controlled Flight Into Terrain

'Controlled Flight Into Terrain' (CFIT) is the polite phrase used by the aviation business to describe an accident caused by a pilot attempting to fly lower than the surrounding topography. Aeroplanes do not make good burrowing machines, and at best they make a big dent in the ground surrounded by broken bits and pieces.

No one ever collided

with the sky

Anon

A walk in the hills was enlivened by an encounter with the result of an aircraft's failure to out-climb the hill at the end of the valley, possibly as the result of a down-draught. The occupants escaped without serious injury

I have classified an accident as caused by CFIT if the pilot was flying (or trying to fly) IFR, so as to differentiate these accidents from those caused by pilots trying to fly VFR in IMC. Sometimes the category into which an accident falls is arguable, but mostly the two causes can be separated. The 'classic' CFIT accident involves a pilot who sets off into IMC without a proper appreciation of the minimum safety altitude (MSA) for each part of the flight. This comes back to basic pre-flight preparation, and often the pilot's failure to do any worthwhile flight planning is often just part of a more general laxity that characterises a particular approach to flying. Time and again the investigation of CFIT accidents – and for that matter VFR into IMC and loss-of-control-in-IMC accidents – reveals lapsed licenses and ratings, ignored maintenance procedures, logbooks left blank, out-of-date charts or even no topographical charts at all, and so on. The accident flights also often feature failure to book-out or talk to *en route* ATC units, getting lost, infringing controlled airspace or flying outside the privileges of licence or ratings. Even if one of these omissions has no direct relation to the accident itself, it does point to a more general failure on the part of the pilot to operate legally and safely.

A fair proportion of pilots involved in CFIT accidents fall into the owner-pilot category. Operating outside the constraints a flying-school environment places on those who rent and fly their aircraft (out-of-currency check flights, checking licences and ratings, etc) these pilots carry the sole responsibility for ensuring that their operation is safe. If the owner-pilot also flies from a private strip or uncontrolled airfield, there are even more opportunities to 'bend the rules' or continue with dangerous practices and with little danger of being caught out – except, that is, by the laws of chance that prey on the unprepared and the foolish. Failing to do proper planning for an IFR flight, and flying in or over cloud without knowing for sure where you are and how much distance there is between your fragile bones and an unyielding rock face, is about as unprepared and foolish as flying gets.

Let's look at this in stages. At the pre-flight planning stage the proper calculation of a Minimum Safety Altitude (MSA) for each leg of the flight is absolutely vital. This figure must give you a *minimum* clearance of 1000ft above the highest terrain or obstacle within five miles of the planned track. If you will be flying at a flight level, remember to calculate the relationship between this and the MSA. The calculation

"Lunch"

of MSA is so simple and yet so vital that it is worth revising. Look along the track line you have drawn on your map and search for the highest point, be it terrain or an obstruction, within five miles of track. If the point you find is an obstruction, round its altitude up to the next 100ft. Then add 1000ft and you have your MSA. If the highest point is terrain, add 300ft (to allow for an obstruction too low to be shown on the map), round up to the next 100ft, then add 1000ft to get the MSA. Now you have this figure, write it down on your flight log. You'll be needing it.

What happens when pilots fly below MSA in IMC: this aircraft flew into the mast in the background

Before moving on, if the basic precaution of flying higher than the ground level between the destination and arrival airfields – especially in IMC – seems too obvious to need repeating, look at these excerpts from CFIT accident investigations:

> *"The computer-generated pilot's log was recovered at the crash site...No en-route altitudes were quoted and the column provided to record Minimum Safe Altitudes was blank."*

> *"The pilot had planned the route using standard half million-scale aeronautical topographical charts, although those recovered after the accident were not current editions... No evidence has been recovered of any calculation of Minimum Safe Altitudes, nor of any calculations to take account of the wind effect on track or groundspeed."*

Once in flight and in IMC, you should be making FREDA checks or the equivalent cruise check every 10-15 minutes. The 'A' stands for altitude, meaning that you check that you are at the height/altitude/flight level you expect to be. Not only that, you check the pressure setting in use. You also check the MSA. If you can't see the surface, the present MSA should be engraved on your heart – because it is only by staying above the MSA that you prevent your aircraft becoming a failed burrowing machine.

Of course, an MSA for the route you are planning to fly can become increasingly irrelevant if you stray from that route. Most IFR flying is done by routing between radionavigation beacons, usually VORs. If you fly like this a lot in IFR, you may have come to realise that having the VOR needle exactly centred is no guarantee that you are exactly on the selected radial. Tolerances in the VOR beacon itself, the receiver and external factors such as the 'bending' of VOR signals at low level in hilly terrain can all introduce a difference between what your VOR needle shows and your actual direction to or from the beacon. There is nothing mysterious about this. Between the signal leaving a VOR beacon and the needle on your instrument panel, an error of up to 5° is by no means unheard-of. Simple arithmetic tells us that for any given track error angle, the further you are from the beacon, the greater the distance off-track. At 15nm from a beacon, a 5° difference puts you 1·75nm off-track. But by 60nm from the beacon, a 5° difference puts you 5nm off-track. Remember that these errors are more likely at the edge of the beacon's range over mountainous terrain and at low level. So if one day you are planning to let-down through cloud to below the MSA, based on nothing more than the radial from a VOR maybe 30 miles or more distant and with terrain or obstructions only a few miles from your planned track, perhaps you should think again…

The further you are from a VOR (or NDB) the greater off-track you may be, despite what the needle says

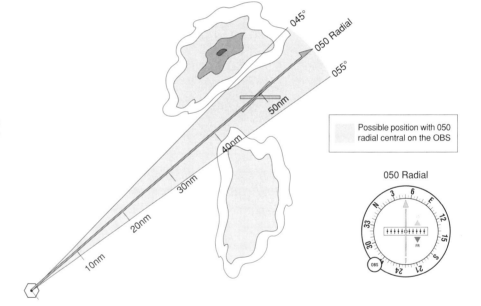

Possible position with 050 radial central on the OBS

050 Radial

Although it is possible to stray off-track with a VOR needle perfectly centred, it is more common for the pilot to make some navigational error or mis-set the cockpit instruments. Aircraft equipped for IFR flying tend to have lots of instruments and dials to play with. They can keep the aviator amused for hours, but they also increase the chances of confusion unless he takes care to ensure that he knows exactly how the instruments are set up. There is no point carefully tuning and identifying a radionavigation beacon on the NAV 1 radio if you then unwittingly fly by reference to a needle driven by NAV 2. By the same token, if you accidentally set your GPS to route you to STORnoway rather than STANsted, the result will belie the display that apparently tells you that you are exactly on track (you're on track all right, but to where?)

Common Causes of Serious Accidents
(and how not to have one)

Above all, knowing where you are and where you are going is a matter of that old favourite, *situational awareness*. Tracking a VOR needle so that it stays fixed in the centre is of limited value if you do not know where you are. It is all too easy to rely totally on one aid to navigation, such as a VOR, and lose sight of the bigger picture. Knowing that you are tracking 142° magnetic towards a beacon that is 32·8 nautical miles away means absolutely nothing unless you can relate that information to the real world beneath you. If you have completed a proper flight log before starting the flight, it should easier to maintain situational awareness by maintaining the log as the flight progresses. Certain key points must be noted, such as the time you pass *en route* waypoints and the ETA at the next one. In this way you guard against the danger of blindly flying on, perhaps waiting to pass a beacon, with no real appreciation of whether your groundspeed is significantly higher or lower than planned. At average light-aircraft cruising speeds and leg distances of less than 100nm, anything more than five minutes early or late on ETA demands further investigation. Likewise, you should be comparing the heading needed to maintain track with that expected. A heading more than 10° different from that planned indicates that something is up. Perhaps the wind velocity is different from the forecast. Headings much more than 20° different require that some searching questions be asked right away. Check first for the obvious. Are you flying the correct heading from this leg? Are the instruments properly set? Confusing 300°, 330° and 030°, or 020° and 200° is easy to do; rare is the pilot who has not made such an error. It is often not appreciated that if you fly properly calculated headings for a properly calculated time, you should be surprisingly close to the intended point. So-called 'Dead Reckoning' (DR) navigation is a much-maligned technique but if you do your sums properly and fly reasonably accurately, it works quite well. Being aware of your DR position based on direction, speed and time since your last known 'fix' is an invaluable backup to all those entertaining and glamorous navigational gizmos that fill up the instrument panel and make it look pretty or the latest model GPS on your knee.

"I'd feel a lot more relaxed if I hadn't seen you panic with the video recorder controls."

Maintaining a proper flight log as the trip progresses will not only improve your situational awareness but also give you a back-up in the event that your primary navigation aid(s) decide to go on strike. Rare though such failures are, they are not completely unknown. A properly maintained flight log and a reasonable level of situational awareness will be invaluable at such times.

So let's imagine that despite your best efforts and good intentions, one day you become lost whilst IFR. Maybe you were trying to become visual with the ground and are below MSA. Maybe a radionavigation aid you were planning to use just doesn't seem to be working. What do you do now? The answer is simple; write it on the back of your hand so you won't forget the three 'Cs':

Climb Get above MSA ***NOW***. If you don't know MSA, start climbing to what seems a sensible figure and then climb some more. Don't hang about: use at least the best rate of climb airspeed, not a gentle cruise-climb. If you think you may be near high ground or obstructions use the best angle of climb airspeed.

Confess Talk to someone and tell them what your problem is. If you are transponder-equipped say so. You will be located a lot quicker. Don't mince your words, and don't pretend to know where you are if you don't.

Comply Do as ATC asks unless there is an exceptionally good reason not to. Your number-one priority is to land safely. You can worry about what went wrong and wounded pride later, when safely on the ground.

So far we have concentrated on avoiding a CFIT accident in the *en route* phase of flight, which is where most such accidents happen. CFIT accidents also happen when pilots begin their descent towards an airfield, and during instrument approaches.

If leaving the cruising altitude to try to regain visual contact with the ground, the MSA should be foremost in your mind. All too often pilots descend when they *think* they know where they are. Rather than descending to a pre-determined MSA, they just keep on going down hoping to catch a glimpse of the ground or perhaps find a break in the clouds. Descending below MSA in such circumstances is simply inviting disaster, as the accident reports show.

Don't descend into this unless you know exactly where you are, where you are going, and your lowest safe altitude/height

Unless you are in good VMC, it is only safe to descend below MSA with the aid of an ATC radar unit or on a proper instrument-approach procedure. Unfortunately it is not uncommon for pilots, especially those flying from smaller uncontrolled airfields, to have their own personal instrument approach 'procedures' into their home airfield. Leaving aside the legal niceties of attempting such things, they rarely amount to much more than descending with reference to a distant radionavigation beacon (or even just a GPS) and hoping to see the ground somewhere in the vicinity of the airfield. There may be no proper calculated minima or vertical profile, no checking of the 'procedure', no missed approach/go-around options. These home-grown approaches are a classic example of pilots flying themselves into dead ends. Often they could easily have made a proper instrument approach at a nearby airfield with the relevant aids and then had the choice of continuing VMC to their destination if the weather permitted or landing off the approach if not. It cannot be repeated too often; keeping your options open and having more than one choice of action available is good flying practice. "I'll just go down a bit further to have a look" is not. Those words, or something similar, are undoubtedly another favourite on the list of famous last words.

Finally we come to CFIT accidents taking place during an instrument approach. These occur when the pilot descends below the minimum safe height for the procedure or flies the procedure incorrectly, often by losing awareness of its requirements and in particular the vertical profile. It is not uncommon for this to happen when the weather conditions were below minima for the approach in any case. All notified instrument approaches have a minimum visibility and minimum height. Descending below the minimum height, or attempting an approach if the visibility is below the published figure, are both illegal and dangerous. Just as in accidents caused by pilots trying to fly VFR in IMC, the pilots who had a CFIT accident during an instrument approach were usually well aware of the prevailing weather. This is a good time to re-iterate that ATC has no power to prevent an aircraft making an approach, even if the pilot is clearly breaking the law. ATC might query the pilot's intentions or drop some heavy hints such as repeating the latest weather report, or reports of suitable diversions. However, if a pilot is intent on risking life and limb and breaking the law at the same time, there is little a controller can do to stop him.

Attempting an instrument approach when the weather is much worse than the procedure minima is not dissimilar to attempting VFR flight in IMC. It's dangerous, it's foolhardy, it's illegal and it carries an exceptionally high mortality rate.

CFIT accidents caused by pilots flying the wrong profile for the approach highlight the fact that an instrument approach can be a demanding task. An instrument approach in

Remember what is under the ocean of clouds: eternity

Wind, Sand and Stars: Antoine de Saint-Exupéry

The ocean of clouds

An instrument approach

IMC should only be attempted by pilots who have the relevant ratings and are in current experience. The type of non-precision approach often available at a smaller airfield (e.g. an NDB approach) is not the easiest instrument approach to fly, especially if you have not flown one for months or even years. In these circumstances a diversion to an airfield offering an easier option, such as a radar or ILS approach, makes a lot more sense than struggling on around a difficult and unfamiliar let-down.

Some 20% of CFIT and 'attempted VFR flight into IMC' accidents occur at night. Whether VMC exists at night is another one of those questions that can keep instructors occupied all day and lawyers for much longer, but that doesn't necessarily help much. In practical terms, if you cannot see the surface – whether that is because of cloud, fog, darkness or whatever – you should be conducting your flight as an IFR exercise. This means observing the minimum altitudes IFR flight entails. Night-time accidents often occur when the aircraft is manoeuvring for the final approach, possibly when the pilot thinks that he has (or is about to have) visual contact with the ground. However, sighting a few scattered lights on the ground is hardly likely to stop a pilot flying straight into a very dark and very unlit hillside. Additionally, at night it is very easy to fly into 'weather' such as a cloud or a shower, for the simple reason that you can't see it coming (clouds also tend not to have lights on). Hence you can quickly go from being able to see the surface reasonably well to no visual reference at all, in a matter of seconds with no warning. If this should happen to you, your first thought must be the MSA; climb to get above MSA at once if at all possible. Nudging the control column forward and hoping to 'duck under' the cloud or weather is a foolish reaction, because you are now descending totally blind towards a surface you may have little chance of seeing until you hit it.

Without going too far into the various facets of night flying, a pilot needs to be aware of two potentially dangerous visual illusions that occur at night. Firstly, lit objects and indeed lights themselves seem to be much closer at night than they really are. This can lead even an experienced pilot seriously to underestimate distances, and therefore descend too soon and too far away from an airfield. Additionally, if the pilot is trying to fly by reference to just a single light or group of lights in otherwise black surroundings, there is a tendency to 'undershoot' during a descent. An aircraft descending towards such lights and apparently (to the pilot) keeping the lights at a constant angle is actually descending on a path that will reach the surface before reaching the light(s). Experiments have shown that in these circumstances, the vast majority of pilots would fly into the ground if they used no other reference. Indeed aircraft flying in clear conditions have been flown into unlit surfaces such as the sea by experienced pilots attempting visual night approaches.

▶ Mid-Air Collision

Of all the major causes of fatal accidents, it is the mid-air collision that comes closest to many pilot's greatest fear – that of a mortal blow that strikes out of the blue, with no apparent warning. Before going any further, it can be said with confidence that there is one single preventative measure which is the best possible insurance against a mid-air collision. This is to use your eyes in a proper, practised lookout scan. Even with modern rules and procedures and aids such as primary and secondary radar, transponders, strobes and the like, it is still a good lookout that gives you the best chance of spotting and avoiding other aircraft.

He who sees first

lives longest

Anon

Common Causes of Serious Accidents
(and how not to have one)

Contrary to what you might think, the majority of mid-air collisions involve pilots who were aware of each other's presence. Indeed around a third of them involved aircraft that were either taking part in an air race or were engaged in formation flying. Air racing is great fun, but it does involve lots of aircraft travelling in close proximity to each other. This invariably heightens the risk of a near-miss or collision, and all pilots who race are clearly aware of this risk. Formation flying also involves aircraft deliberately flying close to each other, but with one exception mid-air collisions in a formation did not involve 'professional' formation flying. Instead the pilots were either 'dog-fighting' (implying that at least one pilot was fooling around) or untrained aviators were attempting to fly in formation.

Formation flying is not a 'teach yourself' activity. There are six Turbulents in this air display formation

Formation flying is rarely part of civilian flying training and it is nowhere near as easy as properly trained pilots make it look. There is nothing in everyday flying to compare it with, and it is emphatically *not* a 'teach yourself' activity. Trying out a spot of formation flying without proper training is **exceptionally dangerous**. No amount of ground briefing or reading of textbooks will compensate for a lack of basic formation-flying skills, and these can only come from dual flying instruction with a suitably qualified and experienced instructor. Military pilots tend to fly in formation on a regular basis. This gives them an acute appreciation of safe closing speeds, relative headings, anticipation and handling skills required for safe formation flying. They are also well practised in what to do when it all goes wrong. Civilian pilots rarely have the same experience and training, and all too often their untrained attempts at formation flying end tragically.

Around a third of collisions occur around an airfield – although this was actually an air display routine

A further 33% of collisions occur close to an airfield when the aircraft involved were either on approach, going around, in the circuit or landing. Obviously aircraft do tend to congregate around airfields, and once there they tend to follow a fairly similar pattern around the same spot – i.e. the active runway. More than once, one of the aircraft seems to have been following an unexpected or non-standard pattern or procedure for the airfield. This took it into conflict with another which *was* following the proper pattern. Standard procedures or patterns mean that all aircraft should be travelling in approximately the same direction and height at any particular place, and their commanders will know what other aircraft ahead or behind can be expected to do. This in itself does not prevent collisions. A number of cases involved one aircraft running into the other from behind, often whilst climbing or descending. Lookout behind is not easy even if the aircraft has all-round vision; not many of us can swivel our head through 180 degrees! It is more practical to exercise a better lookout before and during a descent or climb. Do this by visually clearing the area you will be climbing or descending into *before* starting the manoeuvre.

Once in the climb or descent, weave the aircraft at regular intervals (say every 500ft or so) to view the area ahead hidden by the nose. Weaving may make your aircraft more visible to another because it introduces a relative movement to other aircraft (your wings 'waggle' and your aircraft may move across the windscreen of an approaching aircraft). By the same token, other aircraft may appear to move across your windscreen when weaving, this movement being easier to spot than a stationary dot ahead. When you come to level out, look into the area you will be flying into before, during and after returning to level flight.

It should go without saying that when you're close to an airfield, extra vigilance for other aircraft is essential – even if you are not actually aware of any other aircraft around. Aeroplanes do still fly around without radios after all. It should be an instinctive reaction to clear an area visually before starting a climb or descent, before turning and when reverting to straight and level flight. Make a point also of checking the extended centreline before turning on to finals. Some impatient soul might be sneaking in on a straight-in approach rather than following the proper joining procedure.

On that subject, by the way, know the proper joining procedure and circuit height, (it may not be the standard overhead join) for the particular airfield and *use it*. Apart from safety considerations, a particular airfield's procedure is often designed to minimise noise-disturbance complaints. Visitors who annoy noise-sensitive neighbours tend to be very unpopular at the airfields at which they loudly arrive! Given the heavy workload around the airfield, pilots could be forgiven for complaining that they already have enough to do without extra lookout for non-standard arrivals too.

The final category of mid-air collisions involves accidents occurring in the open FIR between transiting aircraft unaware of each other's presence. As with other collisions, these all occurred in good VMC conditions. In other words, the weather should have been good enough in theory for the aircraft to see and avoid each other. So what's going on?

For one thing, it is worth noting that all the collisions occurred below 3000ft AMSL and that none of the aircraft were flying on a flight level or using the quadrantal rule. Although this might not have been possible in all cases, it illustrates the danger of simply transiting at 2500ft or thereabouts as a matter of habit, when flying at a higher flight level has so much more to offer. As a general rule, flying higher means less aircraft around, better radio range and greater in-flight visibility (cloud permitting). It also gives better visibility on radar, smoother air, increased gliding range, higher true

Common Causes of Serious Accidents
(and how not to have one)

This aircraft made a successful landing at an airfield after a mid-air collision in the 'open FIR' that removed most of its vertical and horizontal tail surfaces

airspeeds and better tailwinds – and, yes, that means stronger headwinds if you're going the other way! Given all this, it seems surprising that even when not limited by cloud or controlled airspace, many GA pilots choose to squeeze into the lowest 3000ft of airspace and ignore the clear and relatively empty skies above.

It also seems surprising that with one exception, the pilots involved in the open-FIR accidents were not making any use of a radar service such as a RAS or RIS – and even in the exceptional case, one of the pilots had been made aware of the aircraft he eventually collided with. Through the munificence of the taxpayer (that's you and me), the full abilities of modern state-of-the-art radar and SSR equipment and its highly trained civil and military personnel are freely available to aviators over most of England and Wales and a smaller portion of Scotland. It seems churlish not to take advantage of this generosity. Indeed, there is a sneaking suspicion that many pilots actively avoid talking to a radar service because they are uncertain of the proper procedures. The answer is simple; there is plenty of literature in the form of textbooks, leaflets and circulars about air traffic services. Grab it, read it and then start making full and free use of all this wonderful equipment and the associated expertise.

Of course, flying high and planning to use a radar service doesn't guarantee the avoidance of other aircraft. And apart from any other consideration, LARS units – most of which are military – have a habit of closing down for evenings, weekends and public holidays even when they are notified as H24 operations. So regardless of the airspace you are in or the ATC service you are receiving, exercising a good lookout is still your best defence against a close encounter of the aeronautical kind.

Develop a lookout scan and then use it. If your eyes are inside the cockpit for more than 10 seconds at a time on a VFR flight, that's too long. Make it a habit to keep your vision outside most of the time. When you have to look in – perhaps to check the instruments or complete a task – do only one job before looking out again.

Looking out of the windows, the best way to avoid an unexpected close encounter

Flying in this way will give you the best chance of spotting other aircraft, and holding heading by outside reference is also generally easier than constantly referring to the HI. In fact, it is preferable to fly by referring mainly to the view outside, checking the instruments one at a time to monitor progress and make minor corrections. This advice might seem a little old-fashioned, especially when modern navigation instruments (and GPS in particular) have given pilots a whole new range of wonderful toys to play with. However, most electronic gizmos including GPS receivers are notoriously difficult to re-program in flight without extended periods of head-in-the-cockpit-and-eyes-down time. Once again, allow me to point out that it's very useful to know your exact range, bearing and groundspeed to a waypoint. However, if you're so absorbed by the readouts that you fly straight into another aircraft whose pilot who is also heads-in and marvelling at modern technology, the information might not be of much use. In the case of GPS, the obvious solution is to do your programming and waypoint insertion *before* flight – which comes back to our old friend, pre-flight planning – and don't become too fixated by the pretty moving map.

Over a quarter of mid-air collisions involved gliders. Most pilots flying *en route* will take care to avoid active airfields and ATZs but gliding sites are not always treated with the same circumspection. This is a shame. Apart from anything else, gliders are often raised aloft using cables that can be carried a good 3000ft above the ground. These are very difficult to spot from the air, but are nevertheless quite capable of inflicting serious and possibly mortal damage on an aeroplane. Away from their launch sites, gliders may congregate wherever lift is to be found. Once one glider finds good lift – underneath a growing cumulus cloud, for instance – and starts circling in it, you can be sure any other gliders nearby will join in. So in a very short space of time there can be a dozen or more gliders circling in one spot.

Now imagine a passing aircraft chancing upon the scene. Despite what glider pilots seem to think, their aircraft can be exceptionally difficult to spot in the air (and they don't 'paint' at all well on radar either, so ATSUs don't always know about them). When viewed directly head-on or tail-on, their slender fuselages and wings are almost invisible at any range and their predominantly white colour blends in perfectly with white clouds and haze. Part of the answer is to avoid gliding sites like the plague, and check pre-flight bulletins for notification of gliding competitions. Whilst in flight exercise a very good lookout and be especially wary of gliders near gliding sites and circling lift in good conditions. Similar observations apply to hang-gliders, parascenders and similar craft; give them all a wide berth.

When looking out during flight, take account of any blind spots caused by the aircraft's design. Struts, windscreen posts and cockpit clutter (compasses, OAT gauges, GPS antennas and the like) will all block an area of sky from your vision. Adjust your lookout to cover these spots. By the same token, in a high-wing aircraft the lower wing will block visibility into a turn when the aircraft is banked. So it is common practice to lift the relevant wing a few degrees to check for traffic before turning. In low-wing aircraft, the higher wing blocks visibility outside the turn. Here again, a good lookout *before* turning is essential.

As with so many other aspects of good flying practice, avoiding a mid-air collision is largely a matter of good preparation before flight and sensible precautions and sound airmanship once airborne. This is no magic formula or astounding insight; it's more a question of common sense and what someone once called "joined-up thinking". So when one day you find yourself flying along without a care in the world, your mind drifting to other things and perhaps somewhat under-aroused – **WAKE UP!** If you're not thinking, you're not concentrating. And if you're not concentrating you are missing something – and that something might be very important indeed.

▶ Other Causes of Serious Accidents

In the foregoing we have covered the common scenarios that account for something like 70% of all serious accidents. Even so, you might be surprised that some of the most commonly publicised hazards to safe flight – such as wake turbulence and thunderstorms – have not been mentioned. Accidents certainly occur as a result of these hazards, but nothing like as often as in the situations we have been looking at. This is not to say that the dangers have been overstated, but perhaps the figures show that good pilot education has worked in these areas. All but the most foolhardy or unfortunate avoid thunderstorms and flying too close behind larger aircraft and helicopters.

Two causes of serious accidents that fall just outside the 'top five' are ditchings and forced landings, and these are worthy of a short mention. Avoiding engine failure is a good start. Simple measures such as monitoring the health of the engine, checking for carb icing and carrying enough fuel to complete the flight are all good ways to avoid a horrible silence from the front end. Ditchings usually follow an engine failure, but are different from forced landings over land in that reaching the surface safely is only the beginning of the story – as we have already seen. When flying over water, carrying and wearing serviceable life-jackets is essential. There won't be time to put them on after the engine has stopped. Likewise, the life-raft (which is as essential as the life-jackets) must be serviceable and must be carried where you can reach it. Having to extract a heavy life-raft from the rear baggage compartment of a sinking aircraft is a scenario to send shivers up the spine, and trying to survive in the cold

"…and the good news is, we'll be able to salvage most of it at low water next Tuesday…"

waters around the UK without a life-raft will also definitely give you the shivers. The message from the accident reports and rescue services is brutal and unequivocal. Bodies are found in life-jackets, survivors are found in life-rafts.

When a prang seems inevitable, endeavour to strike the softest, cheapest object in the vicinity, as slowly and gently as possible

Advice once given to RAF pilots

A serious consequence of an otherwise well-handled engine failure can be due to the aircraft encountering an obstruction of some kind, either during the actual landing or at the end of the landing run. If we dig back into our memories, we can probably all summon up the image of the perfect forced-landing area. It's large, wide, flat, smooth and unobstructed and there's nothing in the undershoot or overshoot area to cause concern. Of course, real-life situations are not always kind enough to provide just such a perfect haven after an engine failure and we have to make do with the best available. The main candidates for ruining an otherwise text-book forced landing are trees and other tall obstructions, buildings, ditches and stone walls. Running into any of these at speed is certain to bring the aircraft to a very rapid halt, and generate forces that will damage it and you much more than if there is at least a clear 100 metres or so to slow down after landing. You might remember the old adage to the effect that it's better to run into the far hedge at taxying speed than hit the near hedge at flying speed.

Despite appearances, both occupants survived this forced landing following an engine failure

We will leave serious accidents here, but let's reiterate what has gone before. If you now understand and are prepared to actively avoid the five common situations which give rise to something like 70% of all serious accidents, you are already well on the way to enjoying safer flying. And you have almost certainly ensured that the best-publicised aspect of your flying career will not be a posthumous appearance in an accident report.

Common Causes of Less Serious Accidents, (and how not to have one all the same)

▶ Introduction

▶ Hard Landings and Loss of Directional Control

▶ Forced Landings

▶ Undercarriage Problems

▶ Performance

▶ Collision with Obstructions

▶ Starting and Taxying

Experience is a hard teacher:

first comes the test,

then the lesson

Anon

Flight Safety

▶Introduction

Thankfully, the vast majority of flying accidents do not involve fatalities. Instead they result in damaged aeroplanes and pilots who are most often uninjured, although frequently severely embarrassed. As with serious accidents, a large number of less serious accidents are avoidable. They occur as a result of a series of events which follow a predictable course to a predictable outcome. All the causes of serious accidents also reappear in the reports of less serious accidents. Indeed, there is sometimes a terribly thin line between an accident resulting in a fatality and an incident resulting in a badly shaken aviator. Pilots do survive mid-air collisions, often by very skilled flying to recover a damaged aeroplane to the ground safely. Some are fortunate enough to survive a loss-of-control or CFIT accident. Nevertheless, lucky as these pilots were, it's a pretty safe bet that they would have preferred not to have been involved in an accident at all.

To look at the common causes of less serious accidents, I examined the reports for one year – an enterprise that yielded just under 200 reportable non-fatal accidents. With the usual caveats that the interpretation of the causes of each accident are sometimes a matter of the balance of probabilities rather than indisputable proof, I established the most common causes as below:

Hard landing and loss of directional control on the ground	34%
Forced landings	20%
Undercarriage problem	12%
Performance	11%
Flight into ground or obstructions	6%
Taxying	6%

It is immediately apparent that the greatest cause of serious accidents is also the greatest cause of less serious accidents – namely pilots mishandling an aircraft close to or on the ground. It is also instructive that in 60% of these, the pilots had less than 100 hours on type. In fact, in half the cases the pilot had less than 50 hours on type. These figures are very close to those for serious accidents. Likewise, 51% involved pilots who had PPLs with no additional ratings and pilots with less than 200 hours total experience accounted for about a third of all the less serious accidents.

The phase of flight during which less serious accidents occurred is markedly different from that involving serious accidents. A full 51% of the former took place during landing, and 20% during take-off. A further 11% of less serious accidents happened in the *en route* phase of flight, with 8% on the ground and only 4% during a go-round. Statistically speaking, it could be said that go-arounds are a lot safer than landings – a theme we will return to shortly.

In keeping with the format of the previous chapter, we will look in more detail at the root causes of each of these most common accident scenarios, and what can be done to avoid them.

Common Causes of Less Serious Accidents,
(and how not to have one all the same)

▶ Hard Landings and Loss of Directional Control

If you talk about this subject to pilots fortunate enough to fly taildraggers (aircraft with tailwheels or tailskids) they may well dismiss the entire topic with a contemptuous snort. Push them a bit further and they might become positively dewy-eyed and nostalgic…

Picture the scene. The goggled aviator, white scarf blowing in the slipstream, leans over the cockpit side and casts an experienced eye at the windsock fluttering in the grassy meadow below. Pulling the throttle back, our hero glides towards the earth, feeding in a touch of 'top rudder' to steepen the descent; the hum of the air through the wires sings out the airspeed. The biplane slips silently over the boundary hedge and, as the wings are levelled, the nose is straightened towards the distant end of the runway. Back, back comes the stick as the nose rises; the wheels and the tailskid brush the grass at the same instant. With a final gentle easing back on the stick, the aircraft sinks softly to the runway in a perfect three-point touchdown. The pilot's feet dance lightly on the rudder pedals as the aircraft slows to a walking pace and a co-ordinated burst of power and a nudge of the rudder bar swings the aircraft towards the clubhouse. As the engine shudders to a stop, a dog runs out to greet its master; a wisp of smoke from the clubhouse chimney means that the kettle is on…

Aircraft such as this Tiger Moth can and do operate perfectly safely without the benefit of nosewheels, brakes, enclosed cockpits, flaps, radios etc

Like all good nostalgia trips, alas, this one will not bear close scrutiny. It is fair to say that aircraft can operate perfectly safely without the benefit of enclosed cockpits, nosewheels and brakes, flaps, radios, ATC, tarmac runways and suchlike luxuries. It is also fair to observe that once the art of landing a taildragger has been mastered (insofar as this rather black art is ever mastered), the general standard of one's landings will probably be improved whether in nosewheel or tailwheel aircraft. That said, taildraggers are not all good news. The reduced view ahead on landing makes the flare and touchdown more difficult to judge and harder to learn, and they are considerably more difficult to keep straight after touchdown. They can be a real hand(foot)ful with even a light crosswind component, so that their realistic crosswind limit is less than a comparable nosewheel design. Take-off is also a more skilled affair. The tail has to be raised at some point during the take-off run, requiring careful co-ordination of elevator and rudder controls. Even when taxying, the view forward is restricted and requires the nose to be swung from side to side to clear the area ahead. And while you're dealing with all these things, a wind from behind may be enough to get under the wing or tail and tip the aeroplane on to its nose.

Taildraggers can be a real hand – and footful to land – especially in a crosswind

These awkward ground-handling characteristics of a tailwheel aircraft are largely dictated by the CG position, which naturally falls behind the mainwheels. It follows that if the aircraft starts to turn or yaw, the motion will continue until a positive force (opposite rudder or braking, or *in extremis* hitting something) is applied. Conversely, the CG of a nosewheel aircraft is ahead of the mainwheels. So if it starts to turn or yaw, the motion will cease quickly unless there is a continuing force applied in the direction of the turn or yaw.

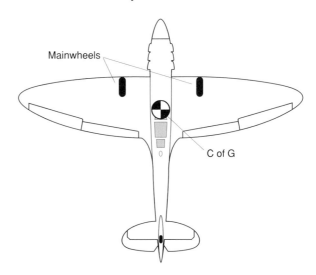

As a taildragger yaws on the ground, the position of the centre of gravity behind the mainwheels increases the yawing moment

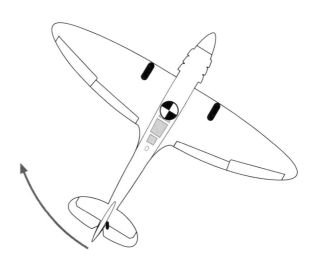

Like many other labour-saving devices, the nosewheel was popularised in the USA. It then spread around the world along with American-designed aircraft, whose nosewheel undercarriage layout was later taken up by other countries. Also, like many new ideas in aviation, the nosewheel was often fiercely resisted by experienced pilots. These might well say that judging by the frequency of landing accidents in modern nosewheel designs, their misgiving were entirely justified. If you're wondering what all this has to do with landing and take-off accidents in nosewheel aircraft, please stay with it – I'm just coming to that.

Common Causes of Less Serious Accidents, (and how not to have one all the same)

Because most early tailwheel aircraft had no flaps, their pilots tended to make glide approaches as standard. So the circuit and approach was flown much closer to the runway. Often the engine was throttled back at the end of the downwind leg and a curving approach was flown until the aircraft lined up with the runway, probably within half a mile or so of the threshold. This steep approach gave the pilot a good view of the landing runway and would keep the aircraft clear of obstructions under the approach path. During the finals turn, the rudder could be used to introduce sideslip and so increase the rate of descent. But without the drag of flaps, the airspeed control had to be precise. If the airspeed became too high, there were only limited ways to slow down without flaps – and airfields and runways used to be smaller and shorter than many are now, giving the pilot less room for a long float.

Airspeed and angle of approach just right – as it has to be in a taildragger

Once over the runway, the aim of the flare and hold-off in a tailwheel aircraft is usually to land in a 'three-point' attitude – that is with the mainwheels and tailwheel touching down simultaneously (taildraggers can do 'wheeler' landings, touching down in a near-level attitude, but that's another story). To make a three-point landing, we gradually pitch the aircraft nose-up in the flare and hold-off to reach the correct attitude whilst the airspeed bleeds off. If we touch down at too shallow an attitude and too fast, the aircraft may well 'skip' and get airborne again. Touching down in the correct attitude will only be possible just above the stalling speed. So the aircraft will settle on to the runway with the control column almost fully back, and will not have enough airspeed to get airborne again. During the flare the aircraft is vulnerable to a gust or crosswind. For this reason we avoid approaching too fast because it prolongs the hold-off, leaving the aircraft floating along nose-high whilst waiting for the airspeed to decline. Approaching too slowly is also not a good idea, not only because it is dangerous but because the high nose attitude ruins the view ahead.

After touchdown, the tailwheel pilot is acutely aware that the landing is not yet over. The aircraft may well try to swing as it slows down, and quick intervention on the rudder pedals (and even some brake) will be needed to stay straight. Turning off the runway at high speed is a definite no-no; it is an open invitation to the aircraft to ground-loop. Likewise there will be no after-landing checks until well clear of the runway because that sort of inattention also invites the aircraft to do its own thing.

Contrast all this with an alternative scenario in a nosewheel aircraft. The downwind leg is flown further from the airfield (probably outside gliding range) and the downwind extended so that the aircraft may even leave the ATZ. The consequent powered approach is flown at a shallow angle, even with the use of flap, because of the distance from the runway. Judgment of the proper approach path may therefore be difficult. The approach may be flown faster than the recommended airspeed for no clear reason other than "...a bit of extra speed does no harm". So even more power is needed, and more neighbours are annoyed by noisy low-flying aircraft. Conversely the airspeed may become too slow if the aircraft is descending short of the runway, and the pilot pitches the aircraft nose-up to trade airspeed for altitude. The shallow approach increases the risk of hitting an obstruction in the approach path, and makes judgment of a precise touchdown point on the runway more difficult.

Once over the runway, the pilot closes the throttle and allows the aircraft to float along in a near-level attitude. Extra airspeed means a prolonged float. But with perhaps 2000 metres of tarmac to use up, the pilot is happy to sit and wait. Certainly there is no pre-decided aiming point for the actual touchdown. Given no proper attempt to 'hold-off', the aircraft may well sink to the runway 10 or 20 knots faster than the stalling speed. If the aircraft touches down almost level, it could well bounce back into the air as a result of this excess velocity. Alternatively, a sudden pull-back on the control column could well make the aircraft 'balloon'. In either case the pilot is left a dozen or so feet above the runway, with rapidly reducing airspeed and equally diminishing options. There might be a temptation to nudge the control column forward to force the aircraft back down to the runway: ***don't do it!*** We'll look at this issue in a moment.

Even if our hero does touch down gently enough, excess airspeed will carry the aircraft much further down the runway than is necessary. But he doesn't appreciate this because as soon as the wheels are on *terra firma* he goes heads-in to do the after-landing checks. Flaps up (oops, there goes the undercarriage instead). Navaids off (dear me, I seem to have missed the turn-off). Non-essential radios off (oh s***, we're not on the runway any more). Crunch, tinkle.

Crunch, tinkle...

Not surprisingly, most landings in both tailwheel and nosewheel aircraft fall somewhere between the two extremes outlined above. But there is no doubt that the basic techniques for a safe landing in a tailwheel aircraft are of more than passing relevance to a nosewheel aeroplane. The problem – if you can call it a problem – is that the nosewheel design is generally much more forgiving of poor or sloppy flying technique and lack of finesse. Therein the seeds of complacency are sown.

Common Causes of Less Serious Accidents, (and how not to have one all the same)

Let's start with the circuit and initial approach. There is undoubtedly an increasing tendency for circuits to become almost mini-cross country trips; the aircraft flies well outside the ATZ even when downwind and turns on to final approach two or three miles from the threshold or even more. Such airliner circuits are rarely necessary and it is difficult to come up with any positive benefits from flying them in VMC. The approach itself tends to become a shallow high-power affair as the pilot drags the aircraft in with lots of power and a poor view of the landing area. Meanwhile other aircraft are being forced to orbit or extend their own circuits while our hero creeps towards the runway. Incidentally, if the runway is fitted with approach-slope indicators such as VASIS or PAPIs, there is no need for light-aircraft pilots to feel obliged to fly the relatively shallow approach slope they mark out. VASIS and PAPIs are intended to be used by large aircraft requiring to fly standard approach angles, but the light-aircraft pilot should be able to judge the approach without reliance on any aids at all. And steeper approaches have many benefits.

With the aircraft established on finals, the landing flap is selected, the airspeed is settled at the proper approach speed and the aircraft is trimmed for this speed. Which begs the question – what *is* the proper approach speed? When you are training, the answer is quite simple; the proper approach speed is whatever your instructor specifies! However, when you leave the nest and start flying new aircraft types or variants, there is a tendency for the approach and landing speeds to be passed down by word of mouth from pilot to pilot. *This is just not good enough for safe aircraft operation.* Whenever you check-out on a new aircraft type, you must spend time with the aircraft's Pilot's Operating Handbook (POH/FM) or equivalent and learn amongst other things the proper airspeeds recommended by the aircraft's manufacturer.

Why the plural? As well as specifying the standard approach speed, the POH/FM or equivalent may state the circumstances requiring it to be increased. There are usually only two safety-related reasons for this. One is the case of a flapless approach, in which a small increase in approach speed (say five knots) may be prudent. The other is in gusty conditions, when an increment of half the gust factor may be added to the approach speed. So if the surface wind speed is 15 knots gusting 25, the gust factor is 10 and five knots is added to the approach airspeed.

SECTION 4
NORMAL PROCEDURES

PIPER AIRCRAFT CORPORATION
PA-28-161, CADET

4.31b Power Off Descent (4.5m)

If a prolonged power off descent is to be made, and icing conditions are suspected, apply full carburetor heat prior to power reduction. Throttle should be retarded and mixture control leaned as required. Power response should be verified approximately every 30 seconds by partially opening and then closing the throttle (clearing the engine). When leveling off, enrichen mixture, set power as required and select carburetor heat off unless carburetor icing conditions are suspected.

4.33 APPROACH AND LANDING (See charts in Section 5) (4.5n)

Check to ensure the fuel selector is on the proper (fullest) tank and that the seat backs are erect. The seat belts and shoulder harnesses should be fastened and the inertia reel checked.

NOTE

If the fixed shoulder harness (non-inertia reel type) is installed, it must be connected to the seat belt and adjusted to allow proper accessibility to all controls including fuel selector, flaps, trim, etc, while maintaining adequate restraint for the occupant.

NOTE

If the inertia reel type shoulder harness is installed, a pull test of its locking restraint feature should be performed.

Turn the electric fuel pump ON and turn the air conditioner OFF. The mixture should be set in the full RICH position.

The airplane should be trimmed to an initial approach speed of 70 KIAS, and a final approach speed of 63 KIAS with flaps extended to 40°. If desired, the flaps can be lowered at speeds up to 103 KIAS.

The mixture control should be kept in full RICH position to ensure maximum acceleration if it should be necessary to open the throttle again. Carburetor heat should not be applied unless there is an indication of carburetor icing, since the use of carburetor heat causes a reduction in power which may be critical in case of a go-around. Full throttle operation with carburetor heat on can cause detonation.

REPORT: VB-1360
4-26

ISSUED: SEPTEMBER 9, 1988

Reference to the Pilots Operating Handbook/Flight Manual (POH/FM) is vital for safe aircraft operation

It is an unfortunate fact that all too often a check-out on a new type involves little or no reference to the aircraft's POH/FM or equivalent. In this way the newly indoctrinated pilot learns that the final approach speed is 75 knots even though the POH/FM recommends 65 knots, because 75 knots is the preference of the pilot providing the checkout. The 'checkee' may then decide that if he flies the aircraft near its gross weight, he will add another five knots – ignoring the fact that the POH/FM figure is probably based on MAUW anyway. Maybe this same pilot then adds a further five knots 'for good luck' or 'for the wife/husband and kids' or whatever. So we end up with an aircraft approaching to land at 85 knots in circumstances where the recommended airspeed is 65 knots. Not good. This particular aviator may also decide to use less than full flap for the landing. There may be a good reason for this, such as a gusty crosswind, or if the aircraft has particularly poor climbing performance with full flap. Alternatively, it may merely be a word-of-mouth technique passed down from pilot to pilot with nobody stopping to wonder why.

An aircraft may end up fast or slow on the approach because of poor speed control (often because of poor trimming), which comes back to pilots paying attention and monitoring the airspeed throughout the approach. More rarely, pilots deliberately use an approach speed slower than recommended, through not knowing the proper speed. The answer is the same as before. Know the proper speeds, apply them and do not accept anything faster or slower. Poor speed control often means the aircraft has not been properly trimmed, so take time to attain the proper approach speed and trim to it at an early stage. Do this and you won't be fighting the aircraft's tendency to fly at the trimmed angle of attack (airspeed) later in the approach.

During the approach, the two most critical parameters are airspeed and approach angle. The pilot must monitor both closely, with the aim of arriving over the threshold at the correct height and the correct airspeed. From this point on there should be no need to monitor the airspeed further as the aim is then to convert a good *approach* into a good *landing*. However, to go back to our original scenario for a moment, we have an aircraft arriving over the threshold from a shallow high-power approach at a higher than necessary airspeed. If the runway is amply long enough, the next observation might be "so what?". Well, let's see what happens next.

Somewhere between the final approach over the threshold and the touchdown, the pilot has to perform a set of manoeuvres which are most often broken down into the 'flare' (or 'round-out') and the 'hold-off'. It helps to get back to basics and understand what each of these manoeuvres is intended to achieve. The flare is done primarily to arrest the rate of descent, and to leave the aircraft flying parallel with the surface a few feet high. The throttle is usually closed during the flare in preparation for the landing and from this point the aircraft will begin to slow down.

Starting the 'flare', leading to the 'hold-off'

Common Causes of Less Serious Accidents, (and how not to have one all the same)

Left to its own devices, it will probably touch down shortly afterwards on all three wheels at once at quite a high speed. This is in fact how many nosewheel aircraft landings end up, but they shouldn't. As the aircraft slows, the pilot should be pitching nose-up and gradually increasing the angle of attack in an effort to stay airborne. In a sense the 'hold-off' is just that. The pilot is holding the aircraft off the ground, using increasing back pressure on the control column to delay the touchdown until the aircraft is almost out of flying speed. It will then sink on to the runway on the main wheels, with the nosewheel still off the ground. At the point of touchdown, the control column can be held where it is initially. Then as the aircraft decelerates on the ground, further back pressure on the control column will prevent the nosewheel contacting the runway too hard. In any event, the gentle arrival of the nosewheel should occur some time after the main wheels touched down. We are now into the ground run where we can use rudder to maintain direction, brakes as required, and concentrate on slowing to a safe speed to turn off the runway. The aim is not necessarily to touch down as lightly as possible – this can be a sure-fire recipe for aquaplaning on a wet runway – but rather to touch down on the main wheels first at a speed close to the stalling speed.

HOLD OFF

The 'hold-off'

So much for how things *should* happen – what actually *can* happen? Flying into the flare at too high an airspeed makes the judgment of the flare more difficult. Back pressure on the control column applied too far or too quickly will allow the aircraft to convert excess speed into extra lift. The result will be a balloon. Even if the flare is successful, carrying too much speed into the hold-off also makes life more difficult for the pilot. It will take longer for the aircraft to slow to the touchdown speed, during which time the aviator has to avoid over-controlling and pitching too far nose-up or allowing the aircraft to touch-down too fast. In either case the aircraft can either balloon from the hold-off or bounce back into the air from a fast landing. Even worse the pilot may become bored in the extended hold-off and move the control column forward in an attempt to force the aircraft onto the ground. The most likely consequence will be the aircraft touching down nosewheel-first – which is, as we'll see, a recipe for mechanical disaster.

So we have three possible scenarios for things going wrong during the landing:

- Misjudged flare, with possibly too much airspeed, leading to a balloon
- Aircraft bouncing back into the air after touching down too flat and too fast
- Aircraft bouncing after touching down on the nosewheel

Three scenarios, but only one recovery manoeuvre:

- Go-around

It is true to say that if a bounce only takes the aircraft a few feet high, it may be possible to recommence the hold-off and make a second and better touchdown – although this is very much a matter of judgment at the time. It is also true that the vast majority of heavy-landing accidents would be avoided if pilots decided to go around at the first sign of trouble. Invariably it is the nosewheel that collapses during a heavy-landing accident, usually because at some stage the pilot moved the control column forward. On average, according to the accident reports, the pilot bounced the aircraft on its nosewheel not once but three times before it gave up the unequal contest and failed. The costs involved in restoring the aircraft to health would pay for an awful lot of flying…

The inevitable results of a hard landing collapsing the nosewheel: curly propeller tips, a shock-loaded engine, a prolonged visit to the engineers and countless forms to fill-out

There is a natural reluctance to go around, almost as if it is some admission of failure (not that stepping out of a broken aircraft is normally a gesture of triumph). Yet landings do go bad from time to time, even for the most experienced pilot. A readiness and preparedness to go around is essential to any good landing because it leaves the pilot with an escape route – an extra option – in the event that things go wrong.

Sometimes approaches and landings go wrong because of distraction or external factors taking the pilot's attention away from the primary task of flying the aircraft at a critical moment. Classic examples include passengers deciding to be sick half-way down the approach, ATC pressures such as a request to orbit on finals or the proximity of other aircraft – either in the form of a faster aircraft behind or an aircraft landing ahead being slow to clear the runway. If you are subject to such pressures or distractions, your Number One priority is to *fly the aircraft*. This must always remain your primary task. If ATC asks you to do something you're not happy with (such as an orbit at low level), don't do it. Tell them you cannot comply, and if necessary go around. Remember that you carry the ultimate responsibility for the safety of yourself and your aircraft – and if you break the aircraft it will hurt you more than it hurts anyone in another aircraft or in Air Traffic, regardless of who is 'to blame'. By the same token, allowing the poor airmanship of another pilot to distract you from your own priorities is dangerous.

If you find your speed control or approach angle going astray in such situations, be ready to go around at an early stage. This will immediately remove you from the source of conflict. A timely go-around is a sign of sound airmanship, *not* an admission of failure. On this subject, there have been a small number of incidents where pilots have got into conflict with each other around the circuit and taken to dubious airborne tactics to assert their point of view. This behaviour is simply dangerous, and ultimately could lead to the first accident directly attributable to 'air rage'. The proper course of action is to avoid conflicts in the air, whether with ATC or other pilots, and concentrate on landing safely – even if it means giving way when you don't want to. Once on the ground you can resolve your differences with others in any way you see fit. If all else fails, fisticuffs in the club car-park are

Common Causes of Less Serious Accidents,
(and how not to have one all the same)

preferable to broken aeroplanes!

A small number of accidents are attributed to pilots landing directly into a low sun, with the consequent glare making judgment of the flare and hold-off difficult. Keeping the windscreen clean and carrying a pair of sunglasses with you will help, but once again – if you really doubt your ability to make a safe landing, go around! It's nobody's fault that the sun is so low, that the runway is pointed straight into it and that you arrived on the scene at just the moment the two lined up. But it *is* your responsibility as pilot in command to sort out the situation and resolve the problem as best you can. Similar situations are possible when landing in precipitation, or in conditions of poor visibility. Here again, we must judge whether or not a safe approach and landing can be made. If in doubt, we go around. Here's another old saying for your collection: if there's a doubt, there's no doubt.

Making consistently good approaches and landings is one of those areas of flying which can only really be learnt from proper instruction and regular practice. It isn't possible to treat it as a learn-by-numbers exercise. Most heavy-landing accidents are preceded by poor approaches (often too fast or too slow) which were not stabilised by the time the aircraft in question passed over the threshold. As we have already said, most heavy-landing accidents would also have been avoided if the pilot had made a go around at the first sign of trouble.

In summary, here's a short list of 'do's' and 'don'ts' regarding landings:

- **DO** fly a light-aircraft circuit and approach in a light aircraft.
- **DO** know the proper approach speeds and use them. Monitor the airspeed all the way to the threshold.
- **DO** aim to have the approach stabilised before reaching the runway.
- **DO** make a proper flare and hold-off.
- **DO** aim to touch down on the mainwheels first, holding the nosewheel off the ground.
- **DON'T** fly an airliner-style approach in a light aircraft in VMC
- **DON'T** approach too fast for no good reason
- **DON'T** try to force the aircraft on to the runway, and don't allow the nosewheel to contact the ground first.
- **DON'T** hesitate to go around if things go wrong, or if you are not happy with the approach.
- **DON'T** begin the after-landing checks until you are off the runway.

In all of this the aim is not to make *perfect* landings, but to make *safe* landings. If you concentrate first and foremost on making a safe arrival, you will automatically acquire the skills to refine your landings. When assessing a student for a first solo, instructors look for consistently safe approaches and landings and the judgment to make a go around when necessary rather than the occasional feather-light arrival. The same safety, consistency and judgment should be the goal of every pilot, no matter how experienced.

Although heavy landings and consequent broken nosewheels are the most common features of landing-accident reports, loss of directional control – causing the aircraft either to exit the runway or collapse the undercarriage – also crops up. Curiously, perhaps, most accidents involving loss of directional control happened when the crosswind component (if any) was nowhere near the aircraft's limit. This seems to imply that poor control of the rudder and brakes was more likely to be the culprit, although the risks of a loss-of-directional-control accident are higher when landing with a tailwind component or when the runway is slippery. In part, these accidents only emphasise that the landing is not over until the aircraft has taxied off the runway.

A loss of directional control on landing and a taildragger sitting on its nose: fortunately the only human casualty is the pilot's pride

It is easy to imagine a scenario where the pilot, perhaps going through the after-landing checks just after touchdown, fails to notice the aircraft drifting off the runway heading. When the edge of the runway looms or the drift becomes excessive, our hapless pilot finally looks up. In something of a state of shock, he kicks in much too much opposite rudder in an over-correction. The aircraft lurches the other way, the pilot tries to counter with too much corrective rudder, and so on.

The fact that around half these accidents involved taildraggers underlines the fact that such beasts are more prone to swinging on landing. Once they do swing, they require a positive opposing force to stop the yaw and bring the aircraft back on to the runway heading. The rudder becomes less effective as a taildragger slows on landing, and it will be necessary to use increasingly coarse rudder and possibly braking to keep straight. The best advice, applicable to both nosewheel and tailwheel aircraft, is to watch closely for any deviations in direction and make small corrections straight away, rather than allowing a bigger swing to develop which will require greater recovery actions. A collapse of the undercarriage due to loss of directional control also demonstrates that although the main undercarriage may be very strong in coping with normal landing loads, it is usually very poor at dealing with a side load. Touching down with drift, or allowing a violent swing at speed, are both guaranteed to impose harsh side loads on the undercarriage. The result is all too often that it folds up under the aircraft, and the expense of the necessary rectification can be awesome.

Loss of directional control on take-off can also occur, and all but one of these events in the sample year involved tailwheel aircraft. In the early part of the take-off run in a taildragger, the combination of full power (the consequence of which is a substantial slipstream hitting the fin) and reduced rudder effectiveness means that the aircraft will want to swing off-heading. Deft use of the rudder and possibly the brakes will be required to deal with this. As the aircraft gathers speed, the increasingly effective rudder makes directional control easier until the tail is lifted – at which point gyroscopic precession via the rotating propeller makes a further attempt to swing a racing certainty. Moreover, even a light crosswind will complicate matters, especially if it comes from the side to which the aircraft normally swings on take-off. So if the aircraft normally wants to go off to the right on departure, a crosswind from the right (which makes the aircraft want to yaw right, into wind) will just add to the fun. Once again, anticipation and reacting quickly to even the smallest swing is the best defence against the aircraft charging off in a direction of its own choosing.

Common Causes of Less Serious Accidents, (and how not to have one all the same)

The vast majority of loss-of-control accidents during take-off afflict taildragger aircraft

A nosewheel pilot reading this may feel a new respect for tailwheel pilots but perhaps not realise that these points are also relevant to take-offs in his preferred machinery. Even in a nosewheel aircraft, if it tends to yaw left with increased power, a crosswind from the left on departure means that more right rudder may be required to maintain direction. The more powerful the engine, the slower the airspeed and the stronger the crosswind, the more pronounced the effect will be.

▶ Forced Landings

When it comes to engine failures, pilots have a habit of reassuring nervous passengers that they are to all intents and purposes almost unheard-of. It is not unknown for instructors to take the same line with student pilots. The accident statistics themselves present a somewhat different picture. They show that around 20% of reportable accidents occur as a result of a forced landing, and that all but a handful of those were precipitated by engine failure. Perhaps the first moral is that engine failures are not as rare as we would like to think, and there is no room for complacency. So, before looking at forced landings themselves, let's look at how to avoid an engine failure in the first place.

Even with 'modern' engine designs, mechanical failures do occur from time to time. Proper maintenance procedures including observance of airworthiness directives and the manufacturers' service bulletins go a long way towards reducing the risk. During the preparation for flight, the aircraft documents should be reviewed to see whether scheduled maintenance has been carried out as required. At the same time, the aircraft's Technical Log or equivalent can be checked for details of any known faults or problems reported from previous flights. There is sometimes a tendency not to report long-term defects or minor faults on the basis that "everybody knows about that one". Of course, not everybody does – and a series of apparently minor snags may display a trend indicating a more serious problem in the making.

During the pre-flight inspection of the aircraft, your ability to check over the engine will be largely dictated by how far the cowlings can be opened to inspect the engine compartment. Even if the cowling does not open fully, you will be able to check the oil level and to some extent also look for oil or fuel leaks, loose cables, wires or belts and blocked or loose intakes or exhausts. Later, the power checks before take-off are an opportunity not just to check the operation of the magnetos, carburettor heat and temperatures and pressures but also to *listen* to the engine. Does it seem especially noisy or rough, or is there any unusual vibration? If you do come across a problem, don't be afraid to cancel the flight and return the aircraft to the parking spot for further investigation. After all, there's no point in checking for anything amiss, finding a problem and then just ignoring it!

Don't be afraid to cancel the flight and return the aircraft to the parking spot for further investigation...

"…when you open his engine cowling I want to hear a long whistle and lots of 'tut tut tut'…"

Proper maintenance procedures...

"…and another big tube of instant superglue…"

Common Causes of Less Serious Accidents, (and how not to have one all the same)

The engine temperatures and pressures can be monitored during the take-off, and you also should confirm that the engine is developing full power. Something like 40% of the engine failures recorded occurred during take-off and initial climb, so it is clear that we should be especially vigilant for engine problems at this phase of flight. If the engine RPM or manifold pressure does not reach the figure you are expecting, or if the acceleration seems unduly slow, there may be a problem. Make an early decision to abandon the take-off if in doubt rather than take a problem into the air. Once in the cruise, regular cruise checks are the best way to monitor the health of the engine and forewarn of impending problems. More than one forced landing has been averted when a pilot noticed a trend such as falling oil pressure and rising oil temperature and diverted for a safe landing before an engine failure occurred.

Problems with fuel account for around a quarter of all engine failures, and this is perhaps the least forgivable cause of accidents. The basic common-sense requirement is that an aircraft should set out with enough fuel not just to complete the flight *given the prevailing conditions* – i.e. allowing for forecast headwinds or realistic routings – but also with enough reserve for reasonable contingencies such as a diversion or hold. Sadly, fuel planning is all too often relegated to a thought process along the lines of: "Well, old Fred reckons it uses about five gallons an hour. It only took 35 minutes to get there last time, so the six gallons he says are on board will be plenty".

Let's unpick this sort of 'thinking' in stages. Firstly, the best guide to an aircraft's fuel consumption comes from the POH/FM or equivalent document – not from old Fred. Spend a little time with this document and you may be surprised at how much the fuel consumption figures vary in different circumstances. For example, one popular touring aircraft uses 2·5 US gallons per hour more at 75% power than it does at 55% power, even with the recommended mixture-leaning procedure. This represents a variation of nearly 30%, which could be closer to 50% if the proper leaning

RPM	PRESSURE ALTITUDE 2000 FEET											
	20°C BELOW STD. TEMP				STANDARD TEMP				20°C ABOVE STD. TEMP			
	% BHP	TAS KTS	TAS MPH	FUEL GPH	% BHP	TAS KTS	TAS MPH	FUEL GPH	% BHP	TAS KTS	TAS MPH	FUEL GPH
	−9°C (16°F)				11°C (52°F)				31°C (88°F)			
2700	92	130	150	10.7	87	129	149	10.0	82	129	148	9.5
2600	83	125	143	9.6	79	124	143	9.0	75	123	142	8.6
2500	75	119	137	8.6	71	119	136	8.1	68	118	135	7.7
2400	68	114	131	7.8	65	113	130	7.4	61	111	127	7.0
2300	61	108	124	7.0	58	106	121	6.6	55	103	118	6.3
2200	55	101	116	6.2	52	98	113	5.9	50	96	110	5.7
	PRESSURE ALTITUDE 3000 FEET											
	−11°C (12°F)				9°C (48°F)				29°C (84°F)			
2700	90	130	149	10.4	85	129	149	9.8	80	129	148	9.2
2600	82	125	143	9.4	77	124	142	8.8	73	123	142	8.4
2500	73	119	137	8.4	70	118	136	8.0	66	117	134	7.6
2400	66	113	130	7.6	63	112	129	7.2	60	110	126	6.8
2300	60	107	123	6.8	57	105	121	6.5	54	103	118	6.2
2200	54	100	115	6.1	51	97	112	5.8	50	95	108	5.6
	PRESSURE ALTITUDE 4000 FEET											
	−13°C (9°F)				7°C (45°F)				27°C (81°F)			
2700	88	129	149	10.1	83	129	149	9.6	79	129	148	9.0
2600	80	124	143	9.2	75	124	142	8.6	71	122	141	8.1
2500	72	119	137	8.2	68	118	135	7.8	65	116	133	7.4
2400	65	113	130	7.4	62	111	128	7.0	59	109	125	6.8
2300	59	106	122	6.7	56	103	119	6.3	54	102	117	6.1
2200	52	98	113	5.9	51	96	111	5.7	49	93	107	5.5

This cruise performance table from a POH shows a variation in fuel consumption from 10.7 gallons per hour (top left) to 5.5 gallons per hour (bottom right) depending on altitude, temperature and power setting.

procedure is not used. Further investigation of the performance charts in the POH/FM reveal that depending on the power setting, altitude and temperature the 'still air' range with full fuel varies from 700nm to nearly 1000nm –a difference of almost 50% even if the POH procedures are used! So when flight planning, establish the fuel consumption for the power setting, altitude and mixture-leaning technique you intend to employ, and use the resulting TAS for your navigation planning. When planning the route itself, make due allowance for any headwind component and its effect on groundspeed. It is a simple fact of life aloft that headwinds always spring up when you are short of time or short of fuel! Finally, establish at least one realistic diversion airfield and account for the fuel required to reach this diversion from overhead your destination – even if the destination is the same airfield from which you took off. Don't forget a further reserve for holding either at your destination or diversion. Even if your flight is planned to be just a short local 'hop', establish the expected fuel consumption depending on what you plan to do. POH/FM figures are often based on simple cruising flight, but fuel consumption in a climb is typically double that in the cruise. So an hour of circuits might use up almost twice as much fuel as an hour spent at best endurance power and mixture setting.

I'm sure all this seems elementary, and you're probably wondering why I'm banging on about it. But it's been expensively and tragically verified all too often that engines run on fuel, not hope. And accident reports suggest that aircraft engines all too often run out of fuel at more or less the point where the POH/FM information suggested they would. It surely must be easier for pilots to work this out for ourselves before flight than have the AAIB do it for us after an accident.

Having established the fuel required, the fuel tanks must be checked to see if there is at least the appropriate amount on board. Even if a bit of clambering is required, a visual check of their contents is essential. Judging the fuel quantity by peering

Don't assume – check

into a dark tank through a small aperture is hardly an exact science, although using a calibrated dipstick helps and is essential for some aircraft, although even dipsticks are not 100% accurate. Not checking fuel contents – either visually or with a dipstick – is not on. And if *you* can't be bothered to check the fuel before flight, you can be certain that *someone* will be checking the fuel tanks **very** carefully after an engine failure. There may also be a fuelling record with the aircraft's documents, so that you can check the last fuel uplift and how much flying has been done since (remember to make due allowance for taxying time too). Once again, reliance on word-of-mouth information ("I'm sure somebody must have filled it up the other day") is no substitute for hard evidence. It's time for that famous motto again – don't assume, check.

It is generally acknowledged that aircraft fuel gauges are never very accurate, and certainly not good enough to be any substitute for proper fuel planning and visually assessing the fuel contents. However, most fuel gauges are normally quite good at indicating whether a tank is completely full or completely empty, even if the in-between readings are less reliable. For this reason a dangerously low reading should *never* be ignored. If in doubt, take the safest option and assume that more fuel is needed.

Common Causes of Less Serious Accidents, (and how not to have one all the same)

After assessing the *quantity* of fuel, the *quality* of the fuel can be checked. The generally accepted rule is that for the first flight of the day and after refuelling, some fuel should be drained into a sampler for checking. Most aircraft will have a fuel drain at the lowest point in each fuel tank, and another drain point at the engine. Draw fuel from each of these points into some sort of clear sampler (there are several proprietary designs around, but even an old milk bottle is better than nothing). You are looking for the proper colour – blue in the case of AVGAS 100LL – and any sediment and contamination or bubbles at the bottom of the sampler. If in doubt, take another sample and keep taking samples until you are satisfied. Assess the risk of contamination: an aircraft that has been standing in the open, perhaps when there has been heavy rain, is an obvious risk. So is an aircraft that hasn't flown or been refuelled for some time. Remember that it may take up to half an hour after refuelling for the fuel (and any contaminates) to settle in the tank, so taking a fuel sample immediately after refuelling is not recommended.

Drawing fuel into a fuel tester

Once in flight, regular checking of contents against expected consumption is the best way to avoid running out of fuel. If the flight is taking longer than expected, or if the gauges are reading too low for comfort, make an early decision to land where more fuel can be uplifted. Additionally, do *not* be tempted to run one tank dry. Most pilots underestimate how long it will take for the engine to regain power if it has stopped after running a tank dry, and several forced landings have resulted from this misconception. In any case, emptying a fuel tank right to the bottom may dredge up an assortment of sludge or contaminates that have collected in a corner and carry them into the induction system. It only takes a very small obstruction to block a fuel jet…

To illustrate the fact that potentially running out of fuel is an easy situation to encounter and avoid, here is a story directly from personal experience. Some years ago, the flying club I worked for organised a fly-out to an air display involving almost the whole school fleet. A number of instructors, including myself, were flying with students or PPLs. After an enjoyable day we set about planning the return trip, and I voiced my opinion that we should make a fuel stop *en route*. Another instructor objected strongly, on the basis that this would only waste time since all the aircraft had just enough fuel for the return leg. The question of payment for the fuel and extra landing fees could also be difficult. This last point was true but I was unhappy with the fuel reserves should we be delayed or have to divert. Besides, I've always been rather fond of having lots of fuel on board.

Any attempt to stretch fuel is guaranteed to increase headwinds, worsen destination weather or close airfields

To cut a long story short, the *en route* fuel stop was made by all including the dissenting instructor, who grumbled and remonstrated about the waste of time throughout. Our destination airfield was in controlled airspace, and although we arrived at the zone boundary in good VMC, the weather at the airfield itself was IMC. With the benefit of the extra fuel uplifted we orbited outside controlled airspace, waiting for an improvement in the weather that came around 45 minutes later. The dissenting instructor and myself made the best of this delay by flying in circles whilst exchanging hand-signals that, to the best of my knowledge, have yet to find their way into any flying training manual.

Fuel in the tanks is limited. Gravity is forever

There is a postscript to this story. Several years later the same instructor invited me along for a flight in the sophisticated modern airliner he now flies. Inbound to the same airfield as before, he invited me to take a bet on the fuel remaining after landing. Foolishly I agreed, and placed my reliance on the figures being displayed on the multi-million-pound cockpit instrumentation. My friend made a calculation based on his hand-written fuel plan. He won.

Above all else, the avoidance of a fuel-related engine failure is a matter of caution and common sense. It was the aviation pioneer Sir Charles Kingsford Smith who said that the only time an aircraft has too much fuel on board is when it's on fire. This is probably true, and it's also a fact that many more aircraft run out of fuel than ever catch fire. In the majority of 'running out of fuel' accidents, fuel was available at the departure airfield; the aircraft had ample opportunity to return or divert for more fuel during the flight; and the fuel ran out at pretty much the point the POH/FM suggested it would. Perhaps the only real mystery is that the pilot should have been at all surprised by the resulting engine failure.

The final significant factor in engine failures is that of suspected carburettor icing. We say "suspected" because carburettor icing doesn't leave any evidence behind. It tends to cause a loss of power whose symptoms could also be those of a fuel or ignition problem, and once on the ground the ice probably melts away in a matter of minutes. All that is left is the fact that the aircraft had plenty of fuel on board, that the engine had not suffered a mechanical failure and later ran perfectly, and that the conditions were 'conducive to carburettor icing'.

Common Causes of Less Serious Accidents, (and how not to have one all the same)

This isn't the place to recap all that has been said in earlier manuals about carburettor icing, except to emphasis that any pilot who flies an aircraft with a carburettor-equipped engine should always be thinking about the possibility of encountering it. The authorities take the matter so seriously that there is always a current pink AIC in circulation specifically about carburettor icing. The basic message is that it can and does occur over a wide range of conditions, high humidity being the prime risk factor rather than low temperature. It should also be appreciated that some aircraft and engine combinations are especially vulnerable to carburettor icing, and regular in-flight checks are the best defence and warning system. Carburettor icing is more likely to happen at a low power setting such as during a descent, when the engine is cooler and the throttle valve is almost closed. The aircraft's POH/FM or engine handbook should give advice about the use of carburettor heat, especially during the approach and landing, and this advice should be heeded. Many pilots who have suffered suspected carburettor icing have been surprised by how quickly power was lost. The best defence is to know the conditions most likely to lead to carburettor icing, know the aircraft/engine characteristics and recommended procedures and stay vigilant – especially during the descent and approach to land. And if you do encounter it, give the carburettor heating time to work and don't be too surprised if the engine takes quite a while to clear its throat and run smoothly.

Having taken all reasonable steps to avoid an engine failure, we are still left with the possibility of encountering one. So one fine day whilst flying along without a care in the world, we might actually be faced with a very quiet engine and a very urgent need to find somewhere to land. All pilots are taught the 'forced landing without power' procedure in basic training. We spend hours practising it and are tested to verify our competence at dealing with the situation. However, it's a fact that once a pilot has a PPL and has left the training environment behind, practising forced landing – indeed practising for any emergency or abnormal situation – becomes a rare or non-existent event.

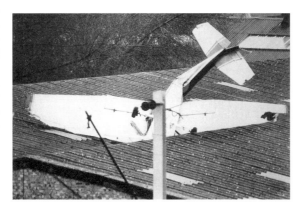

Thankfully, the pilot of this aircraft survived the results of this forced landing at night after an engine failure

The engine of this aircraft failed during a low-level aerobatic air display, and although the aircraft was damaged in the ensuing forced landing, the occupants were uninjured

We learned earlier in this book that what we don't rehearse is eventually forgotten. How many of us could be sure of performing a successful forced landing, including the relevant checks and procedures, if we were faced with an engine failure many years after we last practised for one? Apart from poor field selection and approach planning, a common error is poor speed control – usually caused by not trimming properly for the glide at the beginning of the procedure. A practice engine failure from say 3000ft will only take four to five minutes. It can be conducted over open countryside (don't come too low though) or practised from overhead an airfield so that you can continue right down to the landing. Be honest with yourself; when did you last fly a Practice Forced Landing? If you can't remember, maybe your next flight should include one. The procedure for a PFL is in the Flying Training volume of this series...

You may remember that engine failures during and immediately after take-off account for around 40% of forced-landing accidents. Again, you might not have practised an Engine Failure After Take Off (EFATO) for years. To be fair, airfields often don't like too much EFATO training because it can annoy the neighbours (and it is best practiced with an instructor on-board). Equally, ATC don't like practice EFATOs if they're not warned and may spill their coffee reaching for the crash alarm. Nervous passengers aren't too keen either. Nevertheless, when did you last rehearse the 'drills' in the event of an engine failure at 500ft or below? Have you looked at the area beyond the runways of your base airfield to select a possible landing site? Do you remember the importance of pitching the nose down quickly to the glide attitude, maintaining a safe airspeed and not attempting the 'impossible turn' back to the runway? Above all, when was the last time just before you began a take-off that you said to yourself "If the engine fails after take-off, this is what I will do..."? Being prepared for the unexpected is a basic component of good airmanship. Such practice and rehearsal also makes flying more interesting and challenging – a theme we will return to shortly. It was once said that the difference between test pilots and the rest of us is that if a normal pilot gets airborne and nothing goes wrong, he takes it for granted. But if a test pilot gets airborne and nothing goes wrong, he is surprised.

▶ Undercarriage Problems

It is undeniable that aircraft with retractable undercarriages have the equivalent of aviation sex appeal. They look good and they hold out the promise of better, faster, higher and more sophisticated flying. In reality, the material performance benefit of a retractable undercarriage in many relatively low-powered aircraft, especially single-engined ones, is open to question. It sometimes seems that the extra weight and complication of a retractable undercarriage is not offset by a significant performance improvement, and other fixed-undercarriage designs with a similar engine power are not significantly slower. That said, the retractable undercarriage is here to stay and many pilots aspire to wheels that go up and (usually) come down again.

Got RG (Retractable Gear), the aspiration of many PPLs and the appropriate registration of this Cessna 182 RG

Very broadly, accidents caused by wheels failing to come down or failing to stay locked down occur on landing. They are equally divided between those caused by some kind of mechanical failure and those caused by the pilot forgetting to lower the wheels in the first place.

Common Causes of Less Serious Accidents, (and how not to have one all the same)

A pilot is usually alerted to a mechanical failure when the undercarriage is selected down for landing but one or more of the wheels fails to indicate that it is locked down (usually evidenced by a green light for each undercarriage leg). If this happens, the pilot then has to decide, based on the prevailing circumstances, how to cope with the situation. The POH/FM should detail an alternative undercarriage-lowering procedure. This varies from type to type, so general advice is not possible. However, here is yet another instance where there is no substitute for knowing the proper rules and procedures for the aircraft you are flying, based on the POH/FM or equivalent. Whilst working through these procedures, preferably at a safe height, do not lose sight of your primary task of flying the aeroplane: Aviate, Navigate, Communicate. If there is another pilot with you, it makes sense to split the workload so that one pilot flies, navigates and communicates whilst the other deals with the problem. Most importantly, do not allow a situation to develop where nobody is flying the aeroplane, because even a wheels-up landing is preferable to losing control or flying into the ground.

When faced with an undercarriage problem, pilots often opt to fly past the tower or other ground-based observer for an external view of the situation. Depending on the undercarriage design, this may be best done flying directly towards or directly away from the observer. Once again, retaining control of the aircraft and not flying into anything is still the Number One priority.

If the undercarriage simply refuses to co-operate, you should plan for either a gear-up landing or a landing with whatever wheels have condescended to come down. Depending on the situation, decide whether a diversion to a larger or better equipped airfield is more prudent. Pilots are often either reluctant to declare an emergency, or deliberately turn down the option to have the rescue services in attendance for landing. This is false bravado. In the worst case, the rescue services could save a life; in the best case they get to practice their response times! You might also consider whether you want to land on a hard runway or a grass surface; in principle the latter may result in less airframe damage and a reduced danger of sparks and fire. Whatever you do, take heart from the fact that there are virtually no reported instances of injuries caused by a gear-up or partial-undercarriage landing. Brief your passengers before making the approach, especially on keeping their safety harness tight, the brace position and exiting the aircraft after the landing has finished. Some pilots in this situation choose to shut down the engine(s) when a safe landing is assured, just before touchdown. This not only reduces the fire risk but also minimises damage to the engine(s) and propeller(s), although of course this action should not be taken if it might jeopardise your chance of a safe landing, your primary responsibility is to save yourselves – not the aeroplane. In any case concentrate on making a safe landing, do your best to stay on your chosen landing path and console yourself that you'll probably be dining out on the story for months to come.

A pilot is less likely to want to re-live a wheels-up landing caused by simply failing to lower the undercarriage before landing. To many pilots such an error seems so elemental that it is difficult to believe it could happen to a competent person. In reality, it can be very easy for even an experienced aviator to make this error, especially if the routine of the pre-landing checks is disturbed or if the pilot is distracted in some other way.

A demonstration of a gear-up landing, courtesy of the RAF

Most professional flying operates around a code of conduct known as Standard Operating Procedures (SOPs). Thus it is ordained that at certain set points, certain set procedures or checks will be carried out. So an airline might state that aircraft must not descend below 1000ft unless the undercarriage is down and locked, or must not continue an approach if the aircraft is not fully established at five miles from touchdown, and so on. The value of this disciplined approach to flying an aircraft is that if a check or action is accidentally missed, there is a better chance that the omission will be picked up by a cross-check – or that based on well-established routine, the crew will sense that something is wrong. Flying a light aircraft is generally a less regimented business, with more latitude for varied operating techniques. A pilot might elect not to lower the undercarriage during the pre-landing checks, possibly to keep the speed up on approach. Alternatively the pre-landing checks might be interrupted or missed altogether by unexpected ATC instructions or distractions such as lots of other aircraft in the circuit and on approach. Maybe the aviator becomes preoccupied with one particular aspect of the landing. This might include an aircraft ahead being slow to clear the runway, the wish to make a good touchdown on an unfamiliar or 'challenging' runway or an approach in adverse conditions. Maybe the pilot is fatigued at the end of a long day or a difficult flight; perhaps the aircraft is unfamiliar; or perhaps the pilot in command is expecting the co-pilot to look after the pre-landing checks. Whatever the facts of the matter, our unfortunate pilot may well have no inkling that anything is wrong until the propeller blades start to carve an irregular and expensive path down the runway.

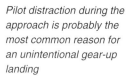

Pilot distraction during the approach is probably the most common reason for an unintentional gear-up landing

By now you may well be thinking that retractable-undercarriage aircraft usually have some sort of warning system to alert the pilot that the gear is not down, like a bell or horn. This is true. However, like any warning system, it will only work in a defined set of circumstances – usually when power is reduced to a certain point or if the flaps are lowered beyond a particular setting with the wheels still up. So if a pilot makes an approach with more power and less flap than normal, the warning system may not be activated until too late. Conversely, if the warning system is too ready to activate, pilots will become used to ignoring it. There have been attempts to develop 'fool-proof' systems, such as undercarriages that automatically lower below certain power settings and airspeeds. These worked fine in most circumstances but could also lower the undercarriage unbidden at a bad moment, such as immediately following an engine failure. The consequent increase in drag could well be just what the pilot did not want at that moment. There was also the danger of becoming too reliant on the automatic system. So if the 'fail safe' decided not to work, or an unusual combination of power and airspeed meant the system was not activated, the aircraft would still end up scraping along the runway. One such system in a popular light aircraft became such a nuisance that eventually the manufacturer permitted a modification to disable the system – which is exactly what most operators promptly did!

There is a wider issue here about how many warnings a pilot needs in an aircraft, and how reliant pilots should be on systems that take over many of their basic tasks. We have already seen that if pilots become under-aroused, their performance of tasks suffers. And if one of the systems fails, the pilot may not be sufficiently alert to spot the fault. Reducing workload without leaving the pilot with nothing more to do than monitor the aircraft flying itself will be an increasing challenge for designers in the years to come. However, for now the challenge is to find a way to prevent aircraft landing without the benefit of the undercarriage provided for that purpose. The closest solution is probably a short 'SOP' that applies to any landing situation. As the aircraft crosses the landing threshold, the pilot should check 'Reds, Greens and Blues', namely;

Reds	Mixture(s) rich
Greens	Undercarriage down and locked
Blues	Propeller pitch(s) fully fine.

If you rehearse this short mantra on every landing, it should become second nature and almost a reflex. For most if not all of your landings, this check should merely confirm actions you carried out during the approach. But one day, perhaps after a rushed and non-standard arrival into a strange airfield in difficult conditions, it might just save you an awful lot of time and expense.

An alternative approach is that of the pilot who, just before landing, always turns to the right-hand seat. Irrespective of whether it contains a highly experienced pilot or first-time passenger, and pointing to the green lights, he states out loud, "I have three greens". His rationale is that should he ever land gear-up, he will have a witness to say that the lights lied to him!

▶ Performance

Accidents attributed to 'performance' when using a runway which was relatively short for the aircraft concerned are evenly split between take-offs and landings. In either case the end result is usually that the aircraft leaves the end of the runway unintentionally. It then collides with some solid object or is damaged by rough ground.

Virtually all performance accidents can be traced back to two basic root causes. Either the runway was simply too short for the aircraft and/or the pilot did not use the correct take-off or landing technique. There is also an argument that not enough emphasis is placed on performance in basic flight training. Either way, we are taken back once again to the aircraft's POH/FM or equivalent.

Let's start, as most flights do, with the take-off. The POH/FM should contain enough information in the form of tables or graphs to allow you to work out take-off distance (the distance from beginning the take-off to reaching 50ft AGL) for varying circumstances. Those factors not covered in the POH/FM can be found in the CAA's own advice on take-off and landing performance. Try using this information to calculate take-off distance required next time you go flying, then comparing the figures with the actual take-off performance you achieve. If the actual take-off distance achieved is significantly different from that calculated, go back to the numbers later to see if you can establish a reason why. Repeat this exercise over several flights (especially if you are relatively inexperienced on type) to establish how closely you can match the 'book' figures – which may have been achieved by a test-pilot flying a brand-new aircraft. Take care to use the operating technique stated; to

Now is not the time to start wishing you had checked the take-off performance figures...

get book figures you must use the book technique, especially with regard to flap setting and rotate/climb speeds. Within a few take-offs you should be proficient at calculating take-off performance and know how closely these figures relate to the real world. You should also have a good feel for how varying factors such as weight, wind component and runway surface affect the take-off distance required.

So, you should now know what performance to expect from your aircraft and how short a runway needs to be before reference to the POH/FM is required. You should be practised in the appropriate take-off technique, and also have a 'rule-of-thumb' figure for the shortest runway from which the aircraft can be safely operated. Once again, part of the key to safe flying is *preparation* and *rehearsal*. Even if you operate from a runway several times longer than the aircraft needs, why not practice a short-field take-off from time to time? It will add interest to your flying and mean that when you do one for real, it isn't the first attempt for many years.

Armed with a working knowledge of your aircraft's performance, you can refer to the POH/FM whenever you intend to operate from a runway somewhere close to the minimum acceptable length. Rather like fuel calculations, if you can't be bothered to do this before take-off, you can be sure that somebody else will be looking at the figures very closely after a take-off accident.

Information about the runway itself may come from a number of sources, and you will have to decide how reliable the information is. Here's another story from personal experience. During a flying holiday I learnt of a grass strip which would be more convenient than the airfield where I had based the aircraft, a Piper Cherokee. A telephone call to the non-flying owner of the land revealed a very vague knowledge of the runway dimensions, although the owner was adamant that other Cherokees had used the strip in the last 12 months and felt that in itself should be good enough for me. Feeling somewhat uneasy, I decided to investigate by surface transport before committing myself to using the strip. It was an interesting experience. The strip was narrow and undulating, bounded on one side by a fence and the other side by a road and there was a significant traverse slope across the runway width. I paced out the runway as being just long enough for comfort, but what really caught my eye was the copse of 50ft trees more or less where the strip ended. I had already decided that any Cherokee I was flying was unlikely to grace this strip, but I was intrigued by some broken trees and debris just inside the copse at the end of the runway. This, landowner explained with no apparent trace of irony, was the spot where the last Cherokee to visit had ended its take-off...

So we've calculated the take-off distance required, and checked that at least this amount of runway is available. We've verified the proper short-field take-off technique, and we're current in flying this procedure. So there is no reason not to

Common Causes of Less Serious Accidents,
(and how not to have one all the same)

attempt take-off from a runway that is shorter than you normally use. After all, aviation should still contain challenges if it is to be interesting, and boring flying is not necessarily safer flying. Start your take-off at the beginning of the runway so as to have the full runway length available and monitor the acceleration during the take-off. As a rule-of-thumb, the aircraft should have reached 75% of its lift-off speed (about half-way between the rotate and initial climb speeds) no later than half-way along the take-off distance available. If it has not, there should be enough runway remaining to abort the take-off safely and then decide what to do next.

In many performance-related take-off accidents, either the runway was simply not long enough for that aircraft on that day or the proper short-field take-off technique was not being used. Often the pilot made the decision to abort the take-off far too late, but at least the aircraft left the end of the runway at taxying rather than flying speed. How much better to know the take-off distance required, use the proper technique and have the chance to abort the take-off early enough to stop within the confines of the runway.

If the take-off is not looking good, an early decision to abandon it will avoid a problem becoming an accident

All these comments about take-offs also apply to landings: try calculating landing distances for the prevailing conditions and then see how closely you can match them. Know the proper techniques, especially the final approach speed: use this speed when necessary. Monitor your approach carefully and choose a touch-down point no further than one-third into the runway. If you are not going to land close to this spot, or if the approach does not go well (perhaps you are too fast or too high) make an early decision to go around and decide whether it is worth making another attempt. More commonly than in take-off accidents, the runway *was* long enough for the aircraft but poor technique by the pilot led to the aircraft running off the end of the runway. If you normally fly from a runway much longer than the aircraft needs, you may not be in the habit of aiming to touch down on a particular spot. So for your next landing, choose an exact aiming point to land on and see how close to it you touch-down. One or two hundred metres down the runway may not make much difference if you have 2000m of tarmac ahead, but will be considerably more crucial in the case of a 500m grass runway.

The aftermath of a performance-related accident, fortunately without serious injury

Reports of landing 'overruns' often include a statement from the pilot that a normal approach and landing was made but a subsequently undetectable brake problem led to the aircraft running off the end of the runway. Witnesses tend to see things slightly differently, stating that the aircraft approached fast (possibly with less than full flap), touched down well along the runway (sometimes more than half-way) and as a result could not stop before the runway ended. We are back with our self-evident truism that to obtain book performance, you have to use book technique. If the POH/FM landing performance is based on an approach speed of 65 knots, you are clearly not going to match the expected landing distance if you arrive over the threshold at 75 knots. The kinetic energy dissipated in bringing the aircraft to a full stop increases with the square of its speed. So a 10% increase in speed will increase kinetic energy (and hence, broadly speaking, landing distance) by 21%. Likewise the landing performance figures assume that the aircraft will touch down in the first third of the landing distance available. It is no more than common sense that a successful short-field landing is more likely following an approach flown in the proper configuration, at the proper speed and with a touch-down within the first third of the runway. It is also fairly obvious that if any of these conditions are not likely to be met, an early decision to go around is required rather than hanging on grimly until the airfield boundary fills the windscreen.

Differing runway surfaces and condition tend to have a greater impact on landing distances than take-off. The worst case is something like a wet grass runway, which not only lengthens the landing distance (because braking is less effective) but also increases the risk of problems with directional control. The moral is that even if you have landed safely on the runway before, conditions may mean that – for this day at least – a safe landing cannot be made. This is when good pilot judgment is essential. Again, none of this is rocket science. It merely amounts to assessing the prevailing conditions and make a safe decision based on what is actually happening rather than what you would like to be the case.

A landing on a hot, windless, day and a short grass strip. Not to be attempted lightly

Common Causes of Less Serious Accidents,
(and how not to have one all the same)

▶Collision with Obstructions

Most pilots do their basic training at licensed airfields complying with certain minimum criteria in terms of obstructions on and around the airfield. Once we start flying into unlicensed airfields, these same criteria may not be applied and we may find notable obstructions surprisingly close to the runway. These may not represent a hazard to an aircraft on a 'normal' light-aircraft approach angle, but could be very dangerous to one which is undershooting or flying a particularly shallow approach path. When accidents do occur as a result of aircraft hitting obstructions during the final approach, it is not uncommon that the pilots' view of the approach was obscured in some way – perhaps by a low sun directly ahead. It is also not uncommon for the pilot to have been attempting a touchdown very close to the runway threshold, possibly with the intention of landing 'right on the numbers'.

If you do not have a good view of the approach and landing runway, for whatever reason, a go-around should be seriously considered. The conditions may change (e.g. the sun may go behind a cloud) or it may be possible to change to another runway. In much the same way, if the aircraft looks likely to touch-down short of the runway, an early correction with power – and if necessary a go-around –

An unlicensed airfield may have significantly worse obstructions around the runways than a licensed one

are infinitely preferable to touching down in the rough with no real idea of what you are landing on. If some part of the runway is unusable or if there is a significant obstruction on the approach, the runway will often have a 'displaced' threshold. If you are landing on such a runway, make sure that you are aiming to touch down beyond the displaced threshold numbers and *not* before them – even if doing so would put you on the physical runway. The danger of colliding with an obstruction (such as trees, power cables etc.) is one reason why manufacturers and instructors tend to discourage shallow 'creeping' approaches to land. In this questionable technique the pilot deliberately flies below the ideal approach path, usually at slow

BEWARE
LOW FLYING
AIRCRAFT

airspeed and with a high power setting. The rationale is that as soon as the aircraft is over the threshold, the pilot can cut the power and drop on to the runway. However, the low height and slow airspeed make the aircraft vulnerable to downdraughts, windshear, turbulence and collision with obstructions. The higher-than-normal nose attitude also ruins the view ahead, making it more difficult to see and avoid obstructions and judge the approach path. All other factors being equal, a steeper approach to land is not only safer than creeping in over the boundary fence but it reduces the landing distance.

▶ Starting and Taxying

Aircraft are generally ungainly machines on the ground. Their rotating propeller(s) or jet intakes represent a considerable hazard to people around them; their long wings and tails combine with uncertain turning circles to make them difficult to manoeuvre in confined spaces. Hence the propensity for pilots to have accidents in this regime.

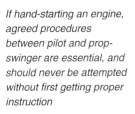

If hand-starting an engine, agreed procedures between pilot and prop-swinger are essential, and should never be attempted without first getting proper instruction

Sometimes a pilot even manages to precipitate an accident within seconds of starting the engine. The aircraft may move forward if the brakes have not been properly applied or an attempt to 'swing' or jump-start the engine goes wrong, especially if there is no one at the controls. Following a proper starting checklist, and working to agreed procedures for hand-swinging or jump-starting an engine, are the best defences against an accident at this stage of flight. Always check the area around the propeller before starting up, and after starting keep your attention outside for the first few seconds to check that the aircraft does not move. Do not leave the controls once the engine is running, and do not allow unsupervised 'running changes' where passengers leave and/or enter the aircraft while the engine is still running. There have been a number of cases of people walking into rotating propellers they did not see, and many passengers do not appreciate the danger areas to avoid. It is also worth noting that a number of larger airfields now require all personnel on the apron or manoeuvring area to wear bright reflective jackets. Although these items are unlikely to become seriously fashionable, they do reduce the risk for being mown down by aircraft – or, more likely, one of the multitude of vehicles to be found ignoring the apron speed limit at most larger airfields.

Common Causes of Less Serious Accidents, (and how not to have one all the same)

Once on the move, you should regulate your speed carefully with respect to the surroundings and conditions. Tailwheel aircraft are very vulnerable to tailwinds that might lift the tail and put the aircraft on its nose, especially when turning with a wind from the rear quarter. Proper use of the flying controls depending on the relative wind direction will help, and is good discipline even in a nosewheel aircraft, beware also of jet-blast or prop-wash from other aircraft. Keeping taxying speed to a minimum in such conditions, particularly in a tailwheel aircraft, is also good airmanship. Rough ground and long grass should be avoided where possible because holes or ruts can easily be hidden from the pilot. Loose gravel and grass cuttings are not kind to engines and propellers, and the latter can clog wheel spats in a remarkably short time if it is high summer and the airfield surfaces have just been mown.

Long wings and tail call for careful judgment when taxying. If in doubt – stop!

The length of the average light aircraft's wings and tail call for careful judgment of distances when taxying close to other aircraft or obstructions. Slow down or stop if necessary rather than charging into a very tight spot. Remember that light aircraft cannot generally reverse under their own power! If in real doubt, stop and get someone to check that you can pass; if all else fails, close down the engine and look for yourself. A low wing may hide obstructions from the pilot, and it can be difficult to judge whether a post or fence will pass safely under the wing. Try not to put a wing over such an obstruction. Taildraggers and runway marker boards have a notorious affinity for each other, hence the standard advice about weaving the nose when taxying to visually clear the area ahead.

On the subject of collisions, there have been some cases where a pilot has had some sort of impact with a solid object on the ground and then gone on to fly without the aircraft being checked by a properly qualified person – such as an engineer. In at least one case, such an action led to a fatal accident after a subsequent catastrophic structural failure. Damage caused by taxying into an obstruction, even at slow speed, can be very much greater than you would expect. In the case mentioned above, the aircraft had hit an obstruction on the ground with the wing, but there was almost no visible damage. Unfortunately, that did not stop the wing coming off shortly after the next departure. As in this case, external damage can be minimal but disruption of the internal structure much more extensive.

If you have a problem of this sort and you're at a strange airfield well away from base, there may be a very strong temptation to continue your planned flight home. If in doubt, ask yourself a question. "If I saw this damage on the aircraft before pulling it out of the hanger at my home airfield, would I still go flying or would I seek advice?" The answer should be enough to tell you whether you should be cancelling the flight and seeking out a qualified opinion.

"If I saw this damage at my home airfield, would I still go flying?" This was actually the result of a bird strike

Accident Reports and
Other Required Reading

Flight Safety

Accident
Reports and
Other
Required
Reading

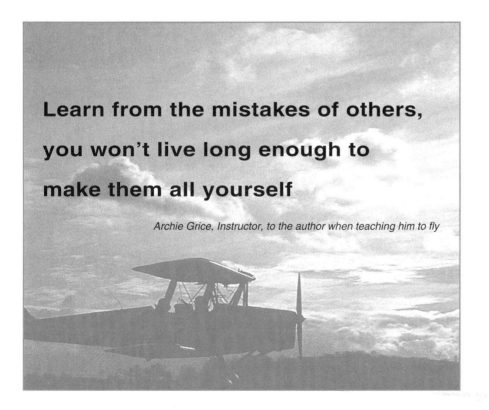

Learn from the mistakes of others,

you won't live long enough to

make them all yourself

Archie Grice, Instructor, to the author when teaching him to fly

Flight Safety

For UK registered aircraft and all aircraft within the UK, any event involving an aeroplane which can be classed as an accident must be reported to the Air Accident Investigation Branch (AAIB). The guidelines for what constitutes a reportable accident are as follows:

An event that occurs between the time that any person boards an aeroplane with the intention of flight and all persons have disembarked, in which:

- Somebody suffers serious or fatal injury as a result of being in the aeroplane, by direct contact with the aeroplane or some part of it or from jet blast

- The aeroplane sustains damage or structural failure affecting its strength, performance or flying characteristics and requiring major repair or replacement

  or

- The aeroplane is missing or completely inaccessible.

There are some exceptions to these guidelines such as self-inflicted injuries or natural causes and 'non-structural' damage.

An AAIB monthly bulletin, as found being used as coffee coasters in many flying clubs and briefing rooms!

The AAIB can also investigate an occurrence other than an accident involving the operation of an aircraft and which affects or could affect the safety of operation.

An AAIB accident investigation may be merely a matter of simple questionnaire for the pilot to complete. At the other end of the scale, it might consist of a detailed examination of the aircraft, the taking of witness statements and the use of relevant material such as ATC transcripts and radar recordings. Much will depend upon the seriousness of the accident. Occasionally an investigation will result in the production of a formal accident report published many months or years after the event. This is rare for an accident involving a general-aviation aircraft. More commonly, the results of the accident investigation will be published as a bulletin report which appears within the monthly digest from the AAIB.

The AAIB makes the point that their reports are intended to establish the causes of accidents, with the express purpose of saving life by preventing future accidents or incidents. There is no remit to establish 'blame' or liability for an accident. Individuals are not identified and the AAIB does not hand-out fines or punishments.

The monthly AAIB bulletin reports are found in most Flying Training Organisations (FTOs) and in the briefing rooms of many airfields. They are usually the most detailed analysis of an accident in general circulation, and to most pilots they make fascinating – if occasionally grim – reading. In most cases the lessons are clear enough, but you should not think that the reports contain merely a litany of human failings. In actual fact there are plenty of instances where they record the good judgment and skill of a pilot faced with an emergency. Accident reports may also identify design or maintenance issues for a particular type, or problems with ATC or other supporting services. Whatever the cause of an accident, it is very rare that there is nothing to be learnt in its aftermath.

Information from AAIB reports also appears in other safety publications. In the UK there is a quarterly magazine called the *Flight Safety Bulletin*. This contains summaries of the recently published AAIB reports, together with articles on safety issues and a lively letters page. The FSB is published by the General Aviation Safety Council, an independent organisation set up to promote flight safety. It is sent to aircraft owners and operators and flying instructors, and is also available by subscription; the address for this and the other publications mentioned here is found in an Appendix to this book. Also available by subscription is a bi-monthly safety publication from the CAA called GASIL (*General Aviation Safety Information Leaflet*). This does include some information relating to accidents or incidents, but also covers a lot of safety information of a more general nature based on current topics and concerns. In particular, GASIL notifies forthcoming airspace and legislation changes and has a section regarding maintenance issues. Even if you do not receive these publications directly, they are normally to be found at most airfields and in most FTOs where they make good browsing.

The CAA also publishes a series of *General Aviation Safety Sense* leaflets, each covering a specific area of flight safety and aircraft operation. These free publications include invaluable advice and information on many important topics, and new issues are normally distributed with GASIL as well as being available on request.

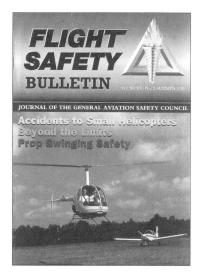

UK's Flight Safety Bulletin

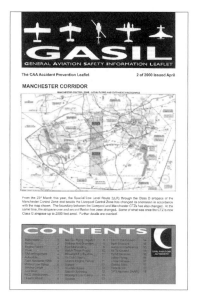

The CAA's General Aviation Safety Information Leaflet (GASIL)

One of the CAA's General Aviation Safety Sense leaflets – full of useful tips and it's free!

One safety publication not generally available to all interested readers is the *Confidential Human Factors Incident Reporting Program,* known as CHIRP. This is sent to holders of professional pilot's licences, Air Traffic Controllers and engineers in the UK and is essentially a system whereby aviation professionals can make totally confidential reports without revealing their identity or becoming involved in formal investigation. This allows them to air grievances, suggest safety improvements, point out potential problems or confess to personal errors. The CHIRP has now been extended into general aviation, with a newsletter called *GA FEEDBACK*. Many larger aviation organisations such as airlines and the armed forces have similar systems for their own personnel (such as the RAF's *Confidential Direct Occurrence Report* or CONDOR) and the reports sometimes reveal a pattern of problems which might otherwise have gone undetected. If you happen to come across any of these, they are very well worth a read.

The confidential reporting system for general aviation in the UK: GA Feedback

Most developed countries with a reasonable level of aviation activity will have similar procedures and publications to the UK, and the safety organisations in each country tend to exchange information amongst themselves. Aviation is after all an international business.

All mainstream flying magazines have regular columns and features on safety matters, usually based on accident reports from the AAIB and overseas organisations. The magazines tend to concentrate on particularly significant events. As you would expect, their stories are written with a journalistic slant and often offer information or opinions not found in the original report. Flying magazines frequently have some sort of pilot 'confessional' feature in which aviators can confess some of their most frightening, most embarrassing or even most funny moments of their flying career. There is a lot to be learnt from these stories and from the pilot's experiences, as indeed there is from the analyses of what went wrong and what went right. The entire spectrum of aviation is covered – from microlights and homebuilt aircraft to military jets and airliners, and from student pilots to airline captains with a lifetime of flying experience. If there is one message common to all these stories, it is that flying is a learning experience. As long as you are flying you should be learning, no matter how many hours you have in your logbook.

The pilot confessional 'I Learned About Flying From That' in Pilot magazine

Flying magazines also report changes in legislation, airspace and aeronautical facilities, forthcoming issues and other important safety matters. Several aviation organisations and associations also publish their own controlled-circulation magazines, which tend to concentrate on issues of direct relevance to their members.

One of the most recent significant developments in publicising aviation safety issues has been the development of the Internet. The AAIB has an excellent Web site which gives access to monthly bulletins going back several years and links to other aviation safety-related sites. Many safety organisations have sites and there are numerous discussion groups covering almost every facet of aviation. The biggest problem is in filtering the flood of material out there to obtain a manageable amount of information! If you have access to the Internet, try entering "aviation" and "safety" into a search engine and go from there.

In conclusion, there is no shortage of safety-related information available in various different guises, both as hard copy and on-line. Reading this should be part of an on-going education programme for *every* pilot. The aviator who thinks that he has nothing more to learn or knows everything is frankly a danger to himself and those around him. Such a person is invariably the one most in need of a little education, including learning from the experiences of others. Many facets of aviation change on a regular basis, in particular legislation, airspace and aeronautical facilities and ATC procedures. We should all have a defined personal education strategy, which may involve nothing more than subscribing to a particular flying publication and taking the time to read each issue.

Incident reports in Flyer magazine

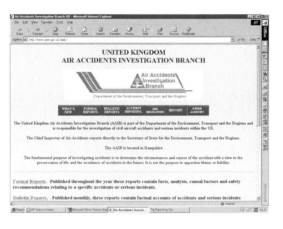

The AAIB website

In a sense, learning from the experiences of others is like gaining extra flying hours for free. It would be impossible for one person to fly long enough to make all the mistakes and experience all the situations that manifest themselves in the various safety reports and publications. By reading everything we can, and taking in the lessons therein, we could save ourselves the trouble and expense suffered by less fortunate, or less well-read, pilots.

When Pilots Get it Wrong
– A Case Study

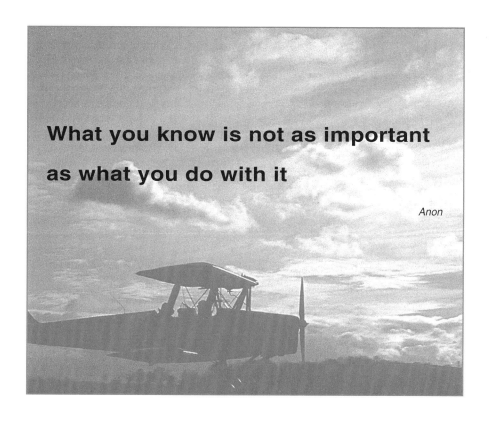

What you know is not as important as what you do with it

Anon

Flight Safety

By now it should be evident that most accidents follow well-worn courses, and have roots in misjudgments and behaviour patterns going back many years. What follows is a short study of one particular accident encompassing many of the common causes of accidents in a single journey. Before reading on, it is worth bearing in mind that none of the following is in any way unique. Similar decisions and judgments have been made many times before and since by many pilots, without the consequence necessarily being an accident. It has been said that an incident happens when two out of three things go wrong but an accident happens when three out of three go wrong.

The intention was to collect a Cessna 150 from an airfield in the south of England and fly it to southern Europe The pilot, a PPL with less than 100 hours total experience, had arranged for a friend to accompany him for this journey to help with navigation. This passenger had been a PPL although his licence had lapsed more than 10 years previously.

A Cessna 150 (not the accident aircraft)

An extract from the C150 Pilot's Guide

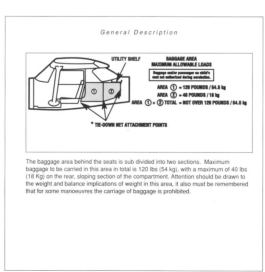

General Description

UTILITY SHELF   BAGGAGE AREA
MAXIMUM ALLOWABLE LOADS

Baggage and/or passenger on child's seat not authorized during aerobatics.

AREA ① = 120 POUNDS / 54.5 kg
AREA ② = 40 POUNDS / 18 kg
AREA ① + ② TOTAL = NOT OVER 120 POUNDS / 54.5 kg

* TIE-DOWN NET ATTACHMENT POINTS

The baggage area behind the seats is sub divided into two sections. Maximum baggage to be carried in this area in total is 120 lbs (54 kg), with a maximum of 40 lbs (18 Kg) on the rear, sloping section of the compartment. Attention should be drawn to the weight and balance implications of weight in this area, it also must be remembered that for some manoeuvres the carriage of baggage is prohibited.

When the two friends met prior to collecting the aircraft, it became clear that the passenger was intending to bring along a considerable amount of baggage – some six pieces. He claimed that the total weight of this baggage was just 55lb and that he had been expecting to fly in a four-seat aircraft (the Cessna 150 has only two seats). In addition to this passenger's accoutrements, the pilot was carrying a further three pieces of baggage. It was later calculated that the combined weight of these items was at least 130lb.

When Pilots Get it Wrong – A Case Study

Having collected the aircraft documents (which, apparently, did not include a weight schedule) the pilot prepared for a flight to a nearby airfield seemingly without making any form of weight and balance calculation. It seems that this gentleman had not flown for at least three months, and had not flown a Cessna 150 for over two years. Nevertheless it appears that no check flight or currency flight took place; the pilot started up, taxied to the active runway and commenced take-off.

Accounts of the proceedings vary, but it is clear the Cessna 150 used all of the 1000-metre tarmac runway to get airborne and climb to about 20ft. To anybody who is familiar with the type, this implies a remarkably dire performance. Indeed, the controller was so concerned by the take-off and subsequent climb-out that he asked the pilot if there was a problem. The pilot apparently replied that the aircraft had a lot of baggage on board and apologised if anybody had been frightened...

GROSS WEIGHT LBS.	IAS 50 FT. MPH	HEAD WIND KNOTS	AT SEA LEVEL & 15°C/59°F.		AT 2500 FT. & 10°C/50°F.		AT 5000 FT. & 5°C/41°F.		AT 7500 FT. & 0°C/32°F.	
			GROUND RUN	TOTAL TO CLEAR 50 FT. OBS.	GROUND RUN	TOTAL TO CLEAR 50 FT. OBS.	GROUND RUN	TOTAL TO CLEAR 50 FT. OBS.	GROUND RUN	TOTAL TO CLEAR 50 FT. OBS.
1600	70	0	735	1385	910	1660	1115	1985	1360	2440
		10	500	1035	630	1250	780	1510	970	1875
		20	305	730	395	890	505	1090	640	1375

TAKE - OFF DISTANCE — FLAPS RETRACTED – HARD SURFACE RUNWAY

NOTES 1. Increase the distances 10% for each 35°f. increase in temperature above standard for the particular altitude.
2. For operation on a dry, grass runway, increase distances (both "ground run" and "total to clear 50 ft. obstacle") by 7% of the "total to clear 50 ft. obstacle" figure.

This sample C150 take-off performance table shows that even on a hot day with no headwind, a C150 at MAUW should be able to take-off on a tarmac runway and climb to 50ft in around 1500ft or 460m

What the pilot thought of the take-off we don't know, but the flight continued as planned to an airfield whose runway was shorter than that from which the aircraft had just departed. The aeroplane arrived at its destination and landed without incident.

After refuelling the aircraft to full tanks and having a meal, the pilot and passenger purchased some life-jackets, charts and airfield guides for the planned flight. They also procured weather information for the intended destination across the Channel. The instructor who obtained the 'actual' (METAR) report remembered that the report included significant cloud at 600ft or below, and he advised that the weather was not suitable for a VFR arrival. However, the pilot apparently telephoned a colleague at the destination to check the weather and arrange overnight accommodation. He then filed a flight plan and was given a comprehensive set of weather forecasts and reports. At the time, the TAF for the intended destination was in essence:

```
1322 20014KT 8000 BR SCT007 BKN020 TEMPO 1322 4000 RA BKN003
TEMPO 1317 1500 RA BKN001
```

(If you aren't confident in decoding this forecast, now is the time to revise your met...)

The folder given to the pilot included an explanation of meteorological codes and formats, although how closely the pilot examined these we do not know. However, his flight plan stated an *en route* time of 1:30 whereas later calculations based on the forecast winds (which pointed to a 30-knot headwind for most of the flight) indicated a more realistic flight time of 2:25. There was no indication that the forecast wind was marked on the pilot's chart or used on his flight log. On filing the flight plan, the pilot allegedly stated that the aircraft would be taking-off overweight and had caused some concern to ATC on his previous departure.

His comments were certainly noted because when the pilot began taxying for take-off, the airfield's emergency services were brought to standby. Once on the runway, the aircraft appeared to accelerate slowly and used most of the 800 metres of tarmac to get airborne. It did not seem to climb or accelerate normally once in the air, but continued flying below the tree line. A quarter of a mile from the runway, the aircraft had still only climbed to about 20ft AGL and apparently had to lower a wing to avoid a tree. When about a mile from the airfield, the Cessna was still only about 150ft high.

It was later calculated that the aircraft was around 230lb overweight at this take-off, an overload of nearly 15% above its maximum allowable all-up weight. The pilot may have believed that aircraft can be loaded with an adult in each seat, full fuel and maximum permitted baggage load and still automatically stay within weight and balance limits. But as we have seen before, this is unfortunately not true. In actual fact there are very few aircraft of any size which offer such wide loading flexibility. Even a passing encounter with the weight and balance information will confirm that for most aircraft from a Cessna 150 to an Airbus 340, it is simply not possible to fill all the seats, carry the maximum baggage or cargo, fill the fuel tanks and still be within the permitted weight and CG range.

Based on a C150 CG moment envelope, the probable loading at the time of the second take-off is marked 'A' – it is not only outside the envelope but off the graph too!

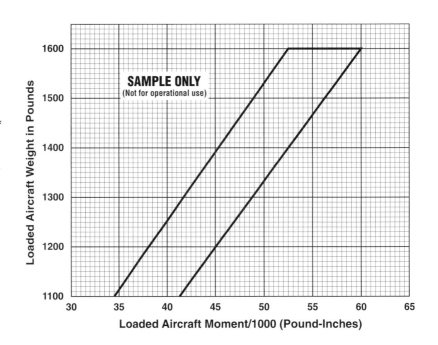

After its eventful departure the aircraft turned *en route* but would not climb above 1500ft. Approaching the coastline the weather, as forecast, began to worsen. As the visibility reduced, the pilot must have reviewed the available options and eventually the decision was made to divert to a nearby airfield. Contact was made with the radio operator at the diversion, and an approach was made. Perhaps because the aircraft was heavy (still at least 200lb overweight at this stage) the approach was made rather faster than normal and with less than full flap. The aircraft was seen to land on all three wheels and bounce back into the air. A series of bounces followed, all but one on the nosewheel. At this stage, and with only about 200m of runway remaining, the pilot commenced a go-around.

In the careful and detailed analysis that follows an accident, events that took only seconds can be dissected and examined in minute detail to the extent that we can make reasonable conjectures about the last moments of the aircraft's flight. Later calculations showed that given the likely loading and flap setting, the overweight Cessna 150 would have descended *even at full power and best rate-of-climb airspeed.* Even with flaps retracted the aircraft would only have been capable of climbing at a marginal 135ft/min.

The aircraft was now flying towards rising ground and was seen to be porpoising and wallowing. At some stage the pilot retracted the flaps and there is evidence that the aircraft was being flown more slowly than the best rate-of-climb speed. Around 200 metres beyond the end of the runway the left wing was seen to drop by 60° followed by the nose as the aircraft probably stalled and entered an incipient spin to the left. At this instant, in the final moments of flight, the occupants of the Cessna used up whichever of their nine lives were left over from the earlier exploits of the day. The aircraft descended into an apple tree, which presumably cushioned some of the impact forces before the aircraft struck the ground. It then crashed through a fence and into a garden, but did not hit the nearby house and did not catch fire. The radio operator saw the crash, alerted the emergency services and arranged for first-aid personnel from the airfield to go to the crash site. Amazingly, and thankfully, both the pilot and his passenger survived the impact.

In order to make sense of any of this, we have to assume that the pilot did not set out with the deliberate intention of having an accident. Indeed, some of his actions – such as making a stop to buy survival equipment and charts and making a diversion when the weather worsened – were sensible precautions. All the same, in the final analysis this accident was avoidable. It need not have happened, and both pilot and passenger were very lucky to survive the experience.

The final word should go to the AAIB. These diligent men and women spend a large proportion of their working lives dealing with the aftermath of human frailties and flaws. Even a casual reading of a number of accident reports reveals a pattern of recurring themes and actions. How difficult it must be to approach every accident with a truly open mind. It must require a rare dedication to explore all reasonable avenues methodically and to eliminate all outside forces only to find time after time that the only thing in the aeroplane not operating properly was the pilot. If the accident investigators do occasionally succumb to frustration or irritation in reporting the same basic accident sequences over and over again, nothing of this shows in their reports which are models of impartiality and factuality. Still, you have to wonder if there wasn't a trace of irony in the report for this accident. It solemnly reported the nature of the damage incurred as "Aircraft, garden fence and wheelbarrow destroyed".

When Pilots Get it Right
– A Case Study

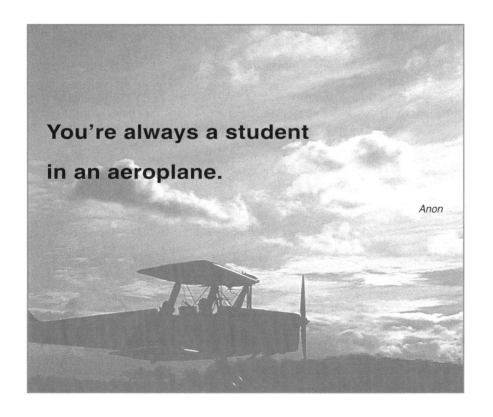

You're always a student

in an aeroplane.

Anon

Flight Safety

It is easy to forget that not all accidents are precipitated by carelessness or serious errors of judgment by pilots. Sometimes aviators truly are the victims of circumstances beyond their control, and then it is their skill and judgment that can make all the difference. There are plenty of instances on record where good airmanship has averted a much more serious incident. In such cases the pilot's licences, ratings and flying hours vary enormously. But the common factors are sound airmanship, good judgment, flying skill and very often a determination to keep flying the aeroplane until the last bit stops moving.

A warm and sunny June afternoon, with a light wind from the south-west, made a near-perfect backdrop for a relaxing flight to the pilot and seven passengers of a twin-engine Piper Navajo. The aircraft was at 5000ft on the return leg of a short round trip; the commander had already flown the same trip that morning. Inbound to base, with a light tailwind and CAVOK conditions, it must have been easy to unwind in anticipation of the end of the working day. Possibly the only factor that could cause some unease was a slight vibration which had occurred during the climb and initial cruise. However, this had ceased and now the pilot was ready to commence a cruise descent towards the destination. Up until this moment the flight was, in every sense, a routine and uneventful trip. But all that was about to change.

A Piper PA-31 Navajo

The description of what happened next comes from the dry words of a formal accident report, but it is not difficult to picture the heart-stopping nature of the moment. As the pilot reduced power to commence the descent there was a loud bang and the aircraft rolled violently into a steep spiral dive or spin to the right. In the two rotations that followed, the pilot – who must have been rather surprised by this turn of events – managed to identify the direction of the spiral or spin, apply full left rudder to stop the rotation and begin easing out of the ensuing steep dive. In short he had, instinctively, followed the golden rule of any emergency; fly the aeroplane.

The sudden and apparently inexplicable events of a few moments were later described in forensic detail in a 100-page report. A propeller blade had separated from the right-hand engine following a massive failure of the propeller hub. The resulting huge out-of-balance forces tore the right-hand engine completely out of the wing, leaving almost nothing forward of the firewall and generating massive drag. Meantime the detached propeller blade passed through the forward fuselage baggage area and into the propeller of the left engine, stopping it instantly.

When Pilots Get it Right— A Case Study

Recovering from the steep dive, it must have been clear to the pilot that a major failure had occurred. He aimed for an airspeed of 100kts, which he estimated to be a reasonable gliding speed. But as speed reduced through 120kts, the aircraft began to roll right despite using full left rudder and aileron. From this the pilot decided to maintain a minimum gliding airspeed of 130kts, which gave adequate control but a steep gliding angle. Fundamentally what the pilot had done was perform a very brief low-speed handling check – a procedure to find the minimum speed at which a damaged aircraft can be controlled. He now knew that at any airspeed below about 120kts he could not be sure of keeping the aircraft under control. Looking out, the pilot saw that the right engine was missing, the left engine had stopped and that there was damage to the nose of the aircraft. Unknown to him the elevator aerodynamic balance horns were also bent out of shape – probably as a result of forces during the rotations and recovery from the ensuing dive – which made elevator control more difficult. In addition, the loss of the right engine had not only wrecked the aerodynamics of the aircraft but also significantly altered the CG position.

At the best of times a Navajo is not likely to win any gliding competitions, and flying *sans* engines isn't the sort of thing multi-engine pilots practice as a matter of course. What's more, in its damaged condition the Navajo in question was presenting its commander with a totally unknown scenario. His situation was certainly not one which could be realistically envisaged or simulated. Nevertheless he had the aircraft back under control, albeit as an unpredictable and inefficient glider, and so was in a position to set up for a forced landing. A suitable large field of standing crops was spotted, although the approach was obstructed by power lines. No better option was available in the limited time available, so the pilot decided to make for that field whilst manoeuvring to avoid the obstacles. During this short descent he also made two brief Mayday calls, although noise and vibration prevented him from hearing the replies. He also managed a few words to the passengers; quite what they thought of events can only be imagined.

No hydraulics were available because the only remaining engine was not turning, and use of the hand pump to lower the undercarriage and flaps was not a realistic option in the time remaining before landing. Besides, the pilot needed both hands to fly the aircraft despite applying full left aileron and rudder trim. The aircraft levelled out just above the standing crop in the chosen field and began to slow down; the pilot just had time to call for the passengers to take up the brace position. He had given the passengers a pre-flight safety briefing before the flight, and suitable briefing cards were available for each passenger seat.

The landing path of the Navajo through the standing crop

The rear fuselage first brushed the standing crop about 300 metres into the field. Over the next 400 metres or so the aircraft gradually sank into the crop until the left wingtip touched the ground. The aircraft slewed left for 100 metres and eventually came to a halt after a total 'landing' distance of about 800 metres. The aircraft was intact and upright, little more than 120 seconds after the violent rolling manoeuvre that announced the right engine separation. The pilot and all the passengers were able to leave the aircraft through the exits; the only injury was a later report of whiplash. Shortly afterwards, the pilot returned to the aircraft and established radio contact to report the successful forced landing. Within five minutes another aircraft located the Navajo and was able to confirm its exact position.

The AAIB later made a number of safety recommendations centred on the propeller hub design. These mostly concerned procedures for giving mandatory status to certain manufacturer's service bulletins, updating airworthiness directives (ADs)

The Navajo after the pilot's successful forced landing

which relate to Service Bulletins and publicising ADs and service bulletins containing safety information relevant to pilots.

This accident occurred in daylight and good VMC. The aircraft was high enough to be recovered from the spiral or spin, and it was over open countryside where a suitable forced-landing area was available. In different circumstances the situation could have been far more serious. This emphatically does not detract from the fact that the skill and judgment of the pilot in command saved eight lives. The accident report commented that the pilot was *"...greatly commended for his very skilful recovery of the aircraft, his concern for the passengers, and for carrying out the subsequent forced landing with such a high level of proficiency."* In the final analysis it was the sheer professionalism of this pilot – from giving a proper safety briefing before flight to the skilful forced landing in circumstances impossible to foresee – that made the vital difference. Although he was relatively inexperienced on the aircraft type, it was his approach to the flight and his professional attitude throughout that meant more than any number of licences or ratings or hours in a logbook.

Ten Ways Not to Have an Accident and Fly Happily Ever After

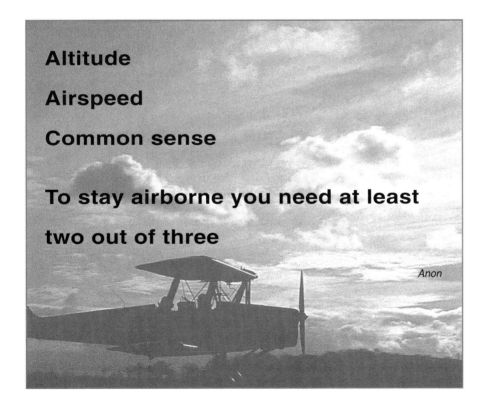

Altitude

Airspeed

Common sense

To stay airborne you need at least

two out of three

Anon

Flight Safety

Flight Safety

*Ten Ways Not
to Have an
Accident*

In talking about accidents and flight safety, it is very easy to produce a long list of commandments containing prescriptive phrases such as 'do not' and 'under no circumstances' and 'it is forbidden to'. This tends to take all the fun out of being a pilot and leave just an academic exercise that is more about form-filling and paperwork than flying aeroplanes. However, safe flying doesn't have to be tedious or boring; there is no reason why it cannot be challenging and adventurous whilst being safe at the same time. Few pilots would disagree that a properly prepared and professionally flown air-display routine can be safe and exciting while the impromptu antics of an unskilled aviator showing-off are frightening and dangerous for all concerned. A challenging arrival to a short runway can be either a stimulating challenge if approached professionally or a stressful ordeal if proper preparations have not been made. The attempted manoeuvres may be similar but the end result is very different. With this in mind the following suggestions are a personal view of how to avoid accidents, enjoy safe aviating and get the best out of your flying.

1 ▶ Aviate, Navigate, Communicate

Wherever, whatever, whenever; the pilot only ever has one overriding priority – *fly the aeroplane.* No apologies for saying it again.

No matter what the situation is, being in control of the aircraft must always comes above all other demands on the pilot's attention. This is simply because if the aircraft goes out of control, knowing exactly where you are or making word-perfect RT calls are of no consequence whatsoever. Above all, flying the aeroplane is never more important than in an emergency. In this situation there will be plenty of distractions and pressures that could lead the unwary pilot to lose control of a basically airworthy machine. In more normal circumstances the flying of the aeroplane also covers basic attention to the aircraft's condition. Are the engine temperatures and pressures OK? What is the fuel state? Is the aircraft in the proper configuration? Proper in-flight checks, such as the 'FREDA' cruise checks should cover those issues.

When we are satisfied that the aeroplane is under control and working properly, navigation becomes an issue. The basic foundation of navigation is dead reckoning (DR). In other words, having flown from a known point in a set direction at a set speed for a set time, we should have a reasonable idea of where we are. DR is backed up with map reading (in VMC) and maybe radionavigation. In IMC, dead reckoning is just as important, allied with radionavigation. To make any kind of informed decisions, we need to have a good mental picture of where the aeroplane is and where it is going. Merely following a needle on a dial, with no real idea of current position or ETA, relegates us to nothing more than an autopilot. Vertical navigation also comes into play. If at any time in flight we do not have a clear idea of the distance between the aeroplane and the surface below and ahead, then we jolly well should.

Don't drop the aeroplane in order to fly the microphone

Anon

Communication comes after flying and navigation. Despite the importance placed by some pilots on sounding imperturbable and professional on the radio, it comes a definite third in the hierarchy. Remember that the ATC organisation is there to aid pilots, not to distract them from their primary tasks. And they don't impress easily, so cut the waffle. They don't need to hear stuff like "4436 coming down sir" or "We're almost abeam the Golf India November at this moment in time".

2▶ Always have a Plan B

Keeping your options open is a basic requirement for safe flying. Time after time the accident investigators are left to clear up the results of a pilot's refusal to consider any course of action other than the pre-determined goal. Weather can be worse than forecast, runways can be blocked and airfields or ATC units unexpectedly closed. Engines and other systems can fail, fuel can be used more quickly than expected. The best-laid plans can and certainly do go awry. And if any of this happens to us one day – tough luck. There's no point complaining about it until we're safely on the ground. As pilots we need to be thinking ahead and keeping one step infront of the aeroplane to avoid sudden surprises. In short, never take an aeroplane anywhere that your brain didn't get to at least five minutes earlier.

Proper in-flight checks such as FREDA will go a long way towards helping us maintain a basic situational awareness – not just in terms of what is happening now but what is likely to happen. It also helps to think of our intentions or objective as a preferred course of action rather than as an absolute must-happen no-argument target. Too many pilots plough on in unsuitable conditions,

Flying is done largely with the imagination

Stick and Rudder, Wolfgang Langewiesche

apparently blinkered like a racehorse with nothing in sight but the intended finishing post. We can think of flying as being rather like playing cards; regardless of what hand you are dealt, you always want to have an ace up your sleeve. In the case of aerobatics and manoeuvring flight involving extreme attitudes, it could be called the Ace of Altitude. But if we are going to perform aerobatic or extreme manoeuvres so close to the ground that there is no room to recover from any error or mishap in handing, all the aces are held by our old friend gravity. And gravity plays to win.

3▶ The Five Ps – or Proper Preparation Prevents Poor Performance

All too many accident investigations reveal that the accident pilot made hardly any sensible preparation for the flight undertaken. The list is a long one; weather not checked (actual reports *as well* as forecasts), out-of-date charts, no fuel plan, weight and balance outside limits, over-optimistic estimates of performance, no safety-altitude calculations or headings and times not based on forecast winds. All are classic examples of an over-casual, unprofessional, attitude to the business of flying an aeroplane. The environment in which we operate really is "...mercilessly unforgiving of any carelessness, incapacity or neglect". I honestly don't want to sound like an evangelist, but we enter into this domain as visitors only; we are always bound to return to our native surface existence. Proper preparation is one of the best ways to ensure that this return is at a place and in a manner of our choosing.

The importance of checking forecasts against recent actual weather reports

TAF 170903Z 171019 21005KT 8000 SCT005 PROB30 TEMPO 1011 1200 BR BKN002 BECMG 1013 9999=

METAR 170920 170920Z 24005KT 0500 FG VV003 03/02 Q1022=

(this day the visibility never improved beyond 1100 metres)

4 ▶ Stay current

Experienced pilots are wont to say that flying an aeroplane is like riding a bicycle; once you've learnt, you never forget and never fall off. To a certain extent this is true; the basic skills of flying an aeroplane tend to be retained even without constant practice. Most ex-pilots would probably have a good chance of landing an aeroplane many years after they last flew. However, piloting skills do deteriorate without rehearsal; standards fall and even the simplest manoeuvre requires much more concentration than when you are in current practice. Moreover, checks and procedures that are second nature when you practice them regularly are easily forgotten or confused when they have to be dragged out of long-term memory. The skills and procedures most likely to be lost and forgotten are those for emergency and abnormal situations. These are the sort of things that by definition do not crop up often (if ever), but when they do they require sure and competent action by the pilot.

The majority of non-professional pilots do not fly as often as they would like because of money or time constraints. Private pilots may not be regularly tested in emergency procedures as professional pilots are, but that is no reason why they should not be current in emergencies. Every flight is an opportunity to rehearse at least one procedure, or to practice a skill not required for everyday flight. Below is a suggested list of such procedures for daylight VMC flight:

- Short-field take-off
- Forced landing without power (including engine fire checks)
- Partial engine failure
- Slow flight
- Steep turns
- Radio failure
- Electrical failure
- Cabin fire
- Compass turns and constant compass heading
- Practice position fix
- Practice diversion
- Glide approach and landing
- Flapless approach and landing
- Short-field approach and landing
- Precautionary landing including bad weather circuit
- Go-around

Ten Ways Not to Have an Accident and Fly Happily Ever After

Some of these procedures may take us no more than a few moments of 'touch drills', with reference to the checklist to see how you fared. Others can be combined, such as engine fire and forced landing, position fix and diversion, electrical failure and flapless landing and so on. By working at least one of the above procedures into each flight, most of us will have practised a complete range of flying skills and procedures in the course of an average year. Practising in this way also allows a margin of error. A short-field take-off and landing on a long tarmac runway allows us to keep in practice and gauge the field performance of our aircraft without causing serious problems if we're having a bad day and miss the intended touch down point by 200 metres!

Practising emergency and abnormal procedures not only keeps the skills current but also presents an extra challenge – which for many pilots was part of the attraction of flying in the first place. Even the most inexperienced aviator is unlikely to be seriously challenged by an aimless 30-minute flight around the local area. Maybe the perceived lack of new challenge is what causes some pilots to lose their enthusiasm for flying in the first few years of holding a licence. At the very least, practising an emergency situation or abnormal procedure may remind us that there can be very much more to flying than a trip round the houses.

Are you current in crosswind landings? This pilot is

For pilots with instrument-flying qualifications, the list of procedures can be expanded to include some situations specific to instrument flying:

■ Limited panel flight, including recovery from unusual attitudes

■ Full go-around from decision height or missed approach point

■ A different instrument approach every couple of months – don't always accept radar vectors to the ILS!

It may well be prudent to carry a safety pilot for some or all of the above.

There are many benefits in practising and rehearsing at least one emergency or abnormal procedure on every flight we make. Not only are we keeping our skills up-to-date but we will probably find that 'normal' flying seems much easier. Moreover we will develop the mindset that treats such situations as possibilities to be prepared for rather than events so unlikely that they are not even worth thinking about.

5▶ Know your aeroplane

Too many pilots take to the air in aircraft that they do not really know or understand. Their knowledge of the machine may have been limited to a brief 'check flight', and everyday vital statistics such as fuel consumption, flying speeds and loading limits are based on little more than word-of-mouth information. We should take time, especially when new to a type, to read and understand the manufacturer's recommended operating procedures, aircraft limits, handling characteristics and performance. Performance such as take-off and landing distances, fuel consumption and climb rates can be calculated and then checked against real life. Even different models of the same basic type can have quite different design features, handling characteristics or limits which are not immediately obvious because the aircraft look the same. Individual examples of the same type and model may have special options or modifications such as autopilots and extra fuel systems, These can materially alter the operation of the aircraft.

> # An aeroplane may disappoint any pilot, but it'll never surprise a good one
>
> *Len Morgan*

Each aircraft type also has its own foibles (not always good ones) with which we must make an effort to become acquainted. Accident and incident reports for the particular type will sometimes reveal problem areas for the unwary. Pilots experienced on type, owner's associations and safety organisations are also good sources of information about the sort of things manufacturers don't always publicise – the so-called 'everybody knows about that' factor. Not everybody does, and learning from the experience and knowledge of others can be a lot less painful than finding out the hard way.

6▶ Know yourself

As far as is known, every holder of a pilot's licence is a human being and we all possess character traits (sometimes rather dangerously referred to as 'strengths and weaknesses') as part of our psyche. Getting to know who we are is a lifetime's work, and indeed some – maybe all – of us will never really know. Whatever our particular personal qualities, and however conscious or unconscious of them we might be, they are not left behind when we get into an aircraft. Instead, they become part of the skill, experience and judgment each of us brings to the art of flying. Good training and sound operating procedures will go a long way towards reducing the hazards induced by certain human frailties and personality traits. However, pilots are humans and not robots and tend to act accordingly.

If we are particularly susceptible to group pressure, we must be especially wary of being led by others into situation with which we do not feel able to cope. If we are easily hassled or panicked by time pressure, we need to take extra care to allow adequate time for pre-flight planning and preparation. If we need a sound eight hours of sleep a night, we probably will not make good piloting decisions after a short and disturbed sleep period. If we have a tendency to resent authority, we should be mindful of this when it comes to dealing with authority figures such as aviation regulators, ATC, instructors and the like. Rather than automatically rejecting their advice or instructions, we should consider whether this attitude is justified or whether perhaps it symbolises something much older and unresolved within us. We may ourselves have unresolved and unconscious authoritarian traits. In much the same way we may have unconscious biases against others based on race, sex, age or even factors such as accent, social class, relative wealth and the like. Leaving aside the wider social implications of such an attitude, it is important to look beyond the messenger and listen to the message without prejudice.

"…I said to myself, 'ah microlight' when I spotted the clip-on bow tie…"

It is equally important to appreciate our own limitations as pilots. It is exceptionally unlikely that any one person will possess identical levels of skill in all areas of piloting technique. A gifted aerobatic pilot might have difficulty with applied instrument flying. A competent airline pilot might not be able to make consistent landings in a single-seat tailwheel aircraft on short grass runways. Even within the standard PPL syllabus, most pilots find that some particular manoeuvre – glide approaches, steep turns, crosswind landings, overhead joins or whatever – seem more difficult or require more practice and training than others.

Ideally we should play to our "strengths" and minimise our "weaknesses" – and have some compassion for the weaknesses of others. If we are aware of our own weaknesses, we can act accordingly in situations where they might manifest themselves. Possibly the most dangerous personality traits in a pilot are those of complacency and over-confidence. Unchecked, these will lead us into situations where we eventually exceed our own limitations or those of the aeroplane. In these cases a little more self-awareness could prevent an accident (breaking that chain again). Knowledge of who we are can be the most valuable wisdom we bring into the cockpit; we are well worth thinking about.

▶7 If in doubt, shout

As pilots, we are privileged to be surrounded by a supporting network of air traffic facilities, meteorologists, engineers, aeronautical information services and all sorts of other things. It is sensible to make use of this network because these professionals are all experts in their own fields; their knowledge and experience can be very valuable to us, provided that we have the common sense to ask for their help. Instead many of us will plough on, even when we know we have a problem, without asking for any assistance from anyone else. This may be caused by misplaced pride – we don't want to admit to 'outsiders' that things are going wrong, or that we don't know something we should. Maybe we're operating in a denial mode; perhaps we're believing that as long as we act as though everything is normal, somehow the situation will sort itself out. It won't. Once things start to go wrong, there is every chance that the predicament will get worse unless we make a positive effort to retrieve the situation. There have been cases where a pilot has damaged an aircraft, or had obvious doubts about the serviceability of an aircraft, but either did not consult an engineer or ignored their advice – with appalling results.

Air traffic controllers can also be worth their weight in gold to us, but once again they can only help if we are willing to accept their aid. There was a recent tragedy when a non-instrument pilot flew into cloud after the weather proved to be significantly worse than forecast. An ATC unit located the aircraft and offered advice about diversions but the pilot apparently decided to change to another frequency, evidently intent on sorting out the situation unaided. For the next 45 minutes the controllers watched their radar with increasing desperation as the aircraft flew steadily towards mountains, apparently not in contact with any ATC unit. Local airfields, other aircraft and even the distress and diversion service tried to contact the pilot, but their calls went unanswered and they were left powerless to help. When the aircraft's return faded from radar, the best ATC could do was direct the SAR services to the location of the crash – some 50 miles off the planned route. Right up to the last few moments, a calamity could have been averted if only the pilot had asked for help.

They are here for you. Call on 121.5 in the UK and you will probably find yourself talking to somebody in the Distress and Diversion cell, seen here

8▶ If it's illegal or it feels wrong, don't do it

The most common contributory factor in serious accidents is that of the pilot operating outside the privileges of his or her licences and ratings. The training and currency requirements required for various situations, such as instrument flying, are there for a good reason. The number of accidents caused by aviators exceeding their licence privileges only underline why these rules exist in the first place. A little excursion into cloud might seem like a good idea, or even a necessity at times. But there is a world of difference between simulated instrument flying 'under the hood' in the company of a soothing instructor and flying alone into real, dark, unfriendly cloud.

You're a long way from home at a foreign airfield and you 'need' to get back today. There's no de-icing fluid around so...should you ignore the frost on the aeroplane and chance it?

As with many areas of human activity, with increasing experience we develop a sense of what is safe in aviation terms and what is not. This may manifest itself as a deep sense of unease, which can be unfortunately overridden by a perceived need or pressure to act against our better judgment. Or it may be simply a nagging feeling that something is not quite right. It is always a mistake to ignore such feelings, even if they amount to nothing more than a 'sixth sense' that cannot be isolated to any particular problem or predicament. The human psyche contains an enormously strong sense of self-preservation, an instinct capable of showing itself in a spectacular variety of different ways. A feeling that we are in some way out on a limb or heading for unspecified trouble is not one to be ignored.

9▶ Enjoy your flying

We all have some kind of motivation for wanting to fly aeroplanes; it's not the sort of activity people get involved in for no reason at all. We should take time to explore what it is we enjoy most about flying, because this is the key to getting the best out of our chosen pursuit. General aviation offers a huge variety of flying experiences. We may enjoy pure aircraft handling, in which case aerobatics and tailwheel aircraft may be our future. We may lean towards instrument flying and complex aircraft, which will lead us in turn towards advanced aircraft and instrument qualifications. The freedom of flying non-radio between small grass strips is difficult to beat, as is the satisfaction of operating safely into a major airport amongst heavy jets.

You may be within an hour's flying time of a breath-taking winter's scene such as this

Humans are generally best motivated to excel at what they enjoy, and for many pilots the enjoyment of flying – in whatever form – is the satisfaction of meeting a challenge successfully. Challenge can be hard to find if we are flying the same aeroplane around the same airfield on the same routine with little variation. It is

There are at least 500 airfields to visit in the UK alone

all too easy for us to fall into the trap of just flying to the same airfields and then wondering why flying doesn't seem to be so much fun any more. Maybe we don't fly any other types because we don't want to go through another checkout. Maybe we only fly to the same airfields we visited in basic training because we lack the confidence to go further afield. Either way, we are hardly making the full use of our piloting potential.

Flying different aircraft types and flying into different airfields is a very simple way of setting ourselves a challenge, widening our skills and putting some fun back into our flying. Even a short flight with a sympathetic pilot or instructor in an aircraft we

This grass strip is a challenging prospect for sure. But with the right preparation and the right aeroplane, it's a challenge that's yours for the taking

have never flown before can be great fun, and far more memorable than any number of hours droning around our home airfield in the usual club machine. There are at least 500 airfields in the UK alone, so if we haven't visited a new airfield for years, there's no shortage of them out there. There are too many different aircraft types to count; Cessnas are different from Pipers, and Robins are different from both. If we've only ever flown nosewheel aircraft, a taildragger might be a real eye-opener. A wood-and-fabric vintage aircraft has a very different aura from a modern machine. Flying into a short grass strip presents a whole different range of challenges from those of a 2000-metre tarmac runway. If we are happy and fulfilled by our regular flying, fine. If not, why don't we fly into a rally or an open day or a fly-in? Flying into an air display might also be great fun; we get to miss the traffic queues and enjoy a good day's entertainment too.

Ever thought of a flight in a hot-air balloon? Or a glider, a microlight, a floatplane, a helicopter...

Even if you have covered this ground, flying has many more challenges to offer. Have you ever considered a flight in a multi-engine aircraft, a floatplane, a microlight, a glider, a helicopter or even a balloon? Any of these will give you a whole new outlook on the wider aviation world and need not be expensive. Arrange for a 'trial flight' experience, tell the instructor about your own flying background and interests and you are likely to get far more 'hands-on' flying than an average 'punter'. You might even gain a new respect for the pilots of some of the other flying craft with which you share the skies.

In short, flying should be fun and should remain a challenge, a task against which to measure our skills and knowledge. A pilot's licence should be the passport to an indulgence, not a millstone around the neck. If we understand what motivated us to want to learn to fly in the first place, we should have the key to keeping our flying enjoyable and worthwhile.

10 ▶ Never stop learning

No one person will ever know everything there is to know about aviation. A pilot has to have a working knowledge of many different subjects, but the syllabus for even the most advanced pilot's licences will rarely make a pilot a true expert in any one discipline. Spend some time with a professional weather forecaster, a lecturer in aerodynamics or an aviation engineer and you will soon realise how much more there is to know about their specialist subject. This is not to say that we have to spend the rest of our flying career studying more and more textbooks. It is more important to appreciate that whatever pilot's licence we hold, it is nothing more than a licence to learn. If we ever come to believe we know it all, we really are in trouble.

Some people believe that all pilots go through stages of overconfidence when they think they know everything worth knowing. It has been speculated that these stages occur at five, 500 and 5000 hours in command. There is no statistical evidence to back up this theory, but it's an interesting idea. It is only human nature that if we are

*...to set ourselves high
standards...*

"...I'm at eight thousand and three feet seven and one thirty second inches..."

flying the same basic task in the same aeroplane type, we will become very skilled over a period of time in dealing with regularly occurring situations. However, there is a delicate line between having a well-founded confidence in our own skills and judgment and slipping into complacency and over-confidence. If we never fly with a pilot more qualified or experienced than ourselves, or if our skills are rarely tested under the eyes of an impartial examiner, it is possible to believe that any landing we walk away from is a good one. It is also possible to believe that as long as we reach our destination, what happens *en route* is not particularly important. If our flying is mostly unmonitored by anybody but ourselves, it is all the more important for us to be self-critical; to set ourselves high standards and expect to attain them. It is a simple matter after each flight to mentally review our performance and decide whether it was up to the standard we set. It is highly unlikely that the flight could be regarded as perfect and flawless, but it is also very rare that it was a complete shambles. Somewhere in between these extremes lie the bulk of our flying experience, and in the minor errors or unforeseen situations that arise are the seeds of the on-going learning curve on which we should all be.

Like so much literature found in the average flying club, this AOPA newsletter is a source of invaluable information

Aviation is not a static environment, and even the pilot of the simplest aircraft flying out of a non-radio grass strip in uncontrolled airspace will be affected by changes which are part of the routine of the flying world. I would recommend that *every* pilot should subscribe to at least one flying magazine and one safety publication. These will allow you to learn from the mistakes of others through accident reports and pilot confessionals. They will also keep you posted about major changes and forthcoming proposals. Other articles will give you a deeper insight into specialist subjects – and the reports of visiting new airfields, flying different aircraft types or attaining new ratings may fire your imagination and desire to stretch your own wings a bit further.

Unless you are exceptionally fortunate, it is likely that on occasion the flights you plan will have to be cancelled because of weather, unserviceability or availability problems. You can use the time that would have spent flying by propping up the bar or going home. Alternatively you could spend the time catching up on some of the reading you might never normally find time for. The literature you might try includes AICs, the aircraft's documents, pre-flight information bulletins, safety publications, accident reports and so on. In doing this, you may have gained as much knowledge as the intended flight would have given you.

Ten Ways Not to Have an Accident and Fly Happily Ever After

Once again, however we approach our flying, the most important element is to treat the whole of our flying life, down to each single flight, as a learning experience. I am taken back to the opening words of this series: achieving the ability to fly an aeroplane is still a special and significant personal achievement. The skills and knowledge we need should not be taken for granted but have to be nurtured and sustained. Once you have obtained your licence, you must be your own sternest examiner and wisest instructor, your own impartial judge and jury: you must always be learning and developing as a pilot.

I fly because it releases my mind from the tyranny of petty things

Antoine de Saint-Exupéry

Good luck; be safe; happy landings.

A

B

C

index

F

G

H

index

I

J

K

L

M

N

O

P

R

S

T

I

U

V

W

index

n

notes

notes

notes

notes

notes

notes

notes

notes